CODE AND CUSTOM
IN A
THAI PROVINCIAL COURT

Sketch Map of **THAILAND** and **CHIANGMAI PROVINCE**

prepared by Elaine Martina

The Association for Asian Studies: Monograph No. XXXIV
Paul Wheatley, General Editor

CODE AND CUSTOM IN A THAI PROVINCIAL COURT

The Interaction of Formal and Informal Systems of Justice

DAVID M. ENGEL

(Frank Reynolds, Editor)

Published for the Association for Asian Studies by
THE UNIVERSITY OF ARIZONA PRESS
Tucson, Arizona

About the Author...

David M. Engel, a research attorney at the American Bar Foundation, received an A.B. degree from Harvard College, a master's degree from the Center for South and Southeast Asian Studies of the University of Michigan, and a Juris Doctor degree from the Law School of the University of Michigan. The author has lived and worked in Thailand as a Peace Corps volunteer and has written about the transformation of the Thai legal system in his study, *Law and Kingship in Thailand During the Reign of King Chulalongkorn* (1975).

The publication of this volume has been financed from a revolving fund that initially was established by a generous grant from the Ford Foundation to the Association for Asian Studies.

THE UNIVERSITY OF ARIZONA PRESS

Copyright © 1978
The Arizona Board of Regents
All Rights Reserved
Manufactured in the U.S.A.

I.S.B.N. 0-8165-0622-1 paper
I.S.B.N. 0-8165-0629-9 cloth
L.C. No. 78-50936

To my mother and father

Contents

LIST OF FIGURES	xi
LIST OF TABLES	xi
ACKNOWLEDGMENTS	xiii
INTRODUCTION	1
PART ONE. COURT, MINISTRY AND PROVINCE: THE SETTING	**11**
Chapter One. The Court and the Ministry of Justice	13
A portrait of the Chiangmai Court	13
Court and Ministry	15
Provincial Thai justice before the Ministry of Justice	18
Transformation of the provincial judicial system	24
Chapter Two. The Court and the Province of Chiangmai	30
Modern Chiangmai and its early origins	30
Incorporation of Chiangmai into the modern Thai state	32
Characteristics of modern Chiangmai	36
Chapter Three. The Court and Its Functions	43
PART TWO. PRIVATE WRONGS, MEDIATION, AND THE TRADITIONAL LEGAL CULTURE	**55**
Chapter Four. The Meanings of Justice	57
Traditional views of the human personality	57

Injuries	61
Responses to injury	63

Chapter Five. Hierarchies of Liability—Channels of Negotiation — 69
- Hierarchy and social organization — 69
- Liability of the entourage to outsiders — 73
- Hierarchy and the negotiation of disputes — 75

Chapter Six. The Levels of Mediation — 79
- Non-official mediation — 81
- Mediation by village chief and *kamnan* — 84
- District level mediation — 90
- Police mediation — 93
- Mediation by private attorneys — 96
- Conclusion — 98

PART THREE. PRIVATE WRONGS IN THE COURT: THE INTERACTION OF TRADITIONAL AND MODERN ELEMENTS — 101

Chapter Seven. Civil and Private Criminal Suits — 103
- Private criminal suits and joint prosecutions — 104
- Civil suits for private wrongs — 111
- The joining of criminal and civil litigation — 114

Chapter Eight. The Interaction of Code and Custom in the Court — 118
- Standing and liability for injury — 118
- Providing a remedy — 126
- Effect of prior settlements — 131

Chapter Nine. Court as Mediator — 133
- The process of mediation — 134
- The "missing *phuyai*" — 137

PART FOUR. AREAS OF CONFLICT: NEW LAWS IN THE TRADITIONAL SOCIETY — 151

Chapter Ten. Rights in Land — 153
- Registration and rental of real property — 153
- Resolution of private wrongs involving land — 160

Chapter Eleven. Women and Men — 166
- Marital disputes — 171
- Other forms of conflict between men and women — 178

Contents

    Chapter Twelve. Private Citizens and Public Officials   186
        Government agents and the public   187
        Private wrongs between villagers and officials   190

CONCLUSION   205

BIBLIOGRAPHY   211

CASE DESCRIPTION INDEX   223

SUBJECT INDEX   225

LIST OF FIGURES

1. Two Symbols of Justice in Thailand — 4
2. The Ministry of Justice and the Thai Judiciary — 19
3. Major Administrative Levels and Chief Administrators in Provincial Thailand — 37
4. Negotiation Between Disputants in Separate Patron-Client Hierarchies — 77
5. Negotiation Between Disputants in the Same Patron-Client Hierarchy — 77
6. Levels of Mediation in Provincial Thailand — 80
7. Relationships Among Participants in Ox Cart Dispute — 121
8. Customary Compensation Procedure in Ox Cart Dispute — 122
9. Proper Legal Procedure in Ox Cart Dispute — 123
10. Schematic Map of Irrigation System in Tobacco Field Case — 138
11. Distribution of *Nai* Wong's Land Among His Descendants — 154
12. Distribution of *Nai* Wong's Land at Time of Dispute — 155
13. Role of Court and Administrative Officials in Obtaining Compromise Agreements in Two Land Disputes — 163

LIST OF TABLES

1. Literacy by Age Group in Chiangmai Province, 1970 — 42
2. Number of Criminal and Civil Cases Processed in Each Division of Chiangmai Provincial Court, 1965-1974 — 44
3. Number of Criminal and Civil Cases Processed in Provincial and Magistrates' Courts per 1,000 Population, 1965-1974 — 45
4. Cases Most Frequently Litigated in Provincial and Magistrates' Courts of Chiangmai in 1965, 1968, 1971, and 1974 — 48
5. Three Modes of Justice in the Chiangmai Trial Courts: Analysis of Selected Civil and Criminal Cases by Outcome — 51
6. Frequency of Litigation and Geographical Relationship of Litigants in Lawsuits Involving Private Wrongs — 143
7. Comparison of Female and Male Literacy by Age Group in Chiangmai Province, 1970 — 167
8. Frequency of Litigation of Private Wrongs by Sex of Litigant in Provincial and Magistrates' Courts of Chiangmai Province in 1965, 1968, 1971, and 1974 — 171

Acknowledgments

A number of people provided suggestions, criticism, and advice during the course of this study. I am particularly indebted to Frank Reynolds, M. B. Hooker, and Jane and Lucien Hanks for their invaluable support. I also owe special thanks to Mary Broadley Gomes, Nidhi Aeusrivongse, John K. Whitmore, Richard L. Abel, Eric H. Steele, and Marc Galanter for their help at various stages in the project.

My research was sponsored by a grant from the Foreign Area Fellowship Program of the Social Science Research Council. I wish to thank them as well as the University of Michigan Law School and the American Bar Foundation for their support.

In Thailand, this study was facilitated by the cooperation of the National Research Council of Thailand and the Royal Thai Ministry of Justice. In addition, a great many judges, lawyers, villagers, government officials, scholars, and personal friends contributed their time and efforts during our stay in Thailand. I wish to thank all of these individuals. I would also like to acknowledge the generous cooperation of three individuals who have served as Chief Judge of the Chiangmai Provincial Court: Justice Tanin Kraivixien, Judge Niwet Cumphong, and Judge Amphai Wichitwetchakan (Acting Chief Judge).

I am grateful to my Thai father, mother, and grandmother, not only for their personal kindness and generosity but also for the insights and suggestions they provided in the course of my research. I am indebted to my sister-in-law, *Khun* Kanyamas Saiprasert, who spent so much of her time helping to make our stay an enjoyable and productive one. I would also like to thank *Ajaan* Nakorn Wasuwat for his indispensable aid in conducting the research.

My own parents were an unfailing source of support, encouragement, shelter, companionship, and advice. As always, I am deeply grateful to them.

Jaruwan S. Engel, through her energy, her intelligence, her love, and her patience, helped to shape this study from beginning to end. Although she cannot be held accountable for mistakes I may have made in writing this book, anything that might be of value here owes its existence in large part to her.

Introduction

A DISCUSSION OF GENERAL THEMES

The establishment of a centralized provincial judiciary and the drafting of the modern Thai law codes were among the most important of the many reforms instituted under King Chulalongkorn at the turn of the twentieth century. Responding to the threat of aggression from the great colonial powers along Thailand's borders and the absence of strong central control over Thailand's own territory, the king and his advisers embarked upon a remarkable program of consolidation and change that helped to ensure Thai independence from external rule. As a result of these reforms, the entire structure of law and government in Thailand was dramatically revised. A new legal system was created, substituting a centralized judiciary and a national system of laws for a traditional legal structure governed largely by local practices and personnel. The transformation of Thai law raised fundamental questions concerning the concept of justice in Thailand and the procedures by which justice was to be achieved. These questions are still very much alive in Thai society, perhaps more urgent during the past decade than at any time since the reign of King Chulalongkorn. Yet the judicial system in its provincial setting, where the idealized legal structure meets the realities of traditional Thai life, has seldom been the subject of study or discussion. Indeed, the concept of justice itself—*khwam pen tham*—is generally treated as a monolithic and readily understood entity rather than a complex blend of classical Buddhism, village customary practices, and western legal and political theory.[1]

---

1. In transcribing Thai words, phrases, and names, I have followed the transcription system set forth in *The Nature and Development of the Thai Language* by *Phraya* Anuman Rajadhon (2d ed., Bangkok: Fine Arts Department, 1963), pp. 32-36, except that I have rendered the vowel "u'" as "ü." I have departed from this system in a few instances, where personal preferences (as in proper names) or popular usage (as in place names or in common terms such as "*baht*") have made an alternative spelling more appropriate. In passages quoted from other non-Thai sources I have, of course, retained their transcriptions rather than substituting the system adopted for this study.

The process of major social, political, and legal change has continued in Thailand for more than a century. Like other countries throughout the world, Thailand has looked to her legal system to guide these changes in directions her leaders have seen as desirable, to propel the society toward a goal they have perceived as "modernity." The transformation of Thai law is thus analogous in many respects to changes in other segments of Thai society, such as the educational system, the Buddhist clergy, the government and administrative bureaucracy, and the economic system. Each of these areas has received its share of scholarly attention, while the subject of Thai legal development has been all but ignored. The omission of Thai law from the literature of "modernization" is particularly striking because Thailand's leaders, from the time of King Chulalongkorn to the present, have regarded the legal system not merely as one of many elements that make up the machinery of modern society, but as the engine that drives the machinery and makes all the other parts work. The law has been used in Thailand as a favored means to change the entire social order, with an almost mystical faith that the promulgation of modern codes, statutes, and constitutions would somehow produce a modern Thailand.

These expectations have never been completely realized. It is true that the transformation of Thai law has provided a powerful symbol of modernity, enabling the central government to extend its power throughout the emerging nation-state, to face foreign powers with greater confidence and strength, and to effect certain changes in provincial Thai society. At the same time, however, the new Thai legal system has been strongly influenced—even subverted—by the persistence of customary patterns of justice in the Thai countryside. While the ruling elite has attempted to implement through legal change its own idealized conceptions of the "modern" state, local citizens and bureaucrats have often responded with a firm and determined insistence upon traditional values, traditional modes of behavior, and traditional concepts of what justice is and how it should be achieved.

In this study, then, while focusing upon the Chiangmai provincial court and its setting, I shall attempt to develop three major themes related to the patterns of change and development in the nation as a whole. The first theme involves the reception in Thailand of a new legal system based largely upon western models. Although the legal reforms were stimulated in large measure by foreign policy considerations, their impact upon Thai society has been extensive and profound. As indigenous patterns of indirect vassal relationships and semi-autonomous local rule gave way to new patterns of legal and political control, there emerged a new concept of the state itself, and a redefinition of the relationships between the state and the individual and between individual and individual. The new Thai law codes, both explicitly and implicitly, articulated a new and radically different view of the private citizen, the family, the social group, the administrative bureaucracy, and the nation as

Discussion of General Themes 3

a whole. These shifting relationships and the role played by the legal system in promoting such changes within the new Thai nation-state are encompassed in the first theme of this study.

The second theme involves the indigenous legal culture in provincial Thailand, the existing network of legal norms and procedures that confronted the new legal system as it spread outward from the capital. Thailand was and remains a non-litigious society. Among most Thais there is still a strong preference for mediation rather than direct confrontation and the adjudication of private disputes. Courts of law are generally avoided, and a low value is placed upon the resort to litigation. The neutral and independent judge, a legal specialist who takes testimony, hears oral arguments, and applies law to the facts, was a figure unfamiliar to most Thais before the establishment of the modern judicial system. Customary procedures for handling disputes have tended to conform to traditional religious and philosophical attitudes towards injuries and private wrongs. Such attitudes and procedures continue to influence the behavior of disputants in provincial Thailand, both in and out of court. Traditional social hierarchies have provided the framework in which disputes are negotiated and liability distributed. Indigenous legal norms are still familiar and congenial to persons living in provincial Thailand, and they exert a strong influence upon the formal and informal handling of legal conflict at all levels of Thai society.

The third theme involves the interaction between the new law codes and the norms and customs that prevailed in provincial Thai society before the reforms were instituted. As the laws and the judicial system penetrated outward from the capital, they came to dominate and destroy many of the traditional institutions that had formerly regulated the handling of disputes. New procedures were established, new rights and duties were articulated, new interests and obligations were created, and new definitions of justice were announced. At the same time, however, local customs began to dictate the ways in which the formal law codes were used and the goals toward which the litigants applied themselves. Codified norms were implicitly modified to conform to customary practices. Formalized procedures were manipulated to pursue informal traditional goals. This interplay between code and custom in a changing social order is the real story of the "modernization" of Thai law. The modern Thai legal system is in practice an amalgam of traditional norms and codified rules of law. Just as the advent of modern Thai law has gradually promoted changes in provincial Thai society, the administration of the law has itself been shaped by indigenous customs. In striking ways, many traditional patterns of justice have established themselves within the very forum designed to transform the adjudication of wrongs in provincial Thailand.

The interaction between traditional Thai legal culture and the new theories of law formulated at the turn of the century can be illustrated by two Thai seals, symbols of justice before and after the transformation of Thai law (figure 1). The first seal was used before the reign of King Chulalongkorn by the *müang* minister, who was responsible for criminal matters and most lawsuits administered in the Thai capital. The seal depicts *Phraya* Yommarat mounted on a lion. Like the royal law codes in use at that time, the first seal reflects the strong influence of Indian traditions upon Thai society. In classical Hindu-Buddhist cosmology, *Phraya* Yommarat is Yama, the god of death and ruler of the underworld. Yama has always been associated with justice.

Seal 1:
Phraya Yommarat
mounted on a lion

Seal 2:
The scales of justice
Source: *Phraya* Anuman Rajadhon (1950)

Figure 1. Two Symbols of Justice in Thailand

Indeed, *thamma (dharma)* is said to be another name for the god of death: he personifies the concept of justice itself (*Phraya* Anuman Rajadhon, 1950:29). When humans die, they appear before the throne of Yama and are forced to account for the merit and demerit they have accumulated through their existence:

> [T]he Yama King then asks that person, "What merit or evil deeds have you done? Quickly now, think back and speak the truth!" At that time the four *devatā* [gods, angels] who prepare a record of the merit and evil deeds which people have done are present, and hold that record in their hands. In the case of a person who has made merit, the *devatā* write the name of that person on a bright golden tablet. The *devatā* raise this tablet on their heads to present it to the Yama King. The Yama King raises the tablet to his head, expresses his praise, and rejoices with them; and then he places it on a golden table decorated with the seven gems which have rays and are beautiful and bright. As for those who have committed evil deeds, the *devatā* put the record on

a tablet made of dog skin, and then put it aside. (Mani and Frank Reynolds, 1978)

Yama proceeds with his interrogation to determine the good and evil deeds that each individual has performed. Those who have attained merit are given the power to recall and recite each meritorious act they have performed. Those who have done evil are struck dumb, and the *devatā* must read their transgressions aloud from the dog-skin tablets on which they are recorded. Justice is a matter of merit and demerit, not in any isolated act but in the aggregate. If Yama determines that an individual's accumulation of merit exceeds his demerit, then he rewards that person by sending him to one of the celestial abodes where he will be served by female *devatā*, dine on heavenly foods, and enjoy happiness beyond description. If, however, evil acts preponderate, then Yama condemns the individual to excruciating torture and agony until the effect of the misdeeds has been exhausted.

According to this emblem, then, Thai justice is rooted in religious cosmology derived from Indian models. Wrongdoing is more than a violation of man-made laws: it is implicated in the cosmic process itself. Justice is thus conceived in cosmic terms, effected ultimately by a god in human form. The essence of justice is not the fairness of its procedures in sifting through evidence of particular wrongs but rather the aptness of its final judgments as to the total value of an individual's existence.

The second seal, like the modern administration of justice in Thailand, is a blend of the modern and the traditional. The seal was adopted in 1913 as the official symbol of the newly established Ministry of Justice and is still in use at the present time. Justice in this seal has become abstract, impersonal, and secular. The god-like figure of Yama has been replaced by the scales of justice, implying a rationalized weighing of evidence to decide lawsuits rather than an invocation of the cosmic concept of merit and demerit recorded on the tablets of angels. The essence of justice now lies in the balancing of equities between two disputants in specific cases, rather than a determination of each individual's accumulation of merit and demerit over the course of his existence. The scales are suspended, moreover, upon the royal sword of victory (*phra saeng khan*), suggesting that the decisions of impartial judges are now supported by the power of the state rather than the god of death.

The second symbol of justice is western and not Indian in origin. It suggests a new emphasis upon judicial procedures rather than cosmic consequences, upon particularized evidentiary questions rather than generalized questions of individual worth, upon the human process of ascertaining truth rather than the divine process of pronouncing guilt for sins which are finally self-evident. Even in this second seal, however, there is a blending of modern and traditional iconography that corresponds nicely to the blending of modern and traditional elements in the system of Thai justice. The sword of victory itself is part of the traditional Thai regalia, a sacred symbol of royal legitimacy and power with origins in Khmer and Indian ritual (Wales, 1931:98-99).

It stands upon a two-level offering tray (*phan sǫng chan*) of the kind that is used to support special sacred objects associated with the king or the Buddhist religion. In short, the impersonal and rationalized conception of modern justice symbolized by the second seal has retained a sacred aura. Justice is founded upon the cosmic power of the righteous ruler as well as the secular power of the new nation-state. This blending of the old and the new, the traditional and the modern, the western and the Indian, into a formula uniquely Thai provides a fitting emblem for the contemporary concepts of Thai justice that are the subject of this study.

A NOTE ON THE RESEARCH

I have approached this study with the conviction that the role of the Thai provincial court is best understood in the context of provincial Thai society and culture as a whole. A narrow view of litigation and court records without reference to the broader environment in which the lawsuits arise could produce a picture of Thai justice unrelated to the realities of Thai life. My primary goal from the beginning has been a study of the provincial court itself and the actual functioning of the centralized Thai legal system. It became clear very quickly, however, that I could not pursue this goal productively unless I attempted to view the formal Thai juridical institutions in relation to the traditional setting in which they were established. While the core of my research, therefore, has been the information I gathered in the Chiangmai provincial court, I have also searched among a number of other sources for materials and insights that would permit a broader consideration of Thai provincial justice.

Research for this study was conducted both in the United States and in Thailand. In an earlier study of official Thai enactments from 1868 to 1910, I attempted to describe the major legislative accomplishments of King Chulalongkorn which marked the beginning of the modern period of Thai law. In this study I have tried to move on to consider some of the consequences of those legal reforms and some of the ways in which the modern legal system itself has interacted with local systems of justice in the Thai countryside.

My research in Thailand extended over an eight-month period in 1975, most of which was spent in the northern province of Chiangmai. Among the several different data sources upon which I relied, the most important were the court records themselves, dating from 1965 to 1974. I used two types of court documents: the court registers and the individual case files. The court registers provided a broad quantitative overview of the caseflow that was processed in the Chiangmai court, while the case files permitted a detailed qualitative examination of particular issues and patterns of litigation.

The court registers listed in chronological order every case that had passed through the provincial and magistrates' courts over the ten-year period, and provided the names of the litigants, the dates of filing, the dates of all hearings and orders of the court, the subject matter of each case, the final outcome, and the names of the judge or judges involved. I recorded the subject matter entry for all cases processed over the ten-year period, and in addition I recorded the complete register entry for every sixth civil case, every twentieth criminal case, and for all cases involving the litigation of private wrongs. The individual case files, on the other hand, contained all papers submitted by both parties in the course of the litigation, together with all documents issued by the court in connection with the case, hand-written transcriptions of all witness testimony, orders and judgments of the court, documents related to appeals, and documents related to enforcement proceedings. I read 222 such case files, selected for the most part on the basis of their subject matter from the ten-year court registers of the provincial court, with primary emphasis on cases involving private wrongs.

Court documents of this kind must be used with some care, for the facts presented in connection with the lawsuits themselves may provide a partial or a seriously distorted view of the legal problems as they actually occurred. In my own research, I took certain steps to reduce the chance that distortions from the case records would lead to erroneous conclusions about provincial justice in Thailand. The following guidelines were observed in dealing with all court documents: (1) Case records were used primarily to study the behavior of the parties in court, to trace legal strategies and formal legal actions, rather than to determine that particular allegations of fact were true or false or an accurate reflection of the actual conflict between the parties. (2) Case records were also consulted when they mentioned the existence of prior attempts at mediation at official levels lower than the court itself. Distortion was not a serious concern here, since documents and admissions by the opposing party verified in most cases that such attempts had actually occurred, and I was interested usually in the fact of the occurrence more than its precise content. (3) In certain cases, however, I was interested in the details of prior negotiations and also in the details of the original conflict that resulted in litigation. In such cases I relied upon facts acknowledged in the testimony of both of the opposing parties. Any facts alleged by one party but disputed, or not stipulated, by the opposing party were either discarded or, if included in this study, have been clearly labeled as the version of one of the disputants only.

In order to discover what changes, if any, occurred in the nature of the legal matter as it passed through the various levels of mediation and adjudication, I frequently observed judicial proceedings in person, and I interviewed litigants, village chiefs, attorneys, and judges. I was able to trace some cases through the entire process of litigation. From these cases I concluded that significant changes in the original legal matter were generally less frequent in the area of private wrongs brought by the aggrieved parties and their lawyers—such cases being the primary subject of this study—than in other areas such as public prosecutions for criminal offenses, which were channeled through the provincial prosecutor's office, the police, and other local authorities. It was difficult to follow such cases from beginning to end, however, because they tended to be spread out over a period of many months or years. Also, after reading an interesting case file, it was difficult to seek out the litigants for an interview. Reliable personal contacts had first to be made. Often the litigation was considered scandalous by the participants, and such interviews would have been regarded as an unwelcome intrusion in a matter that was best forgotten. Nevertheless, when proper introductions had been arranged, I was able to interview a few village litigants, who were then willing to discuss with me the background of their lawsuit and to describe their impressions of the judicial process in general.

I felt that it was essential to examine the process of handling private wrongs at levels other than that of the provincial court itself. I had neither the time nor the resources to make an exhaustive study of this interesting subject on my own. I decided, therefore, to follow a two-pronged approach in my research. On the one hand, I conducted intensive interviews with a relatively small number of officials at all levels of the local administration, including village leaders, district-level officers, provincial administrators, and ministry officials. On the other hand, I relied heavily upon the relevant data gathered by other researchers, including Wijeyewardene, Moerman, Jane and Lucien Hanks, Kingshill, Klausner, Neher, Phillips, and others. From my own interviews, I gathered a great deal of interesting material, which included detailed accounts of a number of disputes that local officials had mediated successfully. I was then able to compare these case histories to the lawsuits that were actually taken to the provincial court. In addition, I was able to learn at first hand about the attitudes of villagers and other laypeople toward conflict and the formal and informal legal systems available to them. My own research in this area was then supplemented by the studies of other scholars, primarily in north and central Thailand. Although little work has been done specifically on the subject of legal conflict and traditional law in Thai society, I did find descriptions of a number of village-level "cases" in the literature and, equally important, discussions of the values, attitudes, and beliefs regarding conflict and litigation. Historical materials were consulted for the the same purpose, including accounts of Thai society by foreign vistors over the centuries and studies by modern historians insofar as they proved relevant. Conversations with lawyers and judges in Chiangmai, some retired and some still active, also proved invaluable in gaining an understanding of the role that the provincial judiciary plays in the local setting.

By relying upon a variety of sources, rather than a single isolated set of data, I have tried to form a reasonably reliable picture of the litigation of private wrongs in a Thai provincial court. What emerges is an image of a complex institution performing several different functions at the same time, linked in many interesting ways to the traditional society in which it was established and which it was designed in part to change. Although litigation is not a preferred procedure in Thai society, it is consistently used by certain segments of the population each year. The way in which it is used, the effect of traditional practices upon litigation, and the effect of litigation upon the society as a whole will be explored further in the study that follows.

Part One
Court, Ministry, and Province: The Setting

> *In the future, after the implementation of the Law of the Provincial Courts, the duties of government officials in the provinces shall be distributed among two clearly differentiated branches: the judicial and the executive.*
>
> *The responsibilities of the judiciary shall include the hearing and deciding of cases, the rendering of verdicts, and the imposition of punishments according to the provisions of the law. This is what is known as the judicial function. It shall be independent of the royal commissioner and the provincial governor and council, who have no duties as judges in any court whatsoever. . . . [They] are not judges but have purely executive responsibilities and may not order the judges to decide matters of law or to conduct judicial proceedings according to their own wishes. Their authority shall be limited to administrative matters only.*
>
> Prince Damrong Rachanupab
> *Explanation of the Establishment of the Provincial Courts (1896)*[1]

---

1. Sutcharit Thawǫnsuk (1964:57). All translations from Thai in this study are my own, except where a listing in the Bibliography indicates that the work in question provides its own English translation.

Chapter One
The Court and the Ministry of Justice

A PORTRAIT OF THE CHIANGMAI COURT

The Chiangmai courthouse is a large square building set in a grassy yard surrounded by a white fence. The neoclassical facade looks directly into the sun and is avoided by the staff and clients of the court. On either side of the building stand plumeria and flame trees, scattering their white and orange blossoms over a broad shaded area. The plumeria blossoms, associated by Thai people with sadness and death, give off a sweet fragrance which pervades the courthouse.

The rear of the courthouse is the scene of real activity. An open veranda provides access to the central administrative offices where a half-dozen clerks, under the direction of the registrar, transact business with those who come to use the court. The veranda is crowded with people: litigants, their friends and relatives, and their attorneys. Farther to the rear is a parking shed for the automobiles of the judges. At one end of the shed is a lockup in which ten or twelve criminal defendants await proceedings. The prisoners talk through the bars to those who have accompanied them from home. The group clustered around the cell consists mostly of country people in faded sarongs. There are two or three Buddhist priests in orange robes. A handful of curious students wearing the uniform of a nearby high school look on from the periphery of the crowd. A push-cart parked nearby sells noodles to the visitors and staff of the court, while a competitor hawks fresh fruit: pineapple slices, pickled guavas, and sour unripe mangoes served with sugar, salt, and ground chili peppers. In the shade a thin pedicab driver in shorts and sneakers sleeps with his feet propped up on his bicycle seat.

From a window on the second floor a policeman in khaki uniform calls down to the guard at the lockup. The guard opens the door of the cell and a young man emerges. He has dark skin, wears shorts and no shoes, and is in leg-irons. A policeman accompanies him up the old wooden staircase in the rear of the courthouse. The officer is a fat, middle-aged man, wearing a gun at his hip, speaking in a friendly manner to the prisoner. The leg-irons make a clinking sound as the two men walk, heavy black shoes and bare feet on the worn steps. At the head of the stairs they stop and the prisoner is directed into one of several courtrooms on the second floor. There he sits and waits for the judge.

The courtroom is a large rectangle with a bare wood floor and five double rows of benches for spectators. At one end is the judge's rostrum. Directly below and in front of the rostrum is a table where a clerk sits, working with a stack of case records and official papers. To the left is the defendant's bench and to the right the plaintiff's. In the middle, facing the rostrum, is the witness stand. In this room the judge is the ruler, and he is identified both explicitly and implicitly with the king. It is known that when the judge dispenses justice he speaks in the name of the king. The judge's seat is called the *banlang*, or throne, the same word that is used for the throne of the king. He is elevated high above the other participants, on a massive wooden structure, aloof and authoritative. On the wall behind him is a large framed photograph of Thailand's king. Directly overhead rotates the only fan in the room.

Conspicuous signs posted at the door to the judges' chambers forbid entry without permission. From this door the judge walks briskly into the hallway, smiling but not stopping to speak to persons with whom he chatted casually not long before. He wears a suit and tie underneath a black judicial robe with a white sash over his left shoulder. The attorneys are dressed in the same way. The judge enters the courtroom through a separate door reserved for his use. As he seats himself he begins to talk informally with the defendant. He discusses the charges and reminds the defendant that if he chooses to confess, the law will permit the judge to reduce his punishment by half, but if he refuses to do so then the judge will be unable to help him. His manner is stern but not harsh. The young man answers quietly in monosyllables. No immediate decision is urged, and the proceedings begin.

The prosecutor calls as his witness the elderly storekeeper whom the young man is alleged to have robbed. He walks hesitantly to the witness stand where the clerk meets him to administer the oath. Raising his hands to *wai*, the traditional gesture of respect, the witness repeats the oath phrase by phrase:

> I swear before the shrine of Doi Suthep and all sacred things that I will testify in this court honestly according to what I know and have seen. If I should testify falsely, may I die within three days or seven days. If I should testify truthfully, may I receive happiness and prosperity.

Completing the oath, he touches his hands to his forehead.

The judge begins by asking the witness his name, address, age, profession, and relationship to the defendant. The judge writes this information on a standard form used to record the testimony of the witness. Then the prosecutor leads the witness through his testimony. After each answer, the prosecutor pauses while the judge transcribes the response by hand. When the answer is not sufficiently explicit, the judge asks for a clarification or suggests an alternative phrasing. If the witness agrees, the judge writes down the better answer. At one point the judge takes over the questioning entirely, pursuing a matter that particularly interests him—the color of the defendant's shirt, the exact amount of cash in the bag. When the direct questioning is concluded, the defense is given an opportunity for cross-examination. The questions are brief, however, and have little effect upon the witness's account.

The judge then reads aloud what he has transcribed: a practically verbatim record of the witness's answers omitting only the questions to which he was responding. Both sides indicate their approval, and the judge hands the transcript to the prosecutor to be signed by his witness and by the defense attorney. Everyone in the courtroom stands as the judge reads what he has written on a second document: proceedings will be resumed in one month when the defense will present its case. The judge gathers his papers together and leaves the courtroom. The defense attorney goes to the back of the room and talks briefly with the parents of his client. The fat policeman enters the room and directs the prisoner back down the stairs. With a clinking of leg-irons, he rejoins the other prisoners in the lockup.

Late in the afternoon, all the prisoners are released from the cell and are formed into a double line behind the courthouse. They squat on their haunches, talking among themselves, watching their onlookers. Most of the prisoners are barefoot, dressed in tattered shorts and soiled shirts. Near the front of the line, however, one large man is conspicuous because he is wearing a suit, a white shirt and tie, and well-shined shoes. He wears his handcuffs with embarrassment, holding his hands awkwardly in front of him. The prisoners are ordered to stand. Flanked by police, they walk beneath the shade trees into the bright street, where motorcycles and trucks are halted to let them pass. Two blocks away a gate in the high wall of the provincial prison opens and the procession moves slowly inside.

COURT AND MINISTRY

The Chiangmai court is part of a national system of provincial courts controlled from Bangkok by the Ministry of Justice. Outside the capital itself, the country is divided into nine judicial regions, each under the administrative authority of a Chief Justice *(athibǫdi phuphiphaksa phak)*. Within these nine regions, eighty-three provincial courts carry on their functions, together with twenty magistrates' courts for the adjudication of minor claims and petty offenses.[2] Each court operates under the supervision of a Chief Judge

---

2. In general, the magistrates' court may try and adjudicate civil cases involving 2,000 *baht* or less and criminal cases "where the maximum punishment provided by law does

(*phuphiphaksa huana san*). In Chiangmai and in two other provinces—Songkhla and Nakhon Ratchasima—juvenile courts have also been established with separate staffs of judges and with associated Observation and Protection Centers that participate in the handling of juvenile offenders. In June of 1975, Thailand's first "mobile courts" began operations in Fang and Mae Ai districts of Chiangmai province, staffed by personnel of the central Chiangmai court but holding proceedings in the outlying areas. This program was to be expanded to other provinces throughout the country.

In Bangkok the courts of first instance include a Civil Court and a Criminal Court, each supervised by a Chief Justice (*athibǫdi phuphiphaksa*). There are also three magistrates' courts and a Central Juvenile Court with an associated Central Observation and Protection Center. In addition, Bangkok is the site of the Court of Appeals and the Supreme Court of Thailand (*Dika* Court), which review proceedings in the courts of first instance throughout the country.

The Public Prosecution Department belongs to the Ministry of Interior, rather than the Ministry of Justice, but is closely tied to the judicial system because of its responsibility to investigate and prosecute violations of Thailand's penal laws. In all provinces outside the capital, staffs of prosecuting attorneys, under the direction of a Chief Provincial Prosecutor, are assigned to the provincial courts, the magistrates' courts,[3] the juvenile courts, and the mobile courts. The provincial prosecutors may also defend government officials accused of wrongdoing in the course of their official duties.

Thai judges, who preside in the courts of law and who fill certain positions in the Ministry of Justice as well, are selected by rigorous competitive examination from qualified attorneys who have already been admitted to the bar. For purposes of promotion and salary, all judges are grouped into nine different ranks:

1. President of the Supreme Court
2. Chief Justice of the Court of Appeals; Vice-President of the Supreme Court
3. Senior Judge of the Supreme Court; Deputy Chief Justice of the Court of Appeals; Chief Justice of the Civil Court; Chief Justice of the Criminal Court
4. Judge of the Supreme Court; Deputy Chief Justice of the Civil Court; Deputy Chief Justice of the Criminal Court; Chief Justice of the Central Juvenile Court; Chief Justice of the Region

---

not exceed three years imprisonment or six thousand *baht* fine, or both, provided that no punishment exceeding six months imprisonment or two thousand *baht* fine, or both imprisonment and fine, both or any of which exceeds the said rate, may be inflicted." Law for the Organization of the Courts of Justice, 1934 [*Phrathammanun san yuttitham, B.E. 2477*], Sections 22 and 15.

3. Responsibility for prosecuting criminal cases in the magistrates' courts was transferred from the Police Department to the Prosecutor's Office by royal edict on October 18, 1974.

5. Senior Judge of the Court of Appeals

6. Judge of the Court of Appeals; Senior Judge of the Civil Court; Senior Judge of the Criminal Court

7. Judge of the Civil Court; Judge of the Criminal Court; Judge of the Central Juvenile Court; Chief Judge of a Provincial Court

8. Judges in the courts of first instance and others holding the title of Judge

9. Judge-trainee[4]

Despite their prestige and power at the local level, the provincial judges—like many other provincial officials—tend to hold positions of inferior status in the over-all system. The Chief Judge of the Provincial Court is on a level equal to ordinary judges assigned to the Bangkok trial courts, and his staff judges at the provincial level outrank only the fledgling judge-trainees.

All matters involving the "appointment, promotion, transfer and removal of judges" must be approved by the king based upon the recommendation of the Judicial Service Commission (Thailand Supreme Court, 1969:378). The Commission stands between the executive branch—specifically, the Ministries of Justice and Interior—and the judiciary. In this position it acts as a shield for the judiciary, as a "Guardian Angel" in the words of a former President of the Supreme Court, assuring judicial independence from direct executive control (Prakob Hutasingh in Thailand Supreme Court, 1969:168). The Judicial Service Commission is composed of twelve persons. Four members hold their position *ex officio:* the President of the Supreme Court, who presides over the Commission; the Deputy Minister of Justice; the Chief Justice of the Court of Appeals; and the Vice-President of the Supreme Court. Four members are elected by the country's judicial officials from among judges of the third rank. The four remaining members, also elected by the judicial officials, are retired judges of all ranks. Elected members serve for terms of two years.[5]

The offices of the Ministry of Justice itself are situated under the same roof as the central Bangkok courts, facing the Phramane Grounds and the gates of the Temple of the Emerald Buddha. The Minister of Justice now has

---

4. This ranking system is set forth in the Royal Edict Concerning Regulations for Judicial Officials, 1954 [*Phraratchabanyat rabiap kharatchakan fai tulakan, B.E. 2497*], Section 12. English translations are those recommended by the Ministry of Justice. The title "Senior Judge" refers to individuals in charge of panels of judges within the Supreme Court, the Court of Appeals, and the Civil and Criminal courts. Such panels have the power to render verdicts in most cases. "Others holding the title of Judge" includes judges performing technical or research functions. "Judge-trainee" refers to persons who have passed the competitive examination for judges and are in training before being assigned to a judicial post.

5. Royal Edict Concerning Regulations for Judicial Officials, 1954 [*Phraratchabanyat rabiap kharatchakan fai tulakan, B.E. 2497*], Sections 29 and 30. If more than one person holds the rank of Vice-President of the Supreme Court, the individual with greater seniority shall serve on the Judicial Service Commission *ex officio*. The other individual or individuals holding the same rank may also serve on the Commission if elected.

authority over three primary administrative units: the Office of the Under-Secretary of State for Justice, the Office of Judicial Affairs, and the Legal Execution Department. The first of these units, the Office of the Under-Secretary of State for Justice, handles matters involving correspondence and public relations, personnel, the preservation of important documents, and financial matters for the courts and ministry. The Office of Judicial Affairs administers technical matters such as statistics and research, training programs and seminars, and is also in charge of the Secretariat of the Judicial Service Commission. The third administrative unit under the Minister of Justice is the Legal Execution Department. This department handles various matters related to the seizure, attachment, and disposition of property under the control of courts throughout the country, as well as the deposit of property with the courts, related financial matters, and other matters related to criminal, civil, and bankruptcy proceedings.

The structure of the Ministry of Justice and the Thai judicial system is depicted in figure 2.

PROVINCIAL THAI JUSTICE BEFORE THE MINISTRY OF JUSTICE

Thailand's system of provincial courts administered directly from Bangkok dates back only to the first decade of the twentieth century. Under the political leadership of King Chulalongkorn, Thailand extricated herself at that time from the threat of colonization by transforming her entire system of government. As pressures increased from the English in Burma and Malaya and from the French in Indochina, the king hastened to recodify the laws and to create a centralized judiciary that was the keystone for his new administrative system. The king was assisted in this task by his brothers and sons, most notably Prince Damrong Rachanupab and Prince Ratburi Direkrit, and by a staff of foreign legal advisers from several different countries including Belgium, the United States, Japan, and England (Saint-Hubert, 1965; Thamsook Numnonda, 1974; Masao, 1908). The king's explicit goals were to strengthen his rule throughout the entire country, to eliminate the extra-territorial jurisdiction of the "international courts," to provide fairness and predictability for the people in their dealings with the Thai judiciary, and to bring progress and prosperity to the country by adopting selectively the best practices of the world's most "advanced" countries (Engel, 1975).

Before King Chulalongkorn initiated his program of reform and centralization, the provincial Thai legal system featured no purely adjudicative mode of procedure as it was later to be defined: an impartial legal specialist making evidentiary findings and applying a set of fixed rules to them. There was no judge figure other than the local rulers themselves to preside over judicial hearings. Although we have only scant historical evidence of the administration of justice outside the Thai capital, there is strong reason to believe that the formal law texts promulgated by earlier Thai kings were not strictly

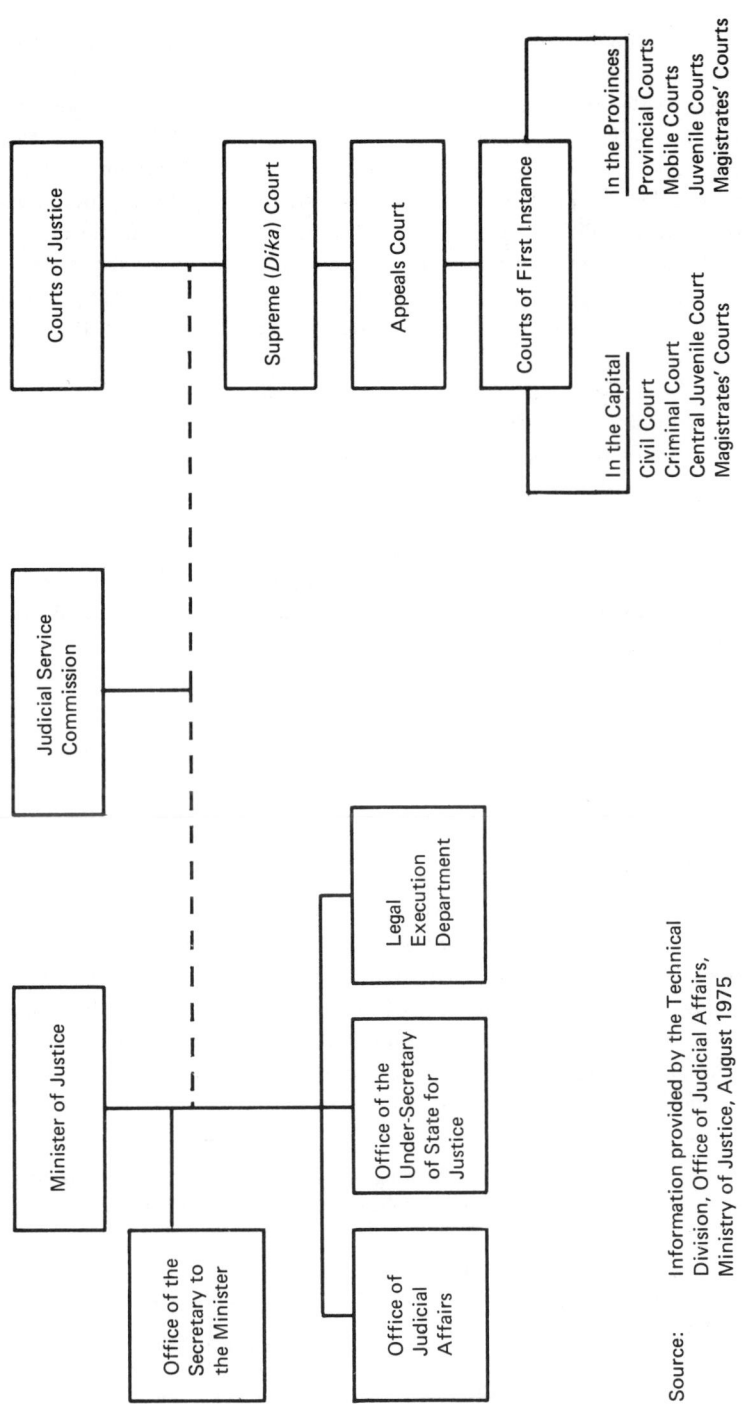

Source: Information provided by the Technical Division, Office of Judicial Affairs, Ministry of Justice, August 1975

Figure 2. The Ministry of Justice and the Thai Judiciary

observed by, or even familar to, many persons living in the provinces.[6] From accounts by foreign observers, by aged Thai villagers, and from other historical sources including the traditional law codes themselves, it is possible to identify at least four methods for handling legal conflicts in provincial Thailand before the reforms of King Chulalongkorn: ordeal and oath, witchcraft proceedings, mediation by elders or persons of high status, and formal judicial proceedings conducted by local political rulers. These four methods were sometimes used independently and were sometimes used in combination or in sequence. A brief account of each procedure will help to set the scene for a description of the new Thai judicial system that was extended into the provinces in the early twentieth century.

Procedure by ordeal and oath drew its legitimacy from an equation of wrongdoing with sin rather than with crime or tort (cf. Derrett, 1968:77 and 182-87). The sinner would suffer pain or death when he underwent an ordeal, was tortured, or falsely swore a sacred oath, but the pure would suffer no injury. The merits of the case were decided with reference to the moral purity of the disputants rather than the rationality of their evidence. Many types of ordeals appear to have been used in Thailand, some of which resemble those appearing elsewhere in Southeast Asia, in India, and in our own Anglo-American past. A fire-walking ceremony was one way to separate the innocent from the guilty. Simon de La Loubère, French special envoy to the court of King Narai in 1687, provides an early description of this procedure:

> In the Proof of Fire they erect a Pile of Faggots in a Ditch, in such a manner that the surface of the Pile be level with the edge of the Ditch. This Pile is five fathoms long, and one broad. Both the parties do walk with their naked Feet from one end to the other, and he that has not the sole of his Feet hurt gains his Suit. (La Loubère, 1969:86)

La Loubère was perceptive enough to see the empirical underpinnings of this religious method of proof. Since a person was far more likely to be burned by rushing quickly across the coals than by walking calmly and steadily upon them, the individual who was confident of his own moral purity may have been injured less often than the individual who was in the wrong and feared the results of the ordeal.[7] An ordeal involving the submersion of the disputants in a stream or a pond was also described in the traditional law texts as well as by

---

6. When King Chulalongkorn's ancestor, King Rama I, founded the Čhakkri Dynasty in Bangkok, he ordered the compilation and revision of all existing legal materials from the Ayutthaya period. The project was completed in 1805. Known as The Law of the Three Seals, this legal code survived largely intact until the major reforms of King Chulalongkorn a century later. The Law of the Three Seals, as amended over the years, contained many provisions that, in theory, controlled the administration of justice even in the outlying provincial areas.

7. "But as they are accustomed to go with naked Feet, and that they have the sole of the Foot hard like Horn, they say that it is very common that the Fire spares them, provided they rest the Foot upon the Coals: for the way to burn themselves is to go quick and lightly" (La Loubère, 1969:86).

foreign visitors.[8] Again, it may have been sensed that shortness of breath would be more likely among persons nervously aware of their own moral guilt than among those confident of their moral purity. The individual who came to the surface first may, in some cases at least, have been the party who knew himself to be in the wrong. Other ordeals involved eating or drinking consecrated food or liquid, the use of pills and emetics, dipping the hand in molten metals or boiling oil, and the swearing of sacred oaths of innocence.[9] Disputants in modern Thailand will still challenge one another to swear an oath on certain occasions. Where the power of such oaths is regarded with fear, it is not unusual for one party to decline the challenge, preferring to suffer temporary embarrassment rather than some more serious and long-lasting consequence (Klausner, 1974:47-48).[10] There is evidence that oaths and ordeals were used in earlier times at the highest levels of provincial proceedings, sometimes supervised by officials of the local government council.

Whereas the ordeal equated wrongdoing with sin, witchcraft proceedings were based upon a concept of wrongdoing as evil magic, as sorcery, or as possession by malign spirits. Wrongs that befell individuals or entire communities were often attributed to magical substances eaten or inhaled by the victim (*Phraya* Anuman Rajadhon, 1968:137-51; Wood, 1965:50), to evil spirits inhabiting the bodies of fellow villagers, or to wrongful acts whose origins could be ascertained by persons learned in the arts of divination. Witchcraft proceedings usually occurred on a less official level than oaths and ordeals, although the subject matter was clearly appropriate for formal proceedings if this should prove necessary. When the wrongdoer was identified by those skilled in the magic arts, sometimes with the help of information obtained from the community or the victim, his wrongful act was countered by magic, by exorcism, or by expulsion from the community. Charges of witchcraft were noted with special frequency in northern Thailand by Christian missionaries who found exiled witches especially amenable to their teachings. Exile was not always required, however, if the witch agreed to submit to an exorcism rite as the price for remaining in the community:

My first son died at the age of seventeen because a witch ate him.

---

8. See La Loubère (87); Gerini (1895:419 and 421-24); Hallett (1890:260). Prani Sirithon Na Phatthalung (1963: vol. 2, 218-20) describes a dispute between two members of the Chiangmai nobility which was decided by a water submersion ordeal in 1881. The results were later disallowed because both sides had hired substitutes and because the loser had submerged himself before the winner, placing him at a disadvantage in the contest.

9. See Gerini (1895:156-58 and 160-62); van Vliet (1910:70-71); La Loubère (1969:86-87).

10. The modern judicial oath, which I have quoted on page 14, is a close relative of the oaths used on such occasions. I was told in Chiangmai that, until recently, the administering of such oaths in court was regarded as a very serious matter, and it was not unusual for one side to pay the clerks a few extra *baht* in order to have them administer a particularly strong version of the oath to the witnesses of the adversary.

He had fallen in love with a girl in this village. People believed that
devils were staying with this girl. When my son broke his word to this
girl, she was very angry and sent the worst devils to kill him. He got
suddenly sick and died the same day. Nobody dared to touch this girl
because they were afraid of her until a shaman came from another
village to drive the devils away from the girl, enclose them in a pot,
and throw them into the Mae Ping River. This girl is still living in Ku
Daeng at the present time, but I do not wish to mention her name.
(Kingshill, 1960:287-88)[11]

Village opinion was easily mobilized against the girl in this case, for the victim's father was village headman. The accused witch was forced to choose between exorcism and exile:

The woman did not like to have the ceremony held, but she had to
submit since it was the will of the majority of the villagers. Otherwise,
she would have had to leave the village, which would have made it
difficult for her to find a new place to live. (288)[12]

A third method to deal with disputes or wrongful behavior was negotiation and mediation by a *phuyai,* a "big person" with sufficient status and authority to command the respect of both parties to the dispute. I shall discuss this procedure in its modern form later in this study. Traditional Thai society, with its formal structure of patron-client relationships, was ideally suited for the mediation of private grievances, and this procedure was probably employed more frequently than any other. The complex hierarchical organization of the entire population by law meant that every individual had above him one or several persons of superior status to whom he owed his services and his respect. In return, such persons were expected to offer protection and security of various kinds. One aspect of the *phuyai*'s role was to intercede with government officials on behalf of his underlings, to settle disputes among persons under his protection, and, if necessary, to institute formal legal proceedings for them (Akin Rabibhadana, 1969:83-84). The organization of pre-Chulalongkorn Thai society thus provided the pattern and the necessary authority figure for resolving most conflicts at the local level.

A fourth method for handling legal conflicts was the formal administrative procedure conducted by the local ruler and his council. This procedure was based upon a concept of wrongdoing as an affront to the authority of the

---

11. Kingshill interviewed the narrator of this incident when she was 73 years old in 1953 or 1954. If we assume that she was approximately 20-25 years of age when her first son was born, then the incident can be dated roughly during the years 1917-22, the period when the modern judicial system was first beginning to function in Chiangmai.

12. See also Hallett (1890: 106-108), for a description of northern Thai witchcraft proceedings. Tambiah observes that in contemporary northeastern Thailand there sometimes occurs a "sudden wave of possessions" in which the victims all name the same malefactor. In such cases, which are not common, the wrongdoer may be forced out of the community by threats or even by stoning (1970:332).

ruler, as a political problem to be resolved by the same administrative personnel who governed the province. The decision in a particular lawsuit was not merely a judgment upon the merits of the case but a means of political control by the governor. The royal law texts directed that different members of the provincial council handle different types of lawsuits.[13] These suits, brought in many cases by the patron of the aggrieved party, were presented orally to the proper official, who recorded them in written form. With the approval of the governor, this official would take the depositions of interested persons and would call both parties to attempt a conciliation (La Loubère, 1969:86; Bowring, 1969:176). La Loubère states that the parties were "summon'd three times, more for fashions sake, than with a sincere intention of procuring the accommodation" (86). If no agreement could be reached, the written material would be reviewed at a meeting of the provincial council, and opinions of the individual councilors would be solicited. The hearing examiner by that time had probably reached his own opinion on the merits of the lawsuit, perhaps with the assistance of ordeals or torture of both disputants. After the council meeting, the case was presented to the governor for discussion and decision. From beginning to end, this procedure was characterized by an emphasis upon documentation, a minimum of oral confrontation, and a method of decision making similar in many respects to that employed in handling other administrative matters.

The administrative mode of dispute processing derived in part from Indian concepts of authority and justice, which required political leaders to promote the universal rules of *dharma* by a stern and righteous application of their power throughout the territory they governed. In India, however, the Brahmins were responsible for interpreting the sacred laws in particular cases, while the political rulers had a separate duty to protect justice through their "temporal powers" of force and punishment (Lingat, 1973:211-23). In the Thai capital, the functions of adjudication and enforcement were also differentiated to some extent, as the kings relied upon their Brahmin legal advisers to assist in the interpretation of the sacred laws (King Chulalongkorn, 1927:16-33; Engel, 1975:60-61). In the Thai provinces, however, the functions of the king and the Brahmins were merged, and the local political leaders were identified both with *dharma*, justice in its most cosmic sense, and *daṇḍa*, the use of force, coercion, and punishment to maintain justice.[14]

Theoretically, both of these functions at the provincial level were subject to the intervention and control of the Thai king. His chosen agent in each province, the *yokkrabat,* was deeply involved in the administration of justice. Pardons and executions throughout the kingdom were officially the preroga-

---

13. See *Phrathammanun* from The Law of the Three Seals, in Sathian Laiyalak *et al.*, comps. (1935-53: vol. 1, 43-65).
14. *Dharma* and *daṇḍa* are discussed by Basham (1963:114-15), and Lingat (1973:211-15).

tive of the Thai monarch. In fact, however, the provincial rulers exercised considerable autonomy in most matters. Even the power to pronounce the death sentence, theoretically vested in the king alone, appears to have existed widely at the local level.[15] In large part, this local autonomy arose from the practice of hereditary succession of local nobility to the governorship of most provinces, contrary to the nominal power of the king to exercise his full authority in appointing new governors (Vickery, 1970:866-72; Arsa Meksawan, 1962:71-72). In addition, provinces were organized by law into four classes, with those of the first three classes responsible for the administration of certain minor provinces, thus making control from the capital even more remote and indirect (Vickery, 1970:866).

The function of local administration was known as *kin müang,* literally to "eat the territory," meaning that the ruler received no salary or maintenance from the central government but was expected to support himself by a portion of the labor, food, goods, and revenues of the people he controlled. When such support came to officials in the course of a lawsuit, it was perceived by many foreigners as simple bribery or corruption, a characteristic of which they frequently complained in the administration of Thai justice (Gervaise, 1928:37; Bowring, 1969: vol. 1, 176; Young, 1907:223-25; Thompson, 1906:62; and others). The prerogatives of the rulers under such a system could lead to serious excesses. Many governors, in their quest for power and authority, formed alliances with the local *nakleng to,* strong men with large and fearsome bands of followers who could enforce the governor's orders against local citizens and outlaws (Chakrit Noranitipadungkarn, 1963:105-106). On occasion, justice must indeed have been eclipsed by the requirements of power in the minds of the local rulers responsible for both of these sacred concepts.

TRANSFORMATION OF THE PROVINCIAL JUDICIAL SYSTEM

The reforms of King Chulalongkorn brought two important changes to the traditional system of justice in provincial Thailand: first, to an extent never before possible, the power of the king was asserted directly in the political affairs of the provinces; and second, a new and independent judicial procedure was established in each of the Thai provinces, unlike any that had previously existed. These two achievements were closely interdependent.[16] The new

---

15. Wenk (1968:28). Akin Rabibhadana speculates that this power existed only in times of war and unrest, when the governor acted pursuant to his powers as army commander (1969:70). Van Vliet, however, wrote in the seventeenth century of the governor's "absolute power and supreme authority over justice, pardons, remittals and other affairs concerning the province and its inhabitants" (1910:60). Power to pronounce the death sentence apparently belonged as well to the Chiangmai ruler in the nineteenth century: see pp. 33-34 *infra.*

16. Compare Weber's observations (1968:809) on the relationship between the rationalization of an administrative hierarchy and the rationalization of judicial procedure:

The more rational the administrative machinery of the princes or hierarchs became,

administrative structure, known as the *thesaphiban* system, gradually divided the entire country into "circles" (*monthon*), each administered by a royal commissioner loyal to the king and directly responsible to the king's halfbrother, Prince Damrong Rachanupab, who was the Minister of Interior. Between 1894 and 1915, twenty circles were established, some of them encompassing areas traditionally remote from central control (Vickery, 1970:875). The separate provinces within each circle were administered by governor and council, who reported directly to the royal commissioner.[17] Provinces were subdivided into districts, districts into *tambon*,[18] and *tambon* into villages. Village chiefs were elected by the villagers; *tambon* chiefs (*kamnan*) were elected by an assembly of village headmen in each *tambon*. All administrative officers above the *tambon* level were appointed from Bangkok.

The transformation of the judiciary was a crucial part of this change from an indigenous system of hierarchical dependencies to a centralized nationstate. The Law of the Provincial Courts created a three-level provincial court system in 1896, consisting of *monthon* courts, provincial courts, and magistrates' courts, each with its own staff of judges, each with a distinct jurisdictional authority (Engel, 1975:70). In 1908, the Law of the Courts of Justice transferred control of the provincial court system from the Ministry of Interior to the Ministry of Justice, thereby unifying the administration of justice throughout the country under a single legal specialist: Prince Ratburi Direkrit, son of the king and widely known as the "father of Thai law." Legal codes were drafted by committees of Thai and foreign experts, first provisional in nature and then final in form: a law of evidence was promulgated in 1895, the provisional codes of criminal and civil procedure in 1896, the Penal Code in 1908, the six books of the Civil and Commercial Code between 1924 and 1935, the permanent codes of criminal and civil procedure in 1935 (Thailand *Yearbook,* 1964:242-45; Engel, 1975:74-75). Even as the *monthon* system dissolved and the absolute monarchy was replaced by a constitutional system in the 1930s, the centralized judicial system emerged intact from the political mold in which it was formed, with a permanent shape and legitimacy of its own.

---

that is, the greater the extent to which administrative "officials" were used in the exercise of the power, the greater was the likelihood that the legal procedure would also become "rational" both in form and substance. To the extent to which the rationality of the organization of authority increased, irrational forms of procedure were eliminated and the substantive law was systematized, i.e., the law as a whole was rationalized.

17. There were some temporary exceptions to this pattern. In the Northwest *monthon,* of which Chiangmai was a part, the major provinces were permitted for some time to administer their traditional dependencies. See Vickery (1970:876); and Chakrit Noranitipadungkarn (1963:242-52).
18. The conventional English translations of *"tambon"*—"sub-district" and "commune"—are both misleading, since a *tambon* is essentially a small number of villages grouped together for administrative purposes. For this reason I have simply used the untranslated Thai term throughout this study, and I have referred to the *tambon* leader by his Thai title: *kamnan.*

The new legal system brought to the provinces a concept of judicial procedure that was foreign to jurisdictions which had hitherto relied upon ordeal, oath, magic and exorcism, mediation, and the administrative processing of legal conflicts. Realizing the implications of this profound change, Prince Damrong Rachanupab drafted an Explanation of the Establishment of the Provincial Courts, which he presented at a historic meeting of the royal commissioners from seven different *monthon* in January 1896. In his explanation of the forthcoming Law of the Provincial Courts, Prince Damrong emphasized the new concept of a judiciary independent of executive control:

> The customs regarding the judges of provincial courts, even to the present day, are such that administrative officials from the rank of governor downwards are compelled to examine and decide legal disputes in addition to their other administrative responsibilities. Nearly every person has his duties mixed together in this way. Because we have established the *thesaphiban* system to improve our country through discipline and strength, it is now necessary to separate these functions. That is, one unit will now be established for political administration while a separate judicial unit will handle lawsuits. In this way we will assure a proper state of affairs in the provinces. (Sutčharit Thawǫnsuk, 1964:40)

Still in doubt, the royal commissioner from the *monthon* of Chaisri, *Phraya* Mahathep (But Bunyarattaphan), asked the Minister:

> If any task needs to be performed as part of the business of the court, will the judges not have to seek the approval of the royal commissioners first?

Again, in his reply, Prince Damrong stressed the distinction between administrative and judicial functions:

> If the matter is an administrative one, the judge will have to seek approval. But if it involves his judicial responsibilities, such as the hearing of cases, rendering of verdicts, and imposition of punishments, then the royal commissioners shall not be involved. (24)

The specialization of function in the new judicial system also extended to the prosecution of criminal offenses. Prince Damrong explained this change by pointing to the drawbacks of the traditional criminal laws under which the prosecution often rested in the hands of the injured party or of the very judge who was to decide the defendant's guilt or innocence:

> If an individual violated any provision of the royal law, sometimes no plaintiff would come forward to bring suit and the issue would be lost through neglect. Or sometimes the plaintiff and defendant would entice one another into reaching a settlement which allowed the wrongdoer to escape punishment. Sometimes there was no plaintiff, and instead an official would arrest the suspect, interrogate him and solve the case, acting both as plaintiff and as the judge who passed final verdict at the same time. (45)

Prince Damrong argued that justice demanded the establishment of a prosecutor who was independent of the judiciary, thus placing the plaintiff and defendant on an equal footing in criminal cases and assuring impartiality on the part of the judge:

> The creation of a prosecutor's office will advance the cause of justice in another way: it will encourage the people generally to see the position of judge as being trustworthy. The judge will be neutral, not involved with either the plaintiff or the defendant in any suit. (46)

The impartial judge was himself to impose sentence upon those he found guilty of criminal wrongdoing. The sentence would depend primarily upon the gravity of the offense and not the social position of the criminal or his victim. The concept of judicial neutrality meant not only that the judge would be independent of both sides in the lawsuits over which he presided, but that he would ignore questions of rank and status that were previously the very essence of justice.[19]

Thailand was not, of course, the first country to attempt the transition from a local system of justice, based upon "irrational" factors such as the rank of the parties and their relationship to the mediator or judge, to a centralized system based upon universal legal norms administered by a neutral and independent legal specialist. Indigenous Indian legal procedures, for example, had traditionally been characterized less by the application of "abstract principles of law" than by a "meticulous attention to the minute adjustments of a prestige society" (Derrett, 1968:224). Under British colonial rule, the traditional system was replaced by a centralized judiciary administering the universal precepts of a newly codified legal regime. The result was a transformation of the very concept of law:

> The [British-instituted] common law courts undertook to deal with the merits of a single transaction or offense, isolated from the related disputes among the parties and their supporters. The "fireside equities" and qualifying circumstances known to the indigenous tribunal were excluded from the court's consideration. In accordance with the precept of "equality before the law," the status and ties of the parties, matters of moment to an indigenous tribunal, were deliberately ignored. And, unlike the indigenous tribunals which sought compromise or face-saving solutions acceptable to all parties, the government's courts dispensed clearcut "all or none" decisions.... The new

---

19. Under The Law of the Three Seals, punishments were determined by a formula based upon the ranks of the wrongdoer and his victim. Generally, punishments were increased in proportion to the rank of the defendant, because persons of higher rank had a greater obligation to behave in a socially acceptable manner. In addition, the higher the rank of the victim, the more severe tended to be the punishment imposed upon the wrongdoer. Phra Wǫraphakphibun (1969:137); Prince Damrong Rachanupab (1933:32). Rank also determined the right of litigants to legal counsel at trial, with persons of 400 sakdina or higher entitled to be represented, while those of lower rank were not. Prince Damrong Rachanupab (32).

courts not only created new opportunities for intimidation and harassment and new means for carrying on old disputes, but they also gave rise to a sense of individual right not dependent on opinion or usage and capable of being actively enforced by government, even in opposition to community opinion. (Galanter, 1968:70)

"Modern law," whether instituted by colonization or by other means, has typically appeared as an important element in the extension of a centralized political power and the consolidation of the administration into a modern "nation-state." In Thailand, as in a handful of other countries, including Japan, Ethiopia, and Turkey, the legal transformation was accomplished by local rulers rather than by foreign governments (see Hooker, 1975). While the end result of judicial centralization in Thailand was comparable in many ways to the process that took place in her colonized neighbors, a greater flexibility and adaptability in the Thai legal system probably resulted from the fact that it was administered for the most part by the Thais themselves.

It has been observed that the establishment of a modern legal system tends to set in motion an irreversible process in which the indigenous legal systems are replaced and destroyed. This process may occur for several reasons. One reason is that the centralized legal system efficiently disseminates its new legal norms throughout the country, presenting a single and internally consistent set of rules to the entire populace, backed by the prestige and power of the central authority that created them (Galanter, 1968:76). Also, certain factions within a changing society may strongly desire the imposition of a rationalized legal order and will cooperate with the political authorities to promote this goal. Among such factions are the "bourgeois interests" described by Weber as seeking administrative stability and the enforceability of contracts (1968:847). Foreign political and mercantile interests may demand physical safety and security in their commercial dealings. Various repressed or embattled segments of the local population may also welcome the arrival of a clear, neutral, and enforceable set of rules to protect them from encroachments by their neighbors and from arbitrary behavior by the privileged classes.

The new legal system possesses certain intrinsic characteristics that enable it to achieve dominance over the indigenous legal systems it is intended to replace:

First, the national legal system is politically superior, to the extent of being able to abolish the indigenous system(s). Second, where there is a clash of obligation between systems then the rules of the national system will prevail and any allowance made for the indigenous system will be made on the premises and in the forms required by the national system. Third, in any description and analysis of indigenous systems the classifications used will be those of the national system. (Hooker, 1975:4).

Traditional legal systems thus tend to disappear or to be consumed by the new law of the nation-state:

... it tolerates no rivals; it dissolves away that which cannot be transformed into modern law and absorbs the remainder; it creates a numerous class of professionals who form the connecting links of the nation-state and a vast array of vested rights and defined expectations which disincline those holding them to support or even conceive drastic changes. (Galanter, 1968:86).

The centralized judicial system of Thailand, administering the codified laws first enacted in the early twentieth century, has indeed asserted its dominance over the indigenous provincial systems in a process continuing to the present day. The process, however, has been one that "absorbed" as much as it "dissolved" of the traditional legal concepts. Modern Thailand has been noteworthy not only for its avoidance of colonial rule, but also for its ability to accept external models while adapting them to purposes uniquely Thai. In this way the pressures for change have been satisfied without destroying many of the deeper impulses toward continuity with the traditional past. As King Chulalongkorn, Princes Damrong Rachanupab and Ratburi Direkrit, and their foreign legal advisers succeeded in extending the new judicial system into the farthest corners of the kingdom, the indigenous culture exercised a profound effect upon the new legal forms. A primary goal of this study is to demonstrate the processes of adaptation and change still at work in the northern province of Chiangmai, a distant and formerly semi-autonomous political entity that played an important role from the very outset of the establishment of the modern Thai judicial system.

Chapter Two
The Court and the Province of Chiangmai

MODERN CHIANGMAI AND ITS EARLY ORIGINS

The Chiangmai courthouse and the provincial government building face each other across a busy street, divided halves of a formerly unified whole. They stand within the old city center, which is enclosed by the remains of the picturesque city walls built in 1801. The walls are set off by a moat in which children now swim and fish. Modern Chiangmai has spread east of the old walled city across the Mae Ping River to the railway station, south through the silver and antique district to the airport, north through a busy market area to the Teachers Training College and the superhighway, and west toward the Chiangmai University campus and the sacred mountain crest of Doi Suthep. The city of Chiangmai is situated in the largest of the many fertile valleys of northern Thailand, each carved into the rough hilly terrain and supported by a network of rivers whose waters flow southward toward the broad open ricelands of the central plain.

According to legend, the original inhabitants of the Mae Ping valley were the Lawa people who now live in the distant forests and mountains. From these early peoples, whom legend made into cannibals, headhunters, and even giants, the guardian spirits of the land were said to be descended and were worshipped by the later inhabitants of Chiangmai province (Kraisri Nimmanahaeminda, 1967; Kunstadter, 1967:640-42). The majority of Chiangmai's modern population are descendents of the Tai peoples who, by the early thirteenth century, had spread throughout the lands to the south of China into much of Indochina, Burma, and Thailand (Coedès, 1968:189-91).[1]

---

1. "Tai" refers to the large ethnolinguistic group spread throughout Thailand and beyond, in southern China and northern Southeast Asia. See LeBar et al. (1964:187-239). "Thai" in this study refers to citizens of the modern state of Thailand within its present geo-political boundaries. For convenience, I shall use the term "Thai" rather than "Siamese" to refer to the people of the central kingdoms of Ayutthaya and Bangkok before the establishment of the modern Thai state within its present boundaries.

Gradually these people grew numerous and strong enough to form independent Tai principalities. One of several powerful Tai leaders to emerge in the region during the latter part of the thirteenth century was King Mangrai, commonly regarded as the founder of Chiangmai, the "new town," which he established in 1296 as a capital for the northern kingdom he had forged by a dramatic campaign of consolidation and conquest (Coedès, 1968:195 and 208-209).

King Mangrai's descendants ruled for many years over the northern kingdom, known as Lannathai, and its dependencies. By the middle of the fifteenth century, Lannathai political power and culture flourished. Some of Chiangmai's most distinctive temples date from this early period. A legal tradition seems also to have developed, recorded in numerous collections known as *mangraisat,* the *śāstras* of Mangrai. Various compilations based upon this tradition are still to be found on palm-leaf manuscripts now scattered among the temples of the north. In the mid-sixteenth century, powerful Burmese forces conquered Chiangmai and subsequently went on to overwhelm the central Thai capital of Ayutthaya. Chiangmai's strategic location made it a prize coveted by both of the warring factions. Although Ayutthaya succeeded before long in throwing off Burmese control, Chiangmai was to remain under Burma's indirect rule until 1774, her local princes selected with the approval of the Burmese court (Davis, 1974:29-31; Hall, 1964:238-54).

The kings of Ayutthaya had long considered Chiangmai to be one of their own vassal states, despite its great distance from the capital and the realities of Burmese power in the north. In the Palatine Law of King Trailok, which David Wyatt dates in the year 1468, Chiangmai was listed among twenty towns that sent the gold and silver flowers of tribute to the royal court of Ayutthaya (Wyatt, 1967). In fact, according to Nigel Brailey, Thai and Burmese ambitions had long been played against one another by the Chiangmai rulers, who often sought to preserve Chiangmai's autonomy by siding with the weaker of the two powers against the stronger. In 1774, seven years after Ayutthaya had been destroyed by invading Burmese armies, the Chiangmai nobility plotted to free themselves from Burmese control and opened the gates of Chiangmai and nearby Lampang to the resurgent Thai armies of King Taksin. At the same time that the Thonburi—Bangkok dynasty was founded by King Taksin and by King Rama I, therefore, we find a significant increase in central Thai influence over Chiangmai (Brailey, 1973:302). In 1775, however, the Burmese staged a short-lived counterattack in the north, driving the local rulers south and depopulating the entire area, leaving the city of Chiangmai vacant for the next twenty years.[2] Only in 1796, under Prince Kawila of

---

2. "... Chiengmai, Chiengrai, Phayao, Chiengsaen, Thoeng, and Lǫ were practically depopulated; the people had either emigrated to other places, such as Lampang, the forests and the hills, or been taken forcibly to Burma. Some had been taken as slaves to reward the higher officers in the Burmese army. And some of the Thai Yuan were swept down to Amphoe Saohai, in the province of Saraburi; Amphoe Sikhiu, province of

Lampang, was the area repopulated during a period known locally as "put vegetables into baskets, and people into towns," a policy which accounts in large part for the make-up of the modern Chiangmai population:

> In an effort to "put people into the town" the *Chao* or rulers of Chiengmai sent their armies to fight various towns to the north in the Thai Yai (Shan) and Thai *Lṳ* country, the Sipsongpanna. All the people in any towns they defeated were taken down to Chiengmai to increase the manpower. Therefore, the Khon *Mṳang* who now make up the inhabitants of Chiengmai are either descendants of Thai Yuan, or descendants of Thai Yai, Thai *Lṳ*, Thai *Yǫng*, and Thai Khoen, who speak with an intonation similar to that of the Thai Yuan of Chiengmai. As time passed, these latter ethnic groups forgot their language and culture and became northern Thai or Khon *Mṳang*. (Kraisri Nimmanahaeminda, 1965b:7)

From that time until the reign of King Chulalongkorn, Chiangmai remained a semi-autonomous state, relying upon Thai assistance on occasion to do battle with the Burmese (see Vella, 1957:92-93) and paying rich tribute to the Bangkok court, but largely independent in its own internal affairs and itself responsible for the supervision of its local dependencies. This traditional tributary relationship was to change only with the increasing penetration of the British into neighboring Burma from the 1850s onward and with the involvement of western teak interests in the great forests of northern Thailand.

INCORPORATION OF CHIANGMAI INTO THE MODERN THAI STATE

Chiangmai has been termed the "birthplace of the modern Thai judicial system" (Sutčharit Thawǫnsuk, 1964:11) because of the reforms in legal procedure which the Thai government instituted in that area during the second half of the nineteenth century. It was primarily the difficulty in administering legal disputes—which involved teak concessions and the safety of British subjects in the north—that led to the expansion of Thai political power in Chiangmai and the ultimate removal of the local nobility from control. Complaints and threats by the British resulted first in a treaty signed in 1874 by the new government of King Chulalongkorn and the British government in India. This treaty provided for the appointment of a Thai Judge-Commissioner in Chiangmai who would, with a visiting British officer in attendance, decide certain lawsuits involving British subjects and would help to regulate local commercial dealings and other legal matters.[3]

Probably, as Brailey suggests, the Judge-Commissioner was viewed by King Chulalongkorn and his young followers as " 'the thin end of the wedge',

---

Nakhǫn Ratchasima; and Amphoe Mṳang, province of Ratchaburi" (Kraisri Nimmanahaeminda, 1965b:7).

3. For the text of the treaty, see 2 Martens (2d Series) 511; 66 B.S.P. 537. For discussion, see Brailey (1974:444); Ramsay (1971:70-71).

gradually to expand Siamese influence into authority, perhaps ultimately by force" (1974:446). Certainly this unprecedented appointment proved the intention of the Thai king to assert the greatest possible judicial and political control in Chiangmai to protect the area from further western encroachment. Although the treaty provisions soon proved ineffective, a new Anglo-Siamese Chiangmai treaty was signed in 1883 which permitted more extensive British involvement in the functions of the Thai Judge-Commissioner. The treaty also created an International Court in Chiangmai over which a permanent British Consul or Vice-Consul was to preside. This court could, at the discretion of the British authorities, acquire jurisdiction over any lawsuit arising in the locality in which the defendant alone or both the plaintiff and the defendant were British subjects.[4]

Within the next twenty years, the policies of the Thai government led to the effective incorporation of the northern dependencies into a system of centralized Thai rule which the king now saw as essential. A slow process was initiated whereby the local rulers were gently squeezed from power by representatives of the Bangkok government. In 1900 the Phayap *monthon* was established for the northern vassal states with its center in Chiangmai. At first the *monthon* administration was modified to reflect local traditions and political realites. Instead of dividing the territory into provinces (*müang*) of equal status, each supervised directly by the *monthon* government, the new administrative structure retained the traditional hierarchy of local dependent states.[5] Within six years, however, the northern circle was reorganized to conform to the system used elsewhere in the country. The local nobility remained in their traditional offices, but real power was now vested in the officials of the central government and the judicial officers (Vickery, 1970:876; Ramsay, 1971:260-66). The Law of the Courts of Justice (1908) was enforced in Chiangmai, as it was throughout the country, and so were the legal codes of the early twentieth century. In 1932, constitutional government came to Chiangmai and to the nation of Thailand. In 1933 the *monthon* system was abolished, and Chiangmai joined the ranks of Thai provinces administered directly from Bangkok.

For the people of Chiangmai these changes in the administrative and judicial structure had varying implications. Justice was no longer administered by the provincial councilors and the local ruler, the *čhao chiwit ao*, "lord of life," with power to condemn a person to death merely by uttering the word

---

4. 10 Martens (2d Series) 570; 74 B.S.P. 78.
5. "Within the *monthon* the traditional title of *nakhon* was retained for Lampang, Lamphun, Nan, and Chiengmai, the last two retaining their own traditional vassal *muong*. As a coordinate member with the four *nakhon* there was *muong* Phrae, which still had its own ruling family. Official titles were established in the local dialect. In each *nakhon* there was a ruling council consisting of the hereditary ruler and two Royal Commissioners, and orders of the central government officials were issued through it. In spite of the effort to preserve appearances, little real authority was left to the local rulers . . ." (Vickery, 1970:876).

*"ao."*⁶ Oaths and ordeals—including the ordeal by submersion in water, which is most frequently mentioned—were no longer considered acceptable procedures to distinguish the innocent from the wrongdoer. Would-be litigants were disappointed to find that the new courts refused to hear certain allegations of wrongdoing by magic, which previously had entitled them to a remedy:

> A Shan British subject actually entered a case against his Chinese neighbour for causing the death of his wife by burning sesame seeds; these, when burnt, give forth a rather pungent odour. The plaintiff's wife was in childbirth, and his contention was that the defendant burnt the seeds well knowing the woman's condition, and knowing also that the smell was likely to kill her.... Another Shan sued a neighbour for causing the death of his little son, who was suffering from fever, by frying sausages next door. (Wood, 1965:50)⁷

Witchcraft cases were also rejected under the new laws. A story recounted by Daniel McGilvary, a missionary and long-time resident of Chiangmai, reveals how the new courts began to reflect and to reinforce new power relationships within the community. McGilvary begins with a description of widespread witchcraft proceedings in the north, exaggerated in certain respects, but probably accurate when he implies that such procedures were often a means for one faction in the society to win dominance over another:

> From the time of our first arrival in Chiengmai we were continually amazed to find what multitudes of people had been driven from their homes for supposed witchcraft. All the northern provinces and towns, as has already been mentioned, were largely peopled by that unfortunate class. Accusations of witchcraft had become one of the most dreaded means of oppression and persecution. It was a favourite way of getting rid of an envied rival or of a disagreeable neighbour. (McGilvary, 1912:204)

In 1878, with the first Anglo-Siamese treaty more or less in effect, McGilvary was asked by a local prince to provide protection for a family that had been accused of witchcraft. McGilvary agreed immediately, for he wished to prove the Christians unafraid of witches, and the prince had agreed to assume "all legal responsibility" for adverse local opinion. McGilvary notified the newly-appointed Thai Judge-Commissioner of the situation.

Later, the anger of the local community towards the family surged up once again as they were suspected of causing a local epidemic of fever. Unable to withstand the public pressure, the prince now demanded that the missionaries

---

6. Phornphun Chongvatana (1974:56). She refers specifically to the reign of *Phračhao* Kawilorot, 1856-1870.

7. Wood, the British Consul-General in Chiangmai, sat as judge in the International Court of Chiangmai for cases involving British subjects, such as the Shan litigants described in these two examples.

release the family. McGilvary refused and the prince threatened to take the matter to court. Under traditional law the prince would have won an easy victory, because of his status and because his case was a popular one supported by substantial evidence. McGilvary, however, realized that the treaty had already begun to change the local power structure, and that witches and Christians now had access to political leverage which had never been theirs in traditional Chiangmai society:

> I replied that I was perfectly willing that the case be tried; but it should not be tried before a Lāo [northern Thai] court, but before the Commissioner. If they could convince him that the sickness in the village was caused by a malicious spirit resident in that family, they should be sent off immediately. (206)

When McGilvary added the condition that the accusers should themselves be expelled from the community if their suit failed, the matter was dropped. McGilvary recognized that his victory was possible only because of the slowly shifting power relationships which were centered in the changing legal system:

> Before the arrival of the Commissioner such an outcome would have been impossible. No Lāo court would have refused to expel persons so accused. (206)

His victory, moreover, was crowned by the acquisition of a new set of converts: "The family of Pā Sêng Bun proved to be a treasure, becoming one of the most influential and valuable in the Chiengmai church." (206)

The political enclaves of the local princes were gradually subsumed by the larger enclave of the Bangkok government, and the courts became sources of power to many who had previously been outsiders, exiles, or aliens in the community. This process was not necessarily hostile to the interests of the local population, although many traditional causes could no longer find a remedy in the courts of justice. Some communities that had been subject to the arbitrary power of greedy or corrupt rulers—who were also the highest judges—welcomed the new commissioners for providing solutions to their plights which had never before been available.[8] The new judicial procedures, strange indeed to local inhabitants, nevertheless opened new avenues for pressing claims against abuses of official power, against bandits who were sheltered by the local rulers, against uncertainty in commercial dealings previously dominated by the interests and power of the local princes. Some segments of the society recognized that they could now oppose the local rulers by

---

8. See Hallett (1890:406-11). Elizabeth Colson points out that, even under colonial administrations, local communities often looked favorably upon the coming of centralized political control and the establishment of centralized judicial systems. Despite the many causes for resentment which they created, the new courts and administrators often proved capable of resolving conflicts and grievances at the local level that had previously resisted solution (1974:69-73).

invoking the interests and power of the central government when their own goals were more congenial to the national authorities than to the local princes.

The process of change thus had its positive as well as its negative aspects. The local princes, who at their best embodied the distinctive customs and ideals of Chiangmai, were replaced by civil servants who often spoke with strange dialects, ate strange foods, were unaware of local traditions and sometimes looked down upon the local people. The local identity was slowly submerged in a national identity, often with resistance and resentment by that portion of the society which was proud of Chiangmai's historical independence and distinctive culture. At the same time, certain forms of oppression under the traditional system were brought to an end, and rights were vested among a number of people who had previously been powerless in the face of authority exercised by the ruling nobility. Wide-ranging social changes and shifts in the location of political power produced a series of smaller adjustments in the social structure from the highest to the lowest levels. In this changing environment, the centralized judiciary continued to play its role, re-allocating power and participating in the modern quest to redefine the concept of justice itself.

CHARACTERISTICS OF MODERN CHIANGMAI

The province of Chiangmai today contains more than one million persons, of whom approximately 84,000 reside in the municipal area of the city itself.[9] The province is governed by an administrative hierarchy directly descended from the *thesaphiban* system of Prince Damrong and King Chulalongkorn, but lacking the *monthon* as an intermediate level between the provincial government and the Ministry of Interior (see figure 3). Leadership at the village level is determined by local elections among the villagers, who choose their own village chief. The *tambon* leaders, or *kamnan*, are elected by an assembly of village chiefs from the *tambon*. District officers and the provincial governor are Bangkok appointees, although their original home is sometimes in or near the area to which they are assigned.

The population of Chiangmai is distributed, generally speaking, among three environments: the urban setting of Chiangmai city and several smaller towns, the lowland farming communities, and the hill communities. The city of Chiangmai is one of the most populous and sophisticated urban centers in Thailand outside of the metropolis of Bangkok. Its physical beauty and local handicrafts and culture have attracted tourists from other parts of the country and from foreign countries as well. A few modern hotels, movie theaters, night clubs, and bowling alleys have been opened. Other side effects of "modernization" can also be observed in Chiangmai city: clothing and hair

---

9. Population figures are from the *1970 Population and Housing Census; Changwat Chiangmai.*

styles have followed fashions set in the capital, and privately owned automobiles, generally a luxury in Thailand, increased from 1,276 to 7,553 in the ten-year period from 1960 to 1970, while motorcycles multiplied from 1,002 to 32,618 (Chakrit Noranitipadungkarn and A. Clarke Hagensick, 1973:16).

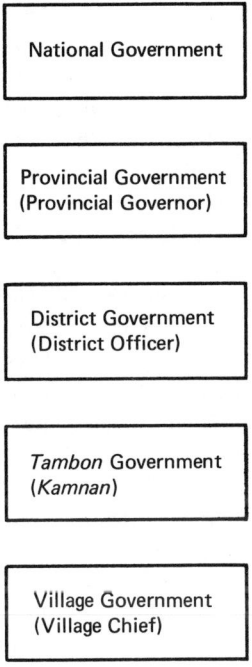

Figure 3. Major Administrative Levels and Chief Administrators in Provincial Thailand

Chiangmai has become the commercial center of the north and is linked to the rest of the country by air, rail, and bus routes and by a modern communication system (*ibid.*: 19). The city is also the site of several reputable secondary schools, the Chiangmai Teachers Training College, the Technical Institute of the North, and Chiangmai University with its many excellent departments and research centers and its sophisticated medical facilities.

The lowland farming communities subsist upon a wet-rice economy supplemented often by the cultivation of secondary crops such as garlic and onions, tobacco, beans, and potatoes. Of Chiangmai's economically active population over eleven years of age, according to figures contained in the 1970 census, approximately 77 percent are engaged in farming activities of some kind.[10] The land for the most part is rich and fertile, and an effective irrigation

---

10. *1970 Population and Housing Census; Changwat Chiangmai*, table 20. Hill tribe populations are excluded from these figures.

system refined over the centuries provides an ample supply of water. A few villages in the lowland area are also known for handicrafts such as silk weaving, teak carving, silverwork, and umbrella making.

The hill communities are generally composed of non-Tai peoples belonging to the groups referred to collectively as "hill tribes." These groups—the Karen, Meo, Lahu, Lisu, Yao, Akha, Lawa, and others—are distinguished from the Tais by custom, language, and appearance, and are isolated from lowland society by formidable hills and forests. They are excluded from the normal census procedures, but their numbers within Chiangmai province were estimated by the Tribal Research Centre of Chiangmai University at 92,919 in the year 1974 (Tribal Data Project, 1974). Their livelihood is derived mainly from slash and burn, or swidden, agriculture, a technique requiring the use of large forest areas and regular migrations of entire villages. This manner of life has proved increasingly difficult in recent years, as expanding hill tribe populations have put too great a strain on the available land. The situation has been complicated by the cultivation of opium poppies, an activity which is strongly opposed by American and international agencies. Because of opium suppression activities, occasional allegations of insurgent support among some of the hill tribes, and their own problems with population expansion and shrinking resources, the isolated hill tribes are beginning now to come into greater contact with the lowland peoples.

The population of Chiangmai, with the exception of the hill tribes, is closely related ethnically and culturally to the population of Thailand as a whole. The vast majority are linguistically and ethnically Tai and are Buddhist in faith—although usually the Buddhism is mixed with some form of animism. Cultural similarities between northern Thai society and that of other regions are usually said to be far more noteworthy than the local differences.[11] There are, nevertheless, certain characteristics of northern Thailand which differentiate it from the other parts of the country. Among these are diet—sticky or glutinous rice is preferred over ordinary rice—dialect, and the strong sense of a unique historical tradition. Even the Theravada Buddhist tradition in northern Thailand was set apart historically from Buddhism elsewhere in the country by differences in ritual, in the organization of the clergy, and in the customs relating to pilgrimage sites (Keyes, 1971 and 1975a). Davis writes that the people do not refer to themselves as "Thai" when they speak among themselves, reserving this term for the administrative officials who are outsiders to their society (1974:24). Neither do they use the term "Lao," although this was

---

11. *E.g.,* de Young (1966:7): "The Thai-speaking peasants of the two northern areas... are as Thai as the central and southern groups, all having drifted into Thailand from the Yunnan provinces of China between the first and fourteenth centuries A.D., bringing with them a tropical wet-rice paddy culture adapted to the lowlands. Over the centuries, owing partly to geographic isolation and partly to external forces, minor cultural differences among the various Thai peasant groups developed—differences in dialect and costume, for example. In recent times, many of these have been erased...."

long applied to them by Europeans and central Thais. The northern Thais refer to themselves as *khon müang,* which Davis translates as "the people of the principalities," and they refer to their dialect as *kam müang,* the language of the principalities (21).

Chiangmai and the north form an area ecologically distinct from the rest of Thailand in several important respects. According to figures presented by Wijeyewardene, the average size of land holdings in Chiangmai is the fourth smallest of the country's seventy-one provinces. In 1963 Chiangmai contained 807,389 *rai* of cultivated land, yet there were 106,795 individual holdings.[12] The average holding was therefore only 7.6 *rai.* The north as a region averaged only 8.6 *rai* per holding, whereas the average holding in central Thailand was 25.9 *rai,* in the south 23.0 *rai,* and in the northeast 21.6 *rai* (Wijeyewardene, 1967:75-79).[13] Although the average holdings in the north were roughly one-third the size of those in the rest of the country, the average yield of rice in kilograms per *rai* was much higher in the north (302.5) than in the central (216.1), south (210.6), or northeastern (169.2) regions *(ibid.:* 78).[14] Rice in the north is cultivated more intensively, with a more sophisticated irrigation system, than it is elsewhere in Thailand *(ibid.:* 78). The high rice yield from these smaller holdings accurately characterizes the north as a relatively prosperous area, less subject to the droughts of the northeast and the indebtedness of farmers in the central region (Moerman, 1968:84). Yet the size of the harvest is also more urgent in the north where the population is much more numerous in proportion to the riceland under cultivation. In the north this ratio of persons per cultivated *rai,* which Moerman calls the "nutritional density," was 114 in the year 1960, whereas it was only 55 in the central region, 47 in the northeast, and 82 in the south (Moerman, 1968:85).[15]

The north differs from the central region in the availability of virgin land, the absence of landlessness as an important social problem, and the generally even distribution of land among the rural population. Although the vicinity of Chiangmai town resembles the central region in its higher degree of tenancy

---

12. One *rai* is equivalent to 0.4 acres.
13. "North" in the figures I have quoted is defined to include only the seven provinces of Chiangrai, Chiangmai, Nan, Phrae, Maehongson, Lampang, and Lamphun. Wijeyewardene favors this definition both for geographical reasons and because it marks off the area where northern Thai dialect predominates (1967:78).
14. These figures are drawn from table 3.8 in Wijeyewardene (1967:78). They apply to the year 1963 and are based upon the *Census of Agriculture 1963* (National Statistical Office, 1965).
15. Figures are for 1960, drawn by Moerman from table 27 of the *Annual Report on 1962 Rice Production in Thailand,* Department of Rice, Ministry of Agriculture (Bangkok, 1965). Presumably "north" is more broadly defined than in the Wijeyewardene figures cited above (see note 13). On Wijeyewardene's basis, the ratio could be even higher in the north. Comparisons, nevertheless, are difficult, as Moerman points out, because certain areas—including the Chiangmai plain—use double cropping while other areas do not.

and landlessness, for the most part land in the north appears to be cultivated by the owner or by relatives of the owner.[16] Precise statistics on this matter, however, are difficult to obtain. The rental of land is very common, yet this does not necessarily indicate landlessness since it may often occur within a single family—the children, for example, working the land of the parents on a sharecropping basis—or it may last for only a few months, during which secondary crops are grown on small portions of some larger holding (Kingshill, 1960:24; Marlowe, 1969:17-18). In most cases, rental arrangements are transacted in kind rather than cash. Cash rentals, on the other hand, are more common in central Thailand, penalizing the tenant "since he always finds it difficult to save money and usually finds it impossible to withhold his crop from the market and wait for the best price" (Moerman, 1968:114). In the north, the tenant generally divides the crop fifty-fifty with the landlord, with adjustments made according to whose buffalo or bullock was used in the harvest (Wijeyewardene, 1965:256; Kingshill, 1960:24). Moerman contrasts the northern landlords with those of the central region, who are often townspeople, appearing remote, wealthy, anonymous, and demanding to their tenants. In Moerman's northern research area, on the other hand, the "absentee landlords" were merely prosperous peasants: "They are members of the same economic and social stratum as their tenants; they are subject to the same social controls and share the same aspirations" (Moerman, 1968:113). Because of the absence of "economic stratification" and of landlord-tenant conflict, and because land was generally available, Moerman found few disputes arising over land (1968:104). My own research, however, revealed that disputes over land do appear with some regularity in the Chiangmai court, and I shall examine the causes and outcomes of such disputes later in this study.

Conflicts over rights in land and contracts for its rental are by no means the only occasions on which disputes may occur in Chiangmai society. One common source of conflict is the practice of multiple marriage and divorce. The incidence of divorce and subsequent remarriage appears to be quite high in the rural areas of northern Thailand (Wijeyewardene, 1967:67-68; Marlowe,

---

16. Moerman emphasizes the availability of riceland in north Thailand for those who wish to cultivate their own land rather than rent. He suggests (1968:85) that the north has relatively fewer landless tenants than does central Thailand: "In Ban Ping, and probably throughout the north, the ownership of land is far more evenly distributed than in central Thailand." Wijeyewardene, on the other hand, speculates that such comparisons between north and central Thailand may be overstated. He cites a survey of northeastern Thailand, which also reported that few farmers were without their own land. In that survey, however, many of the farmers considered to own and cultivate their own land actually owned less than one *rai*, which included the house site. Some of them had to work in fields owned by other farmers in return for a share of the crop. Wijeyewardene suggests that such a situation does not pose the striking contrast to central Thai landholding patterns that is often asserted. His own findings in his northern Thai research site (which he does not necessarily claim to be representative of the north as a whole) indicate that over one-half of the households in 1966 did not own their own land (1967:79n).

1969:17). Official registration of these transitory alliances is not necessarily obtained by the couple, who are more likely to perform rituals to notify village spirits of changes in legal status than to perform the less familiar rituals of the distant government registrars.[17] These factors, taken together with the unusually high mobility of northern villagers,[18] mean that there will frequently be conflicting claims between husband and wife over marital rights, the division of property, and the responsibility of caring for children. In addition, the children themselves may eventually compete with their half-siblings for the resources of the parents. This area of conflict will also be examined in more detail later in the study.

The high mobility of the population in itself may prove to be a factor in the frequency of disputes, for it means that individuals are coming into contact with persons from other villages, strangers not subject to the same social constraints nor respectful of the same authority figures. Improvements in roads and motor vehicles have vastly increased such contacts over the past ten or twenty years and have led, I shall suggest, to greater conflict among total strangers. Economic and technological changes have also brought new ways of thinking and new sources of conflict into the village itself:

> If one compares earlier times with 1960 and plow farming with tractor farming, one finds that wages, haggling, task specificity, tit-for-tat reciprocity, and the hope of immediate profit have become more important. (Moerman, 1968:141)

Traditional forms of reciprocity are frequently replaced by a new contract-mindedness, a new set of expectations that often conflict with the old.

The norms of the society are themselves changing, and an important promotor of such change has been the modern educational system which injects "outside" teachers and ideas into the traditional setting. One indication of the impact of the educational system is the fact that the literacy rate among the younger generation is much higher than among the older generation in Chiangmai province (table 1).

With increased literacy and mobility among the younger generations, and a rapidly changing social setting, there has been an inevitable clash between old

---

17. Registration of marriages by customary and official procedures will be discussed in chapter 11.

18. The phenomenon of high mobility in northern Thailand is often mentioned. See, for example, Wijeyewardene (1967:69) and Davis (1974:43). Some indication is given by table 9 of the 1970 Census, purporting to show migration into Chiangmai from outside the province as well as migration within the province, during the five years preceding the census. These figures show migration by a total of 86,381 individuals five years of age and older—approximately one person in every 10.5 who was five years of age and above. Since mobility appears to be most pronounced among younger people, particularly young men, we might anticipate a much higher figure in a study confined to a particular age group of northern Thai men ranging, for example, from middle teens to 30 or 35 years of age.

norms and new, between the different expectations of older and younger generations, between village views and the views of the broader social system.

TABLE 1
Literacy by Age Group in Chiangmai Province, 1970[a]

Age Group	Population	Number Literate	Percent Literate
10-19	264,157	233,954	88.6
20-29	125,654	103,325	82.2
30-39	134,174	97,485	72.7
40-49	105,567	63,656	60.3
50-59	54,760	19,074	34.8
60-69	43,828	9,598	21.9
70 and over	25,804	4,576	17.7
Unknown	1,368	300	21.9

Source: 1970 Population and Housing Census; Changwat Chiangmai (table 12).

[a]Literacy defined as the ability "to read and write simple statements in any language. If a person can read but cannot write, then he was classified as illiterate." (XVI).

These points of conflict have involved the provincial judiciary in several significant areas of social change, as competing groups have looked to the courts and to the neutral precepts of the law codes to mediate and resolve their differences. This process shall be a central topic in the chapters that follow, as we trace its impact upon the legal system, upon the contending groups, and upon the pattern of social change itself.

Chapter Three
The Court and Its Functions

In the first two chapters of this study I have described some of the settings—administrative, historical, political, and social—in which the Chiangmai court functions. In this third introductory chapter I shall present a final kind of overview: a broad look at the business of the court itself. We shall be dealing primarily with statistics gathered from the court registers for the years 1965 to 1974. The view provided by these statistics is comparable to the view of a landscape from an airplane: useful for ascertaining the broad contours of the land but sometimes inadequate for making the fine discriminations which give us a real knowledge of the setting. The primary unit of measurement is the individual lawsuit, but some distortion is inevitably introduced by assigning equal weight to each of these units. The court can process minor criminal misdemeanors daily in the hundreds, while a single complex civil suit may require months of hearings and debate. There is no indicator here to show us the relative importance of each of these cases to the individuals involved or to the society as a whole. Moreover, the numbers themselves can be misleading, since a casual decision by the private plaintiff or public prosecutor to join actions against many defendants in one suit may yield a single statistical unit instead of 10 or 15. The calculation of litigation rates in proportion to the total population of the province is also a very rough kind of approximation. It is fairly clear that the litigants are not distributed evenly among all segments of the population, and that some plaintiffs—and defendants—appear again and again in the court, collecting debts or paying fines for gambling or prostitution on a regular monthly basis. Many of these unavoidable distortions will be corrected in later sections of this study, where individual cases and legal issues will be examined in detail. For the present, this broad overview will be useful in moving us from the introductory historical and social materials into a consideration of the functions of the court itself, providing us with a high altitude view of a landscape we shall soon explore on foot.

The broadest overview of the flow of litigation in Chiangmai province shows that it is channelled into four separate streams: civil and criminal cases, processed in the provincial court and the magistrates' court. Table 2 shows the number of cases involved in each of these streams over the ten-year period from 1965 to 1974.[1] A few points are worth noting with regard to this chart.

TABLE 2
Number of Criminal and Civil Cases Processed in Each Division of Chiangmai Provincial Court, 1965-1974

	Criminal Cases[a]			Civil Cases			
Year	Provincial Court	Magistrates' Court	Total	Provincial Court	Magistrates' Court	Bankruptcy Court	Total
1965	2,450	992	3,442	628	51	38	717
1966	1,935[b]	1,016	2,951[b]	608	108	27	743
1967	2,094	781	2,875	628	54	44	726
1968	2,108	1,058	3,166	677	32	29	738
1969	2,292	1,066	3,358	732	16	11	759
1970	2,264	758	3,022	820	37	11	868
1971	2,244	945	3,189	660	31	8	699
1972	1,733	869	2,602	647	19	8	674
1973	2,091	851	2,942	800	24	3	827
1974	2,985	881	3,866	727	16	8	751

Source: Court Registers of Chiangmai Provincial Courthouse.
[a]Criminal cases processed by Military Court for Region 7, of which Chiangmai is a part, are not included.
[b]Figures are incomplete: third volume of court register is missing.

Although I have referred in general to the "Chiangmai court," we can see that there are technically two trial courts at the provincial level, one for major criminal and civil matters and the other to handle petty misdemeanors and civil claims on a limited geographical basis. The jurisdiction of the magistrates' court was, until October of 1974, restricted to cases originating in the *Müang* district of the province—the district of the city of Chiangmai itself. Minor cases originating in the other 16 districts[2] were sent to the provincial court, even if they were otherwise within the competence of the magistrates' court— that is, civil cases not exceeding two thousand *baht* (approximately $100), and criminal cases with a maximum punishment not exceeding three years imprisonment, six thousand *baht* fine, or both.[3] In October 1974, the territorial jurisdiction of the magistrates' court was extended to include five other districts in the province: Sankamphaeng, Sansai, Sanpatong, Saraphi, and Hang Dong.

It should be noted that the criminal cases listed in table 2 do not include prosecutions decided by the provincial judges sitting as a "military court," a tribunal whose jurisdiction varied considerably over the ten-year period from

---

1. Table 2 also follows the record-keeping system of the court itself by listing bankruptcy cases separately.
2. Plus one sub-district. Later a total of 18 districts and one sub-district.
3. Law for the Organization of the Courts of Justice, 1934 [*Phrathammanun san yuttitham, B.E. 2477*], Sections 22 and 15. See chapter 1, note 2.

1965 to 1974. These cases have been excluded because the records are maintained by region rather than by province. Chiangmai is one of five provinces in the seventh military region, the others being Lampang, Chiangrai, Lamphun, and Maehongson. From 1965 to 1974, the criminal cases decided each year in the court for the seventh military region numbered 402, 355, 409, 486, 403, 404, 204, 893, 1,246, and 493 respectively. The sharp increase in the number of cases from the end of 1971 to 1973 resulted from an expansion of jurisdiction during a period of rule by martial law following a coup d'etat led by Field Marshals Thanom Kittikachorn and Praphat Charusathien. In all other years, the military courts handled primarily narcotics cases, with a scattering of arson and robbery prosecutions. During the period of martial law, however, prosecutions were brought in the military courts for bodily injury, theft, homicide, sexual offenses, and various other criminal violations. As these cases were tried by the military courts, we may note a corresponding drop in the rate of criminal litigation in the provincial and magistrates' courts.

The figures contained in table 2 suggest that the citizens of Chiangmai generally avoid bringing disputes to the provincial court. The proportion of criminal to civil cases is approximately four to one, suggesting that the courts are used far more frequently by the authorities—in their historical function of suppressing crime and preserving the peace—than by private individuals or groups who wish to resolve conflicting claims. This non-litigious tendency is underscored by the relatively low litigation rates per 1,000 population shown in table 3.

TABLE 3
Number of Criminal and Civil Cases Processed in Provincial and Magistrates' Courts per 1,000 Population, 1965-1974

Year	Population[a]	Criminal Cases	Civil Cases	Criminal Cases per 1,000 Pop.	Civil Cases per 1,000 Pop.
1965	909,958	3,442	717	3.78	0.79
1966	931,357	----[b]	743	----	0.80
1967	948,760	2,875	726	3.03	0.77
1968	968,738	3,166	738	3.27	0.76
1969	985,920	3,358	759	3.41	0.77
1970	1,002,295	3,022	868	3.02	0.87
1971	1,023,223	3,189	699	3.12	0.68
1972	1,049,702	2,602[c]	674	2.48[c]	0.64
1973	1,073,833	2,942[c]	827	2.74[c]	0.77
1974	1,086,203	3,866	751	3.56	0.69

[a]Population figures for Chiangmai Province obtained from the Chiangmai Provincial Offices. Comparison with the more reliable 10-year census of the National Statistical Office for 1970 suggests these figures may be understated by 2-3%. Hill tribe populations, which numbered 92,919 in 1974, are not included.

[b]Figures unavailable: third volume of court register is missing.

[c]Decline in criminal cases attributable to expanded jurisdiction of Military Court for Region 7 during 1972 and 1973.

The Chiangmai litigation rates stand in sharp contrast to those available from the study of courts in societies outside East and Southeast Asia. The

Chiangmai civil litigation rates vary between 0.64 and 0.87 cases per 1,000 population. We have figures from a small town in Turkey which suggest a civil litigation rate of approximately 21.8 cases per 1,000 population in the year 1967 (Starr and Pool, 1974:550).[4] A preliminary study of courts in Kenya shows a range of roughly 4.3 to 6.2 cases per 1,000 population from 1959 to 1969 (Abel, 1973b: table II).[5] In Alameda and San Benito counties of California, the local superior courts alone handled 11.0 and 10.2 civil cases per 1,000 population respectively in the year 1970 (Friedman and Percival, 1976:277).[6] The Chiangmai rates for criminal litigation vary from 2.48 to 3.78 cases per 1,000 population. The comparable figure from Turkey is 13.7 cases. In Kenya, the figures range from 11.2 to 26.7 criminal cases per 1,000 population.[7]

As low as the modern Thai litigation rates are, however, they are approximately double the comparable rates of litigation for the period shortly after the founding of the modern Chiangmai court. During the year 1918,[8] for example, ten years after the enactment of the original Law of the Courts of Justice and the Penal Code, there were only 1.77 criminal cases processed per 1,000 population in the "circle" of Chiangmai, and a mere 0.35 civil cases.[9] The citizens of Chiangmai were initially hesitant to take their legal matters to the new courts, unlike the citizens of India and other nations, who responded immediately to the establishment of local courts as part of their newly centralized judiciary, producing an apparent "flood of litigation" at the local level (Galanter, 1968:69; also Rudolph and Rudolph, 1967:259-62). Although the new courts served some purposes of the Thai people, there was—and still is—a tendency to avoid the entire process of formal litigation.

---

4. In the year 1967, Starr and Pool noted a total of 655 civil and 410 criminal cases in the four courts of first instance in the district of Bodrum. They give population figures of 5,137 for the town of Bodrum (date unspecified) and about 25,000 for the villages in the district. I have therefore used a population figure of 30,000 to compute approximate litigation rates from these data.

5. These figures are part of the data contained in a preliminary draft study of local court use in Kenya. Litigation rates were calculated by Professor Abel from nationwide population and litigation statistics for the years 1948, 1959, 1962, and 1964-69.

6. As a measure of the litigiousness of the residents of the two counties in California, these figures are clearly understated. Disputants had other judicial forums available to them, including the federal court system, for litigating complaints that arose in Alameda and San Benito counties.

7. The California study by Friedman and Percival dealt only with civil and not with criminal litigation.

8. Strictly speaking, the year was April 1, 1918 to March 31, 1919, according to the calendar then used in Thailand.

9. Thailand, Ministry of Finance, Department of General Statistics (1922:29, 222, and 238). These early figures are based upon the entire Phayap *monthon* of which Chiangmai was then a part, together with the provinces of Chiangrai, Maehongson, and Lamphun. No breakdown by individual province is provided.

If we examine the four main streams of litigation in slightly more detail (table 4), we see, with regard first to criminal cases, that there are two important categories: public and private prosecutions. The distinction will be an important one throughout this study. Public prosecutions are criminal suits brought by designated agents of the government acting in the name of the state. Private prosecutions, on the other hand, are criminal suits brought by private individuals who are vested by law with the power to sue in particular cases for alleged criminal violations. Not all private individuals have this right. The plaintiff must show that he or she is either the person injured by the alleged criminal act or a person entitled by law to proceed in the place of the injured person, either as (1) the legal representative or custodian of a minor or incompetent person; (2) "the ascendant or descendant, the husband or wife, in respect only of criminal offenses in which the injured person is so injured that he died or is unable to act by himself"; or (3) "the manager or other representative of a juristic person" (Criminal Procedure Code, Sections 28 and 5). Table 4 shows that public prosecutions are far more numerous than private prosecutions. Many of the public prosecutions, however, represent the routine processing of minor misdemeanors resulting in fines of 50 or 100 *baht* (approximately $2.50 to $5). Among the ten most numerous public prosecutions, all are basically of this type. Many of the private criminal actions, on the other hand, are more serious matters, more time-consuming, and more important to the parties involved.[10]

The civil suits listed in table 4 show a heavy preponderance of contract cases, many of which are brought by commercial enterprises. Second most numerous among the civil suits are cases arising from wrongful acts. Hidden among the wrongful acts, however, are a substantial number of disguised contract cases, for the Civil and Commercial Code defines "wrongful acts" to include unlawful injuries, either willful or negligent, to "the life, body, health, liberty, *property or any right* of another person" (Section 420, emphasis added). A number of cases classified as wrongful acts in fact arise from violations of contractual relationships between the litigants. Most of the remaining civil suits also involve the assertion of contract rights or property rights which give rise to the eviction of tenants or squatters, the collection of rent or damages involving real property, and actions to decide rights in and access to land and water. A final portion of the civil suits consists of uncontested petitions to the court regarding wills, the establishment of legal guardians, and other routine matters.

---

10. This characterization of private criminal actions is probably less true of the check cases than of other alleged violations. Many of the check cases are routine collection actions for loans secured by future-dated checks. This type of action is discussed on page 108 ff., *infra*.

TABLE 4
Cases Most Frequently Litigated in Provincial and Magistrates' Courts of Chiangmai in 1965, 1968, 1971, and 1974

Frequency of Cases

Subject Matter	1965		1968		1971		1974		Aggregate	
A. Public Criminal Prosecutions	No.	% of Yearly Total	No.	% of Yearly Total	No.	% of Yearly Total	No.	% of Yearly Total	No.	% of Total
1. Theft	593	17.8	434	14.4	409	13.6	374	10.1	1,810	13.8
2. Possession of firearms	355	10.6	345	11.4	415	13.8	511	13.8	1,626	12.4
3. Gambling	347	10.4	320	10.6	277	9.2	550	14.8	1,494	11.4
4. Prostitution	292	8.8	377	12.5	156	5.2	99	2.7	924	7.1
5. Bodily harm	197	5.9	199	6.6	280	9.3	233	6.3	909	7.0
6. Violations involving slaughter and distribution of livestock	243	7.3	259	8.6	202	6.7	154	4.1	858	6.6
7. Marijuana, opium, narcotics violations	2	0.1	4	0.1	269	8.9	547	14.7	822	6.3
8. Forestry violations	131	3.9	176	5.8	159	5.3	300	8.1	766	5.9
9. Illegal alcoholic beverages	297	8.9	162	5.4	90	3.0	9	0.2	558	4.3
10. Violations concerning workshops	396	11.9	11	0.4	8	0.3	7	0.2	422	3.2
11. Homicides	82	2.5	109	3.6	119	4.0	76	2.0	386	3.0
12. Traffic violations	18	0.5	57	1.9	128	4.3	96	2.6	299	2.3
13. Receiving stolen property	1	0.0	133	4.4	37	1.2	89	2.4	260	2.0
14. Sexual offenses	39	1.2	73	2.4	84	2.8	60	1.6	256	2.0
15. Misappropriation of property	81	2.4	63	2.1	50	1.7	51	1.4	245	1.9
16. Trespass	25	0.7	19	0.6	36	1.2	46	1.2	126	1.0
17. Robbery	26	0.8	29	1.0	24	0.8	34	0.9	113	0.9
18. Gang robbery	29	0.9	33	1.1	26	0.9	20	0.5	108	0.8
19. Offenses against officials	17	0.5	16	0.5	14	0.5	54	1.5	101	0.8
20. Violations involving protected lands	9	0.3	17	0.6	12	0.4	58	1.6	96	0.7
21. Others	156	4.7	182	6.0	214	7.1	346	9.3	898	6.9
Total	3,336	100.1	3,018	100.0	3,009	100.2	3,714	100.0	13,077	100.3

48

TABLE 4—Continued

Frequency of Cases

Subject Matter B. Private Criminal Prosecutions	1965		1968		1971		1974		Aggregate	
	No.	% of Yearly Total	No.	% of Yearly Total	No.	% of Yearly Total	No.	% of Yearly Total	No.	% of Total
1. Violations involving checks	36	34.0	58	39.2	126	70.0	110	72.4	330	56.3
2. Offenses relating to justice	17	16.0	22	14.9	12	6.7	8	5.3	59	10.1
3. Cheating and fraud	7	6.6	11	7.4	7	3.9	7	4.6	32	5.5
4. Defamation	6	5.7	7	4.7	4	2.2	7	4.6	24	4.1
5. Misappropriation of property	6	5.7	7	4.7	4	2.2	3	2.0	20	3.4
6. Homicide	6	5.7	8	5.4	5	2.8	1	0.7	20	3.4
7. Trespass	7	6.6	5	3.4	6	3.3	1	0.7	19	3.2
8. Bodily harm	3	2.8	7	4.7	3	1.7	0	—	13	2.2
9. Theft	1	0.9	2	1.4	3	1.7	2	1.3	8	1.4
10. Malfeasance in public office	3	2.8	1	0.7	0	—	3	2.0	7	1.2
11. Others	14	13.2	20	13.5	10	5.6	10	6.6	54	9.2
Total	106	100.0	148	100.0	180	100.1	152	100.2	586	100.0

TABLE 4—Continued

Frequency of Cases

Subject Matter C. Civil Suits	1965		1968		1971		1974		Aggregate	
	No.	% of Yearly Total	No.	% of Yearly Total	No.	% of Yearly Total	No.	% of Yearly Total	No.	% of Total
1. Contracts										
a. Loans, checks, promissory notes	192	26.8	190	25.7	235	33.6	280	37.3	897	30.9
b. Sales, hire, hire-purchase	146	20.4	123	16.7	142	20.3	123	16.4	534	18.4
c. Employment, commisisons, production and transportation of goods	18	2.5	15	2.0	12	1.7	12	1.6	57	2.0
d. Suretyship	3	0.4	10	1.4	18	2.6	22	2.9	53	1.8
e. Compromise agreements	11	1.5	11	1.5	15	2.1	10	1.3	47	1.6
f. Other contracts	34	4.7	38	5.1	57	8.2	45	6.0	174	6.0
2. Wrongful acts (*lamoet*)	74	10.3	87	11.8	55	7.9	66	8.8	282	9.7
3. Inheritance-related actions	24	3.3	36	4.9	46	6.6	73	9.7	179	6.2
4. Evictions, actions for rent and damages	30	4.2	60	8.1	34	4.9	43	5.7	167	5.7
5. Rights in, access to, land and water	21	2.9	40	5.4	36	5.2	29	3.9	126	4.3
6. Bankruptcy	38	5.3	29	3.9	8	1.1	8	1.1	83	2.9
7. Divorce, related marital matters	13	1.8	23	3.1	16	2.3	23	3.1	75	2.6
8. Others	113	15.8	76	10.3	25	3.6	17	2.3	231	8.0
Total	717	99.9	738	99.9	699	100.1	751	100.0	2,905	100.1

The Court and Its Functions

A different kind of overview is provided in table 5, which classifies the litigation flow with reference to outcome. This form of classification reveals with some clarity three distinct functions that the Chiangmai court now performs. All three functions, or "modes of justice," derive from the historical and social setting of the court which I have sketched in the preceding chapters. The first "mode of justice" is the suppression of crime, a direct descendant of the traditional responsibility of the provincial ruler (who was also the highest judge) to use force and punishment to maintain order in the society.

TABLE 5
Three Modes of Justice in the Chiangmai Trial Courts: Analysis of Selected Civil and Criminal Cases by Outcome

	MODE I		MODE II				MODE III	
	State Prosecutions for Criminal Offenses ($N = 643$)[a]		Lawsuits Alleging Private Wrongs				Enforcement of Contracts & Property Rights ($N = 684$)[d]	
			Private Criminal Prosecutions ($N = 586$)[b]		Civil Suits ($N = 114$)[c]			
	No.	%	No.	%	No.	%	No.	%
Completely favorable to plaintiff[e]	621	96.6	18	3.1	23	20.2	441	64.5
Completely favorable to defendant	15	2.3	66	11.3	2	1.8	16	2.3
Compromise verdict or settlement in court	---	-----	---	-----	57	50.0	76	11.1
Suit withdrawn	4	0.6	496	84.6	24	21.1	119	17.4
Outcome unknown	3	0.5	6	1.0	8	7.0	32	4.7

Source: Court Registers for Provincial and Magistrates' Courts, Chiangmai Province, for 1965, 1968, 1971, and 1974.

[a]Sample drawn from records of every twentieth criminal suit processed in 1965, 1968, 1971, and 1974.

[b]Sample includes all private criminal suits processed in 1965, 1968, 1971, and 1974.

[c]Sample drawn from records of every third civil suit processed in 1965, 1968, 1971, and 1974. For Mode II, only civil suits involving "wrongful acts" and "divorce and related matters" are included.

[d]Sample drawn from records of every third civil suit processed in 1965, 1968, 1971, and 1974. For Mode III, only civil suits involving contracts, evictions, and land and water disputes are included.

[e]In criminal suits, a finding of guilt as charged; in civil suits, plaintiff wins full amount in controversy.

Outcomes in these cases are overwhelmingly favorable to the state. The conviction rate in public criminal prosecutions is 96.6 percent. In the vast majority of these cases, the defendants formally confess guilt to the charges brought against them, knowing that they may thereby reduce their sentences by half because of their "repentance of wrongdoing and attempt to minimize the consequences thereof" (Penal Code, Section 78). Only 2.3 percent of the criminal defendants in public prosecutions succeed in establishing their innocence.

The second mode of justice involves the litigation of private wrongs. I include in this category all private criminal prosecutions and those civil suits grouped under "wrongful acts" and marital disputes.[11] The second mode of justice is characterized by negotiation rather than adjudication and punishment. Traditionally, private wrongs in Thai society were often mediated by *phuyai*, "big persons," who could exercise authority over the disputants to help them resolve their differences. In modern Thailand, as we shall see in later chapters, mediation is still preferred by most people over litigation. When these disputes do come to court, therefore, the court itself is likely to provide a forum where mediation takes place. Rather than a clear-cut decision on the merits, designating one side the winner and the other side the loser, the outcome is more likely to be some form of compromise. This pattern is clearly reflected in table 5. In the private criminal cases, out-of-court compromises are reached between the parties in 84.6 percent of the cases. The defendant usually pays plaintiff a stipulated amount, and plaintiff then withdraws the prosecution. In the civil cases involving private wrongs, the result may be either an out-of-court compromise followed by plaintiff's withdrawal of the suit (21.1 percent) or, more typically, a compromise agreement formally announced in the court and recorded by the judge as a legally enforceable agreement for future performance (50.0 percent).

The third mode of justice involves the enforcement of contracts and property rights. The outcomes of these cases indicate a great judicial deference to written forms and to officially certified documents. The court tends to enforce such obligations strictly, ensuring that commercial transactions follow the letter of the contract and that official registration forms take priority over informal customary practices. Acting in this way, the court fulfills its original mandate to provide certainty for entrepreneurs and government officials in provincial Thailand. Defendants win only 2.3 percent of these cases; 64.5 percent result in verdicts wholly favorable to plaintiffs, while another 17.4 percent are withdrawn. Litigation in this third mode of justice produces results strongly favorable to persons who hold the relevant legal documents, as opposed to persons whose claims are based upon other less legalistic expectations and behavior. The outcomes of such cases reveal the power that the provincial courts have vested in those who understand and pattern their actions according to the norms of the Civil and Commercial Code and the administrative procedures of the central government.

Throughout the remainder of this study, it will be the second mode of justice—the negotiation of private wrongs—that will occupy most of our attention. All three classes of litigation raise interesting questions about continuity and change in the role of the provincial courts. It is in the second

---

11. Marital disputes are included with the other private wrongs because such lawsuits usually allege some form of wrongdoing or injury by one of the partners, comparable to the legal wrongs alleged in private criminal suits and civil "wrongful acts." This subject will be discussed further in chapter 11.

mode of justice, however, that we see most clearly the dynamics of the interaction between code and custom in the Chiangmai court. In the litigation of private wrongs we come closest to a free-wheeling assertion of claims, where the outcome of the lawsuit may be genuinely in doubt. As we shall see, however, this very uncertainty creates anxiety and uneasiness among the participants. The sooner a resolution can be achieved the better; the greater the control which the participants can exert over the outcome, the more desirable is the process of negotiation itself.

In the chapters that follow, we shall descend into the landscape that we have now viewed from above and explore the work of the court in some detail, particularly with regard to the litigation of private wrongs. From these explorations may come a sense of the various meanings of justice in provincial Thailand and the role that the judiciary plays in defining this elusive concept.

Part Two
Private Wrongs, Mediation, and the Traditional Legal Culture

When the waters rise, fish eat ants; when the waters recede, ants eat fish.

*Walk behind the **phuyai**, and the dogs won't bite.*

Thai proverbs

Chapter Four
The Meanings of Justice

A proper consideration of the litigation of private wrongs in the Chiangmai court must take into account the broader social attitudes towards conflict and the informal patterns of mediation that divert many disputes from the provincial court itself. The establishment of the Chiangmai court brought a new and unfamiliar forum to the traditional setting, and even today there is a general reluctance to take disputes involving private wrongs to this forum. In the preceding chapter we saw that private wrongs were not often litigated in the Chiangmai court. Table 4 shows that only 586 out of 13,663 criminal cases (4.3 percent) were private criminal prosecutions. Among those 586 cases, 330 were based upon violations involving checks, a cause of action as deeply rooted in the law of contract as it is in the law of private wrongs. As for civil litigation, cases that I have classified as private wrongs numbered only 357 (12.3 percent) of the 2,905 civil actions noted in table 4. Even this small figure is inflated by a substantial percentage of lawsuits that are actually enforcement actions for hidden contractual obligations, more properly grouped with the third than the second mode of justice. In this chapter, then, we shall begin to consider some of the factors that account for the low rate of litigation involving private wrongs in the Chiangmai court. In later chapters, however, having examined the complex structure of mediation in Thai society and the social values that discourage individuals from asserting private rights in court, the question will be reversed and we shall be forced to ask why such cases reach the court at all.

TRADITIONAL VIEWS OF THE HUMAN PERSONALITY

The Thai perception of the human personality is a complex blend of Theravada Buddhism, Brahmanism, and animism. While acknowledging that there are significant forces that predetermine human behavior, most Thai people would also emphasize the capacity of the individual to choose between good and evil acts. Even at the time of birth, many of the crucial factors that shape the personality have already come into play. The newborn child already possesses both *khwan* and *winyan*, two "vital essences" that lie at the core of human existence (Jane R. Hanks, 1965:77). The *khwan* is the spiritual essence or soul found in all humans and in certain other animate and inanimate entities, such as elephants, water buffalo, rice fields, and towns (Phraya Anuman Rajadhon, 1968:202). Weak and tender during the first years of life, the *khwan* is strengthened by the passing of time and by the occasional performance of propitiatory rituals. Yet the *khwan* remains flighty throughout life, subject to fright and shock. When this occurs, the *khwan* flies out of the body (*khwan hai* or *khwan ni*) and must be recalled ceremonially.

The *winyan*, on the other hand, is securely anchored in the body, and its loss occurs only with death. The *winyan* regulates the mental and physical activities essential to human life:

> Living in the upper part of the body close to, and governed by, the heart, the winyan is the "leader," or "organizer" of the other thirty-one parts [of the body]. It puts desired actions into effect, e.g., "if you wish to put on a coat, it orders the proper muscular activity." It also produces emotional reactions, such as anger, love, and hate. (Jane R. Hanks, 1965:78)

A strong *winyan* will endow its owner with an independent or assertive personality, while a weak *winyan* will result in passivity (*ibid.:* 79). Upon death, the four constituent parts of the *winyan*, the *čhetaphut*, leave the body and join the world of ghosts (*phi*) which live in constant contact with the human world:

> The chetaphud-turned-phii wander aimlessly for three or more days near their old home, appearing to the living as frightening ghosts. They walk on the tops of their feet, i.e., with the foot turned over, and their heads are turned around backwards. Then one by one these phii fall down flat. When the last one falls, "the person knows that he is dead." His phii "become good" and cease to trouble people. One or more of the chetaphud, after falling, returns to dwell near its former home in the spirit house as a beneficent protector. These become the interested "souls of the ancestors" to whom are addressed prayers for a blessing at marriage, for help if children are sick, and at other times. (*ibid.:* 79, n. 6)

Besides the *khwan* and the *winyan*, other constituent elements of the personality also exert their influence at the time of birth and before. Most important of these are the merit of the individual and the influence of the stars. Merit is determined by the individual's good and evil behavior in his or her life and in previous lives. The newborn child possesses a store of merit and demerit from previous incarnations to which he or she may add or subtract in this existence. The accumulation of merit, attained by the individual's own volition, influences both fate and personality. The relationship between merit and fate was explained by one provincial abbot in the following way:

> "Our merit is the result of what we do, say, and feel. The good that we may do and the reward we receive is merit (*bun*). Evil choices and the punishment they bring us is demerit (*baab*)." This moral process of receiving rewards and punishments continues throughout the endless karmic cycle of rebirths. (Ingersoll, 1966:72-73)

Merit and demerit not only guide the fate of the individual, determining the rewards and punishments that he or she receives, but they also influence the personality of the individual so profoundly that observers can clearly perceive their effects:

> The people of Bang Chan felt they could discern even of themselves who was meritful and who was not according to human circumstances, constitution, and behavior. A meritorious person was healthy, happy, and successful in all undertakings. He enjoyed good health and long life, a kindly personality, many fine children, wealth, high status, intelligence, and luck. . . . He who lacked merit, because of sins committed perhaps many ages ago . . . suffered early death, deformities, unhappiness, poverty, and had a cruel nature. Illness . . . struck as part of the suffering brought on by former sin. It was accepted in the conviction that whoever suffered had brought it on himself. (Jane R. Hanks, 1963:28)

Both of the preceding descriptions, it should be noted, stress the power of individuals to add to their store of merit and thereby alter their own fate and personality for the better.[1]

Merit mixes with "habit" and with the composite "elements" found in each person to determine the "heart" (*čhai*)—the character and disposition—of the individual. Habits are accumulated through many existences and are considered an important source of character distinctions among people. The elements—earth, fire, water, air, and also gold, iron, wood, and others—are blended in different proportions in each individual, producing basic personality traits and helping to determine compatibility or incompatibility in personal relationships (Jane R. Hanks, 1963:19-20). These factors all contribute to the nature of the "heart," a term used frequently to describe character and temperament. People may be "hot-hearted" (*čhai rǫn*) or "cool-hearted" (*čhai yen*), "black-hearted" and merciless (*čhai dam, čhai rai*) or "good-hearted" and kind (*čhai di*), generous and "wide-hearted" (*čhai kwang*) or "narrow-hearted" and stingy (*čhai khaep*), "tender-hearted" and pliable (*čhai ǫn*) or

---

[1]. Of all the activities to increase one's store of merit, the most effective—at least for men—is to become a monk, an option which many men have traditionally exercised at some point in their lives, even if only for a few months.

"hard-hearted" and unyielding (čhai khaeng), daring and "bold-hearted" (čhai kla) or timid and hesitant (čhai sǫ). All of these characteristics are formed by the particular blend of merit, habit, *winyan,* and the elemental make-up of the individual.

Even the influence of the stars upon the personality is not wholly fortuitous. A favorable astrological configuration at the time of birth can be a sign of merit and will help to endow the individual with good character and good fortune. During the individual's lifetime, the stars dictate the rise and fall of one's fortunes, sub-cycles within the greater cycle of this life and of an existence spanning many lives. Thais speak of strong or weak stars as permanent and immutable influences upon one's fate *(duang khaeng* and *duang ǫn),* yet from time to time one's stars will rise and fall, bringing wealth and good fortune and taking them away.

Luck, with its indirect relationship to individual merit, is central to the consciousness of Thai people. There are many ways to ascertain and strengthen one's luck at any given time, and these various methods have long been popular in Thai society. *Phraya* Anuman Rajadhon describes how bamboo poles of varying lengths and with varying numbers of segments were once used to bring luck to the persons who found and carried them (1968:296-301). At most shrines there are containers of sticks which are shaken until one stick falls out, bearing a number that indicates the fortune of the individual. The Thai love of gambling in its hundreds of forms—from cock-fighting to card-playing to participation in lotteries—is also a form of luck-measurement, for a rise in one's fortunes will be indicated clearly by victory and sudden riches. Most people try to determine the auspicious days for engaging in important activities (*ha loek*), and a monk learned in astrology will usually be consulted for advice in such matters. Careful attention to favorable and unfavorable configurations of the stars can bring the individual simultaneous success in all his undertakings—luck in the lottery may be associated with luck in love and in a business transaction all at the same time.

We have seen that theories of the individual personality in combination with the more or less transitory influences of the stars can help to explain behavior and to explain why the individual may suffer misfortune from time to time. The actions of non-human beings may also contribute significantly to these matters. Wijeyewardene, speaking specifically of northern Thailand, describes a cosmological hierarchy in which man occupies a middle ground, with the gods (*thewada*) above and the ghosts (*phi*) below. Gods, such as the Earth Mother (*maenang thǫrani*) and the Rice Goddess (*mae phosop*), live "in one of the heavens, beings enjoying the rewards of their good deeds in previous lives, but according to dogma, not immortal" (1970:249). Ghosts, on the other hand, may be spirits rising from dead persons or from other sources. They can be dangerous and occasionally helpful to humans:

> ...*phi* may either be unequivocally dangerous—and where these are

human spirits the ideology tends to identify them by the nature of their death, in pregnancy, in childbirth or by violence—or they may be both benevolent and dangerous—these are the ancestor spirits. (*ibid.*: 250)

This hierarchy, as Wijeyewardene emphasizes, is not necessarily held clearly in the mind of the villager, and the classification of certain supernatural beings, such as the Lord of the Place (*čhao thi*), is ambiguous. Such discrepancies need not concern us here. What I wish to stress is man's middle ground in the cosmic hierarchy and the crucial influence upon his life of the gods and spirits around him:

... man is at once superior in terms of potential salvation, and inferior in terms of effective power. Incorporeal beings are all pervasive. There is neither place nor act which is necessarily not subject to their interference. For the individual then the domain of non-corporeal beings can provide the explanation for suffering, hope for the future, a scapegoat among his fellows, a focus of fear or a staff of reassurance. (*ibid.*: 250)

The intervention of the gods and the spirits, then, combines with the constituent elements of the individual personality and with the influence of the stars to explain who individuals are, how they behave, and why it is that good or bad fortune befalls them.

INJURIES

The concept of an injury in traditional Thai society is an elusive one, emerging most clearly from a consideration of the remedies commonly sought by the victim. I shall describe four such remedies, hoping to provide an insight into the ways in which injuries are perceived and the interaction between the victim and the wrongdoer understood. These remedies will also suggest an interplay between several philosophical and religious sources—Buddhism, Brahmanism, animism, and western "rationalism"—linking the concept of an injury to some of the views of the human personality that have already been discussed.

One remedy, now on the wane in modern Thai society, is a payment to the spirits of a particular household or village who have been offended by some wrongful act. The wrongdoer is required by village authorities to make a payment or to perform a ceremony to placate the offended spirits. When a community or an individual suffers from a malevolent influence, whose origin may be unknown, a specialist can be called upon to determine the source and to recommend a way for the wrongdoer to make amends. By this process the community mobilizes itself against the wrongdoer and imposes its sanctions.[2]

---

2. See generally Klausner (1974:46-47 and 57-58) and Keyes (1975:196) for discussions of village disputes and spirit intermediaries in northeast Thailand.

The injury is not merely a wrongful act inflicting damage or suffering upon an individual. It is, rather, an offense to the supernatural beings who are vital to the welfare of the household or the entire community. The injury must therefore be remedied by the payment of a fine or the performance of a ceremony in which all the villagers have a vested interest. Failure to obtain an appropriate remedy may have dangerous supernatural consequences for the entire community. The offense against an individual takes on the broader characteristics of an antisocial act.

A second type of remedy looks to the victim rather than to the offended spirits: this is the *kha tham khwan,* or payment to propitiate the *khwan.* This expression is found both in common speech and in the official language of the courts of law. It is well known that if the *khwan* soul is lost the individual will die. Since the *khwan* is delicate and easily frightened, it may leave the body whenever the individual suffers a shock, injury, disease, or other unpleasant experience. When this occurs, a ceremony must be performed to call the *khwan* back and secure it in the body. A silver offering tray is prepared with balls of rice, a banana, a boiled egg, flowers, incense and candles.[3] A learned officiant then chants in a melodious voice to revive the spirit of the person for whom the ceremony is performed:

> The recitation goes on for ten to fifteen minutes. Then the officiant binds the hands [with a piece of string tied around each wrist]. The left hand is tied first. He says, "Bind the left hand and the *khwan* will come. Bind the right hand and the *khwan* will stay. Return, *khwan,* stay with the flesh, stay with the body. Do not float away again. Lead a long and secure life." Thus the ritual ends. Both hands must have string tied around them. Some people wear the string as long as three days, but children can sometimes be seen wearing the unbleached white string until it turns black. (Sanguan Chotisukharat, 1969:267)

This ceremony, Brahman in origin, restores the vital essence of the injured person. It is the responsibility of the wrongdoer to pay the expenses necessary to perform the ritual, in order to repair the damage he or she has done. In many cases the concept of such a payment to revive the spirit of the victim has remained, even when no ceremony is actually performed.

Closely related to the "payment to propitiate the *khwan,*" but Buddhist rather than Brahman in origin, is the "funeral payment," or *kha tham sop.* The wrongdoer makes this type of payment when the victim dies and a ceremony must be held to create merit for the dead person and to cremate his body. The wrongdoer must pay the price of food, candles, incense, flowers,

---

3. I am basing my description upon the ceremony as it is performed in northern Thailand, as described in Sanguan Chotisukharat (1969). Other descriptions of the same ceremony in the north and elsewhere in Thailand may be found in *Phraya* Anuman Rajadhon (1968:202-254); Jane R. Hanks (1963:24 and 68); Kingshill (1960:153-56); Tambiah (1968:108-110); Ingersoll (1966:53).

money and other implements provided for the monks who officiate at the ceremony, transportation costs for the monks, food and drink for the guests, and other expenses associated with preparation of the body for cremation. Like the payment for the *khwan*, the payment of funeral costs defines the responsibility of the wrongdoer with reference to the spiritual or psychic state of the victim. An injury, in these terms, is an act that does damage to the vital essence of the individual and perhaps brings death. The remedy for such an act is to restore the spirit of the victim if possible. If this is no longer possible, then the wrongdoer must help to perform those meritorious acts which will enable the victim to lead a pleasant and successful existence in future lives.

A fourth type of remedy, the *kha siahai*, or "payment for the loss," is also a part of traditional speech as well as the language of the law. This remedy, however, suggests a totally different kind of obligation and a distinctly different concept of injury from the three already discussed. Legalistic in nature and perhaps less traditional in origin, the "payment for the loss" defines injury in materialistic terms. It looks not to the psychic or spiritual state of the victim or the local supernatural beings, but to the value of the property or income that the victim has lost as a result of the wrongful act. The wrongdoer has an obligation to pay the victim an amount sufficient to restore the material loss. The payment is unrelated to the impact of the injury upon the victim's spiritual essence. Indeed, payment of this kind would be appropriate even if the victim were totally unaffected personally or unaware of the injury at the time of its occurrence. In this sense the "payment for the loss" represents a "rationalized" departure from remedies predicated upon cosmic or supernatural factors that have been central to the traditional conception of an injury in Thailand.

RESPONSES TO INJURY

It is most characteristic of Thai people to absorb injuries done to them, to contain their response and to avoid public insistence upon their "legal" rights. Public anger or strongly expressed resentment may be seen as immature, excessive, reflecting poorly upon the victim rather than the wrongdoer. Such an attitude has great significance for the role of the courts and the mediation mechanisms in Thai society. Several related concepts contribute to this seemingly passive response to injury. A discussion of some of these concepts may provide further insights into Thai perceptions of luck and justice and suggest why it is that many Thai people avoid the public litigation of their disputes in court.

A technical legal term for "injured person" is *čhao thuk*, which translates roughly as "the person who suffers." The word *thuk* is of special interest. Derived from the Pali word *dukkha*, its Thai translation is given as "trouble; pain; affliction; sorrow; distress; unhappiness" (McFarland, 1944:417). The concept of *dukkha* is central to the teachings of the Buddha, for it lies at the core of the Four Noble Truths which the Buddha articulated in his sermon at Benares:

> Now this, monks, is the noble truth of pain [*dukkha*]: birth is painful, old age is painful, sickness is painful, death is painful, sorrow, lamentation, dejection, and despair are painful. Contact with unpleasant things is painful, not getting what one wishes is painful. In short the five groups of grasping are painful. (Burtt, 1955:30)

The Buddha explained that the way to end pain, or *dukkha,* was by bringing to an end the cravings and desires that are a part of human existence, through "abandonment, forsaking, release, non-attachment" (30). This could be achieved by following the Eightfold Path of "right views, right intention, right speech, right action, right livelihood, right effort, right mindfulness, right concentration" (30). In short, *dukkha,* whose doctrinal meaning is not merely pain but "imperfection, impermanence, emptiness, insubstantiality" (Rahula, 1959:17), is an inevitable fact of existence. The way for a *"čhao thuk"* to find release from his suffering is not through an insistence upon his rights, but through a meritorious course of action founded upon the Eightfold Path.

Blended with this concept of an idealized Buddhist response to suffering is the Thai social ideal of "coolness," politeness, and non-assertiveness. The person who possesses a "cool heart" is able to retain his psychic equilibrium in the face of all kinds of adversity. By remaining tranquil when his rights are infringed upon, he reveals not only his maturity but his merit, for equanimity is an outward sign of the meritorious person. In legal briefs it is usually maintained that the injury to the *čhao thuk* has made him *"düat rǫn"*—"boiling hot." That is, the injury has disrupted the victim's composure and made him unable to remain "cool." Even when this occurs, however, the Thai value system still restrains the victim in several ways from making any overt response. One of these is by a strong social insistence upon an outwardly polite manner, even in the face of outrageous behavior. The various forms and even the proper language of social intercourse make politeness an extremely important social value, and its absence for whatever reason is usually considered embarrassing and even repulsive. Also, there is the significant and pervasive concept of *"krengčhai"*: "to have consideration for; to be reluctant to impose (upon)" (Haas, 1964:39). Feeling *krengčhai* towards others will make a person non-assertive even where his interests could be seriously jeopardized. A polite and respected man whose land was occupied by a squatter tried to explain to me his unwillingness to take any sort of action, even when he knew he could lose part of his holding by adverse possession:

> This man came to me several years ago and said, "Sir, please don't have any quarrel with me or take me to court. I would lose face. Just tell me when you want me to get off your land." This made me feel *krengčhai* towards him, and now I will just let him stay.

Although many factors in Thai society work to inhibit overt responses to injury, the victims of wrongful acts may console themselves with the knowledge that cosmic or supernatural justice will ultimately be done. According to the Thai Buddhist conception of *dharma*, virtuous acts and acts lacking in virtue will eventually produce their own appropriate results:

> In external terms, *dharma* is the action which, provided it is conformable to the order of things, permits man to realize his destiny to the full, sustains him in this life, and assures his well-being after death. By its own virtue that act produces a spiritual benefit for him who has performed it, which will necessarily bear fruit in the other world. Conversely, an act contrary to *dharma*, called *adharma*, necessarily involves a sanction, a "fall" for the one who does it, which will strike him in his future existence if not actually in his present life. (Lingat, 1973:3-4)

Clearly the term *dharma* implies far more than "justice" in any narrowly juristic sense. It refers to a cosmic law of existence governing all substances and beings in the universe according to their intrinsic nature. The person who has been injured by a wrongful act can rely upon the working of *dharma* ultimately to mete out a proper punishment. Ideally, the injured person should seek to maintain a course of meritorious conduct, leave the wrongdoer to his own fate, and thereby gain power and control over the situation:

> Speak gently, and they will respond.
> Angry words hurt, and rebound on the speaker.
>
> Nirvana:
> When the agitated mind is as still as
> a broken gong.
>
> Like a cowherd with his staff pushing cattle into new pasture,
> old age with death pushes the world's creatures into new lives.
>
> How will a fool doing evil deeds know this?
> He learns the hard way, burning in the fire of his deeds.[4]

On a less exalted level, the animistic beliefs and practices of Thai villagers can sometimes help to dispense justice without requiring injured individuals to assert their own rights directly. Justice at this level, as we have seen, conceives of the village or household spirits and not the individual as the party injured by the wrongful act. It is the spirit doctor and not the victim who identifies the wrongdoer and declares the necessity of some propitiatory act. In this way both the injury and the response to the injury are depersonalized, and the

---

4. From "Punishment" in *The Dhammapada*, P. Lal (1967:83-84).

wrongdoer can be brought to terms with little damage to the smooth fabric of social relationships.[5]

Another factor that may inhibit injured persons from responding directly and personally to wrongs they have suffered is the implicit recognition that both they and the wrongdoer occupy ambiguous moral positions. The ambiguity with regard to the wrongdoer may be illustrated with reference to the term usually applied to bullies or ruffians: *"nakleng."* This term has both negative and positive connotations, referring on the one hand to a "rogue, rascal, gambler" and on the other hand to a "bold person, sporting person" and even to a "big-hearted person" (Haas, 1964:261). A *nakleng* commands respect and sometimes admiration because he is a person with power and often attracts a group of followers through his authority and his generosity. He would not possess these attributes had he not acquired a store of merit in some previous existence. Thus the exercise of power by the *nakleng* may have implications reaching beyond the disreputable or criminal nature of his act. That he possesses such power at all says something for his own special status. That he uses it in the way that he does says something for the status of his victims. However appalling their injuries, they would never have suffered had their own time not been ripe and had their own *karma* not required the result which transpired:

> Everyone who is killed, even if not by sword, gun or hangman's knot, is receiving his due for crimes that he does not even know, that may have been committed in previous lives as well as past decades and years.... The victor with the blood of his own and enemy soldiers on his hands enjoys cosmic backing because of his virtues. His enemies are the cosmic enemies killed for their trespasses, and his judgment, coinciding for a short period with celestial justice, leads to its realization. (Lucien M. Hanks, 1976)

This vision of the village bully meting out cosmic justice for the sins of ages past must, however, be tempered with a more mundane consideration: fear for one's own safety. When injured persons hesitate to press valid claims against bullies too vigorously, it may well be that they fear physical retaliation by the wrongdoer and not that they recognize him as an agent of justice. The cosmic considerations of cause and effect may then serve primarily to rationalize a decision made out of fear.[6] Victims may indeed respond to injury, but by indirect or symbolic means, not wishing to expose themselves to the threat

---

5. See William J. Klausner's essay, "The Cool Heart," in Klausner (1974), especially pp. 46-47.

6. "The villager thus allows himself to be bullied, whether it be a case of a boundary dispute, theft, or payment of a loan. The villager will rationalize his action or lack of it by stating that the wrongdoer will reap what he has sown. Harm and misfortune will befall the latter because of the sinful action." From "Popular Buddhism in Northeast Thailand," Klausner (1974:86).

of retaliation. In this way they can express their displeasure to the wrongdoer without presenting the matter publicly and explicitly. Klausner describes one typical form of indirect communication known as *prachot*:

> I once observed a rather involved example of this indirect method of expressing anti-social emotions. One woman was slapping a dog and speaking angrily to it, but the words were actually directed at another woman who was punishing her own children and reprimanding them with the same words. The only ones who didn't know what was going on at the time were the dog, the children, and myself who had not yet become familiar with this game of what I have termed "projected vilification." (1974:49)

A more spectacular example of *prachot* occurred during the police strike of August 1975, in which thousands of police massed in the northern province of Lamphun to protest the government's release of nine political activists shortly before they were to be tried. The police expressed their displeasure by occupying public buildings and setting up illegal card games in which they gambled before the cameras of news photographers. The symbolism of the police publicly flouting a law that they normally enforced was a dramatic and effective means of communicating their discontent.

Fear of retaliation may deter victims from asserting their rights explicitly. When the injury proves truly intolerable, however, revenge may become the only way in which the victims themselves can give vent to the "heat" which has built up inside them. When the victim is pushed too far, when the wrongdoer's behavior is too outrageous to tolerate, then an act of revenge by the victim is not only understood but even condoned by the community. I was told of one such incident by the headman of a small village in Hang Dong district of Chiangmai. In his village some years ago there was an individual who liked to steal coconuts of a very small variety, which make tasty curries and can also be planted. He was known to steal whole trees on occasion, and every household in the village—including that of the headman himself—had been his target at one time or another. One day this individual was found shot dead in his own house. Revenge had finally been taken. I asked the village headman if he had ever determined the identity of the murderer. He answered emphatically, "How could I learn who had killed him? Everybody had been his victim, and we were all glad to be rid of him." When the provocation is great enough, revenge becomes a socially acceptable way of responding to injury.[7]

This chapter can be concluded with a brief observation about the rights of victims. An injury produced by a wrongful act does not usually stimulate a consciousness of violated rights in any legal sense, and Thai people are

---

7. Revenge may also be taken in other ways, which are less overt but nonetheless dangerous and effective, such as magical spells, charms, and amulets.

generally reluctant to insist openly and vigorously upon their rights. In a different sense, however, a set of rights is violated by such acts: the right of individuals to maintain their coolness and psychic balance, the right to pursue a meritorious existence without being agitated or obstructed, the right to view oneself as a person respected by the community and worthy of that respect. The response of victims will be shaped by the extent to which they feel such rights have been violated. Ideally, they will continue on their own path without allowing themselves to be unduly shaken or diverted. If the suffering is too great, however, if their coolness changes to heat or their *khwan* soul takes flight, then some kind of response may prove to be in order. The response, whether it comes in the form of an indirect verbal or symbolic expression or in the form of a revenge murder, will be understood and even tolerated if it is seen to correspond to the actual disturbance inflicted by the wrongdoer upon the victim. On such occasions, the strength of human passion is implicitly acknowledged to be superior to the moral ideals that otherwise pervade Thai society.

Chapter Five
Hierarchies of Liability—
Channels of Negotiation

The abstract concepts of justice described in the preceding chapter do not exist in isolation but are part of the fabric of Thai society. The patterns of Thai social organization will themselves determine how justice is implemented in many cases. We have seen that the ideal response to injury is no response, and that Thai people are notable for their reluctance to insist publicly and openly upon their own rights. And yet, the realities of human nature being what they are, it often happens that individuals will seek a remedy for injuries they have suffered. The manner in which they proceed, and the individual or group that assumes liability, will be determined by the social hierarchy to which the victim and the wrongdoer belong. The concept of hierarchy is generally cited as the primary organizing principle of Thai society, supported by the twin and sometimes contradictory principles of kinship and individualism. In this chapter we shall examine the nature and the social function of hierarchies and shall then relate these hierarchies to the concept of liability for private wrongs and of negotiation as a means to resolve such wrongs.

HIERARCHY AND SOCIAL ORGANIZATION

Most observers of traditional Thai society have been impressed with the relative weakness of organizational units that are prominent in other societies: caste, community groups, and even kinship. Individualism is mentioned again and again as an outstanding trait among Thai people, and choices based upon individual preference will typically join persons together into flexible and transitory social groupings. Kinship by itself is inadequate to explain the formation of alliances and reciprocal relationships in Thai society. It is not that kinship is unimportant to Thai people. Far from it, the categories of kinship pervade the consciousness and speech of Thai people at all levels of the society. Affectionate relationships are compared to the love between siblings, and the parent-child relationship is a universal symbol of tenderness and generosity on the one hand and an almost unspeakable debt of love and obligation on the other. Kinship terms are a part of everyday speech, used to express friendship or intimacy even among non-relatives who come to know one another through work, through school, or through other circumstances. Kinship relations, however, are like other relations in that they are nurtured largely by the voluntary preferences of the individuals involved. Even the parent-child relationship is subject to the choice of the participants, and it is common for a child to be reared, for one reason or another, in the household of a relative or friend, or in several such households:

> Individuals of all ages recurringly move in and out of families; families splinter, in full or in part, sometimes permanently, but more frequently to be formed again with the same or new members. What is perhaps most distinctive of this flux is the sense of uncertainty that surrounds it—a state that is easily tolerated by the villagers. (Phillips, 1965:29)[1]

Kinship, then, should be considered in the context of other bonds formed through shared experience, through reciprocation, and through a compatibility resulting from causes more profound than mere biological relationship:

> What then does kinship mean? Certainly it does not specify the duties and expectations within a fixed group bound together as flesh and blood. According to the Thai, who draw on Buddhist tradition at this point, the body is mere nails, bone, hair, fluids, and so forth. Only the soul, which enters during the period of gestation, gives distinguishing characteristics. What is registered as amiable by two souls binds them together. Mutual experience begins with child and mother, first within the mother's body, then in the time of nursing and rearing. Growing up in the same household brings mutual experiences to the household members; so can attending school or serving in the same military company. When husband and wife feel particularly compatible, some say that they have shared experiences in a previous existence. Yet to fix and hold these possible connections requires some special expression of love, the giving of a gift and its reciprocation. The mother, giving her own food and body to a child, shows her love. So a sibling or a schoolmate with some smaller gift may also capture and hold the love of another. Then, depending on the relative age, sex, nature of the gift, and feeling of mutual confidence, the two, bound by amiable experience, are called parent and child, uncle and nephew, older and younger brother, or husband and wife. Kinship is psychic rather than physical. (Lucien M. Hanks, 1972:87)

Reciprocal exchanges can lead to the formation of a bond between two

---

1. Similar observations about Thai kinship relations appear in Evers (1969), Moerman (1966a), Wijeyewardene (1967), and others.

individuals, but this alliance will seldom join persons who are equal in age and status. From the beginning of a relationship there will be a delicate probing to determine who is older, who graduated first and from what school, what are the respective family backgrounds and social positions. Once these factors are established, the initial uncertainty will vanish and the individuals can settle comfortably into a relationship based upon acknowledged status differences between the two participants. A mistake in this regard, a failure, for example, to establish at the outset an appropriate older sibling-younger sibling relationship, can produce awkwardness and embarrassment and can permanently spoil a potential friendship. The language itself is dependent upon an accurate determination of relative statuses, for the first- and second-person pronouns are capable of dozens of variations to reflect the shadings of relationship between speaker and listener. Relationships between individuals are thus founded upon free choice, reciprocity, and hierarchy:

> In the West we consider a reciprocal exchange possible only between cooperating equals; inequality of station seems to constrain us. The Thai, however, because they assume symbiosis to form the basis of reciprocity, deem an inequality to be essential. An aspect of this idea is expressed in the following Thai proverb:
>
>> The earth is good because the grass protects it;
>> The grass grows because the earth is good.
>
> A rich man cannot help a rich man, but he can help a poor man; so a landed man can help a landless man, but not another landed man. The image of the good household reveals parents caring for their obedient children, older siblings tending their less competent juniors, and the able providing for the weak. To these various benefactors is assigned the authority to initiate action, while the recipient dutifully returns appropriate services within the limits of his resources. (*Ibid.:* 84-85)

These two-person relationships, voluntarily formed and subject to termination when either member wishes, are the links which form the chains of larger social hierarchies. The larger hierarchies are in turn joined together to organize great numbers of individuals from the lowest to the highest levels of society. Individual hierarchical groups are typically formed around a single person who exercises authority and who possesses status and resources enough to attract followers. The greater the resources of the patron, the greater the number of clients he will attract and the more worthy of respect he will be considered. Relationships within this "entourage"[2] therefore center upon its leader:

---

2. The term "entourage," as used in this context, was coined by Lucien M. Hanks, and the concept is elaborated in several of his writings. The importance of the entourage in northern, as well as central, Thai society has been emphasized by many scholars. Indeed, Van Roy has called the entourage "the institutional foundation of indigenous Thai (and, I suspect, Tai) economy, society, and polity" (1971:114).

Some one seeking to join an entourage is ordinarily introduced to the leader by a mutual acquaintance who seeks to match the interests of the two parties. The initial relationship may be contract-like and limited, to mend a plow in return for money, or to build a wharf in return for the use of a boat. If trust and affection grow from these beginnings, the liaison passes toward an incalculable exchange of benefits, as if the two had become kinsmen. (Lucien M. Hanks, 1966:57)

Bonds are strong between the leader and each of his clients, but weak among the individual group members. When the life, authority, or resources of the leader come to an end, the entourage disintegrates.

The entourage as a model of social organization appears in Thai society in many manifestations. Lucien M. Hanks has described several: governmental agencies, landowners and their tenants, even the individual family whose members work together to raise a crop of rice (*ibid.*: 58-59). Edward Van Roy has examined in detail the way in which the entourage functions as an economic system in the cultivation and production of *miang* (pickled tea) in northern Thailand (1965; 1967; 1971). Even in Thai politics we can perceive the outlines of the entourage in each of the forty-four political parties that were formed during the first parliamentary elections after the overthrow of military rule in 1973. Each party was organized around a single influential individual. Cooperation among the various leaders to reduce the number of parties was difficult, and parliamentary coalitions among the parties were unstable. Horizontal alliances were weak and transitory, but the bonds within each hierarchy were generally strong and enduring.

Although alliances among different entourages are fragile, however, whole entourages can be joined together vertically, with the patron in one entourage becoming a client in another (see Van Roy, 1971:115). Lucien M. Hanks terms these larger alliances "circles" (1975). In Chiangmai, for example, a circle of dependent entourages was formed under the leadership of the traditional noble rulers. In the early twentieth century, the larger and more powerful circle of the Bangkok monarchy intruded upon this local arrangement, and the local princes became clients of the Bangkok king and participants in the circle of the modern nation-state.

The reciprocal benefits exchanged within the entourage are not narrow, tit-for-tat transactions, but involve the whole life of the participants. While the entourage itself may be organized to perform a specific function, such as operating a business enterprise or cultivating a crop, the patron and client are bound together in a way that transcends the mundane purpose of the entourage. The client performs personal services for the patron wholly unrelated to his formal work responsibilities, and is available at any hour of the day or night. The patron, in turn, offers a broad protection to his client, placing his wealth and influence in opposition to the social forces that might otherwise overwhelm him. Among the forces from which the patron shields his client are the requirements of the government bureaucracy and the mandates of the law. Wijeyewardene has noted that "uncertainty in both the substance and enforcement of the law is one of the main factors in the formation of patron-client relations" (1972:426), and he has also suggested that "such relationships seem to be particularly important when illicit activities are involved" (1967:83). In short, one of the important aspects of the security offered by the patron is protection for his clients from problems with the law. Such protection can range from help in avoiding confusion and delay in the client's ordinary dealings with the local district offices to an attempt to prevent prosecution for criminal activities. The patron is thus the modern descendant of the historical *nai* who, as recently as the late nineteenth century, acted for his clients (*phrai*) as protector, mediator of disputes, and spokesman to intercede with government officials on behalf of his underlings in legal matters.[3] The patron's role, however, represents more to his clients than something that is merely familiar or customary. They welcome his protection as an indispensable benefit in a world still full of legal dangers and uncertainties which they would not like to face alone.

LIABILITY OF THE ENTOURAGE TO OUTSIDERS

The "entourage" provides us with one model that explains the most typical form of social organization in Thailand. The entourage, as we have seen, has survived over the years in large part because it offers security against problems that involve the law. It is possible, I think, to describe this form of protection in greater detail. When a member of the entourage, for example, commits a wrongful act against some third person, it is possible to predict the manner in which the entourage will share the liability or will insure against it. If the wrongdoer is a patron, his clients may voluntarily undergo punishment in his place. If he is a client, the patron will often pay damages to the injured person or provide a loan to the client to be used for the same purpose. Both of these phenomena are qualified, however, by the capacity of client or patron to terminate their relationship at any time, and by the capacity of the law to assign liability to an individual for his acts regardless of the customary rules within the entourage itself.[4]

Various forms of collective responsibility for wrongful acts have existed in Thai society since the earliest times. Lingat has demonstrated that the formal law codes of the Ayutthaya period contained many provisions that assigned

---

3. Significantly, "*nai*" is still used in modern Thai speech to refer to a "boss" or employer.
4. In this section I shall introduce some of the basic features of patron-client liability, as distinct from the obligations imposed by the formal law codes. In chapter 8, I shall discuss the interaction in the Chiangmai court between the customary rules of the patron-client hierarchy and the codified law of agency.

liability to the family, the neighbors, or the fellow villagers of a wrongdoer. Lingat notes that the concept of kinship liability grew weaker as time went on, but the concept of group liability grew stronger until the enactment of the modern law codes by King Chulalongkorn. He attributes this development to the organization of the Thai population into the hierarchical *phrai-nai* structure with its military-like chain of responsibility, which weakened the family as a legally responsible unit (1935:94-106). If Lingat's hypothesis is correct, then the *phrai-nai* hierarchies may have served as a source of modern attitudes towards group responsibility for individual wrongs. The entourage, a modern form of the historical patron-client structure, may have preserved the older system of liability distributed within the organizational hierarchy.

The voluntary assumption of liability for wrongful acts committed by another person can take a number of different forms. One man may injure another in a fight. In order to pay for the damages, the wrongdoer will obtain a loan from his own patron. The loan, however, will be repaid only at some distant time when the patron finds himself in need of cash, and may in fact be forgotten entirely. The wealthy man teaching himself how to drive a car will require one of his followers to sit beside him in the front seat. If an accident occurs, the underling assumes full responsibility. A policeman at a village fair tells a villager that he will arrest him for gambling "unless you can find someone to take your place." The villager speaks with one of his followers, and the latter volunteers to be arrested and, if necessary, to go to jail for his patron.

Substitute liabilities of this kind take place only to the extent that they are supported by the relationships within the hierarchy. The more profound the feelings of reciprocal obligation, the more willingness there will be to perform such services. Where the relationships are shallow, on the other hand, or where the wrongful act is particularly repugnant or indefensible, then the support will be half-hearted or nonexistent. The essence of the entourage is free choice, and the concomitant of free choice is the power of either the patron or client to terminate the relationship at any time. Thus when *Nai* Wira, a low-ranking agent for an illegal lottery system run by *Nai* Chu,[5] was arrested and a payoff was required to avoid prosecution, *Nai* Chu lent the money—but with some reluctance. He complained that the amount demanded by the police was excessive, and he appeared generally dissatisfied with the entire affair. When he finally agreed to give *Nai* Wira the money, he required a future-dated check for the full amount. *Nai* Chu's demand for the check, although he knew that *Nai* Wira had no checking account on which to draw the funds, demonstrated that the loan was for a fixed time only and that failure to repay it would expose *Nai* Wira to criminal liability. *Nai* Wira understood the situation and repaid *Nai* Chu within five days. The patron thus

---

5. These names, and all names used in the cases I shall describe in this study, are fictional.

supported his client in time of need, but with a reluctance that indicated the relationship was not a deep one.[6]

In a second lawsuit from the Chiangmai court, we can see the patron-client relationship completely collapsing as a result of the client's wrongful act. *Nai* Bunsong's careless driving of a minibus full of passengers caused an accident which resulted in the amputation of the arm of a 73-year-old woman. *Nai* Bunsong was convicted of criminal violations in connection with this accident. *Nai* Čhampi, the owner of the vehicle and the employer of *Nai* Bunsong, renounced his relationship with the latter and refused to negotiate with the injured woman, citing a contractual agreement between himself and *Nai* Bunsong that released the employer from liability for his employee's negligent acts. The woman brought a civil action for damages against both men, and *Nai* Čhampi again denied any responsibility for his employee's actions. Perhaps as a result of this attitude, *Nai* Bunsong proved susceptible to overtures from the plaintiff and agreed to testify on her behalf against his former employer. Plaintiff helped to get *Nai* Bunsong released from prison for this purpose. Shortly after these arrangements were made, *Nai* Čhampi capitulated and reached a compromise agreement with the injured woman. In this case the patron initially rejected any form of substitute liability and produced a rupture in the relationship with his client. Probably as a result of this attitude, the client deserted the entourage and allied himself with an individual who offered a more attractive form of reciprocity. The final settlement between patron and injured person was not so much a belated assumption of financial responsibility for his client as it was an acknowledgment by the patron that his legal case was now hopeless.

The voluntary assumption of legal responsibility for wrongful acts is an intrinsic part of the reciprocities that hold the patron-client relationship together. Liability is not automatically shunted from client to patron or from patron to client. Rather, it is seen as one of the multiple benefits that either side voluntarily provides for the other, knowing that he or she will receive numerous services and benefits in return. Through such exchanges, security is provided and advancement attained. If the relationships are not deep enough to support such reciprocities, however, either side has the option to say no. In a slightly different context, Sally F. Moore has observed that *"expulsion is a qualifier of collective liability"* (1972:90). "Expulsion" in the setting of the Thai patron-client heirarchy means simply the exercise of individual choice, the voluntary termination of a relationship established by the participants to last as long as the mutual benefits and affections continue to flow.

HIERARCHY AND THE NEGOTIATION OF DISPUTES

Hierarchical relationships in Thai society can act as channels for negotiation

---

6. Information concerning this case was obtained from the uncontroverted testimony of the plaintiff, *Nai* Wira, and his witnesses.

as well as structures for distributing liability. The method of handling disputes that was mentioned to me most often by Thai people was an appeal to the appropriate *phuyai* ("big person" or status superior) to intercede and mediate. I was told on several occasions that Thai people are far more comfortable following the advice of their *phuyai* than they are "giving reasons" and conducting a rationalized debate with their adversary. The interlocking structure of patron-client hierarchies in Thai society provides an ideal setting for such negotiations. The injured person who cannot simply absorb his injury may seek out the *phuyai* best able to command the respect of the wrongdoer and ask that he use his influence to bring the wrongdoer to terms. In chapter 6 I will show specifically how this system of negotiation works at various levels of the society. My purpose here is to present a basic model of negotiation and to show how this model is facilitated by, and forms an essential part of, the patron-client structure.

Let us suppose that A has a quarrel of a personal nature with B, alleging that B has defrauded him by refusing to register certain documents at the district office. B is obstinate and refuses to discuss the matter with A or with A's relatives when they approach him. B is a relatively high-ranking government official and is unimpressed by the authority of local village figures who might otherwise mediate such matters. A has no leverage, no direct means to resolve the matter. Instead A goes to the house of his own superior, the owner of a handicrafts workshop in which A is employed. This man, X, does not know B, but he is a former classmate of one of B's superior officials, Y. He promises to look into the matter. The next day X visits Y at home. After some polite and friendly conversation, X brings up the subject of A's difficulties with B and observes that A's wishes are really quite reasonable. Compliance on B's part would be simple and painless. Y, because of his personal relationship with X, agrees to see what he can do about it. A few days later B is approached by Y, a superior in his own social hierarchy, who mildly and indirectly alludes to the dispute between A and B and exerts subtle pressure upon B to behave in a reasonable manner. B takes the hint and, because of his obligations to and respect for Y, B finally makes arrangements to register the documents.

The content of the dispute is entirely personal, unrelated to the job relationships between A and X or B and Y. Nevertheless, all participants proceed on the basis of personal relationships and obligations. These personal relationships open channels of communication that would not otherwise exist. Because the relationships are hierarchical in nature, they create pressures that lead the disputants to negotiate and settle their differences. Many high-ranking administrators in Thailand are required to spend a great deal of time on "personal" matters of this kind. The distinction between personal matters and business matters is not necessarily apparent, however, to the persons involved. The relationships within the entourage, as we have seen, are not narrowly confined to one aspect of life, but involve the patron and clients totally. It is naturally expected that the patron will spend much of his time, both at work and at home, ensuring that the entourage functions properly and that the relationships among his subordinates and their own clients remain smooth and harmonious.

The negotiating procedure in our example is illustrated in figure 4.

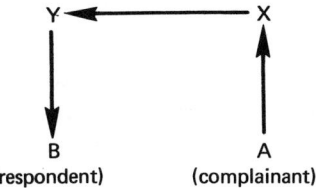

B
(respondent)

A
(complainant)

Figure 4. Negotiation Between Disputants in Separate Patron-Client Hierarchies

This illustration serves as a basic model for the way in which disputes can be negotiated and resolved through the patron-client hierarchies. The complainant moves up in his own hierarchy until he finds a crossover point that will take him into the hierarchy of the respondent, or wrongdoer. In our example, the crossover point was provided by the personal relationship existing between X and Y by virtue of their having been classmates. The message then travels down respondent's hierarchy, reinforced by the status and authority of respondent's own superior, Y. If respondent has a reply or counter-offer that is supported by his patron, it would travel back to the complainant by the same channels. Where A and B are clients of the same patron, the basic model becomes even more simple, for only one intermediary is involved (figure 5).

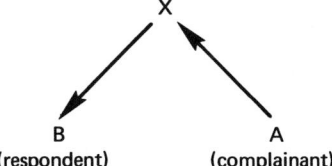

B
(respondent)

A
(complainant)

Figure 5. Negotiation Between Disputants in the Same Patron-Client Hierarchy

In such cases, the negotiations are conducted within a single hierarchy, and X alone provides the crossover point for negotiations between the two disputants.

What will A do if he finds no channel for negotiations with B? It is possible that differences in status, geography, ethnicity, or simply bad luck, will create a situation in which A has no way to send a message through B's hierarchy to B himself. In such cases, A must face the alternatives of abandoning his claim or using some substitute mechanism for negotiation. In the next chapter I shall describe how the official administrative structure provides a ready-made hierarchy in which negotiation can and often does occur. Such negotiations are most successful when the formal hierarchy corresponds closely to the real hierarchical relationships that exist naturally in the society. The village chief and the *kamnan,* for example, are often men who occupy positions of real status and authority in their communities, commanding the respect and loyalty of their villagers. The role of mediator is therefore a common and an effective one for them. Other officials, particularly those more remote from the villagers, are less frequently consulted, even when they are specifically empowered by law to mediate and help resolve disputes. Finally, for the determined complainant who lacks any other effective channel for negotiation, the provincial court itself offers a crossover point to every person within its jurisdiction and backs its powers of mediation with the authority of the state.

Chapter Six
The Levels of Mediation

We have seen that the negotiation and mediation of private wrongs is a natural method for handling conflicts that are not otherwise resolved, abandoned, or ignored by the participants.[1] This mode of procedure is natural in the Thai setting because of its subtlety, indirection, and its close relationship to the system of hierarchical organization that typifies Thai society. In this chapter I shall sketch the various levels of mediation, both official and unofficial, that are available to disputants. As we move higher up the ladder of mediation, we find an increasing recognition of these procedures in the formal laws of Thailand. The provisions concerning mediation in the Thai legal codes, however, do not necessarily coincide with the functions that the mediators perform in fact, nor does official approval of certain mediators make them more attractive to the disputants. Indeed, in many instances the more "official" these mediators become, and the more distant from the village society of the disputants, the less they are valued by persons who might use their services. Official status can increase the legal powers of potential mediators without vesting them with the attributes that are desired by ordinary Thai people.

Figure 6 illustrates in schematic form the various levels at which mediation can take place in provincial Thailand and traces the alternate courses that a

---

1. I am using the term "negotiation" here to suggest a two-way process of communication through which complainant and respondent or their representatives attempt to adjust their respective claims. "Mediation" implies, in addition, the involvement of a third person (or persons) who attempts to "resolve a dispute without imposing a binding decision" (Cohen, 1966:1201). Cohen's study of Confucianism and mediation in China suggests many parallels to the situation in Thailand. Further comparisons could be made with other Asian countries, such as Korea and Japan, in which mediation and compromise are strongly favored over litigation. See Hahm (1969 and 1971); Henderson (1968); Kawashima (1963); Sawada (1968). In short, the attitudes we are describing appear to have a broad regional basis extending beyond the boundaries of Confucianism, with which they have often been associated.

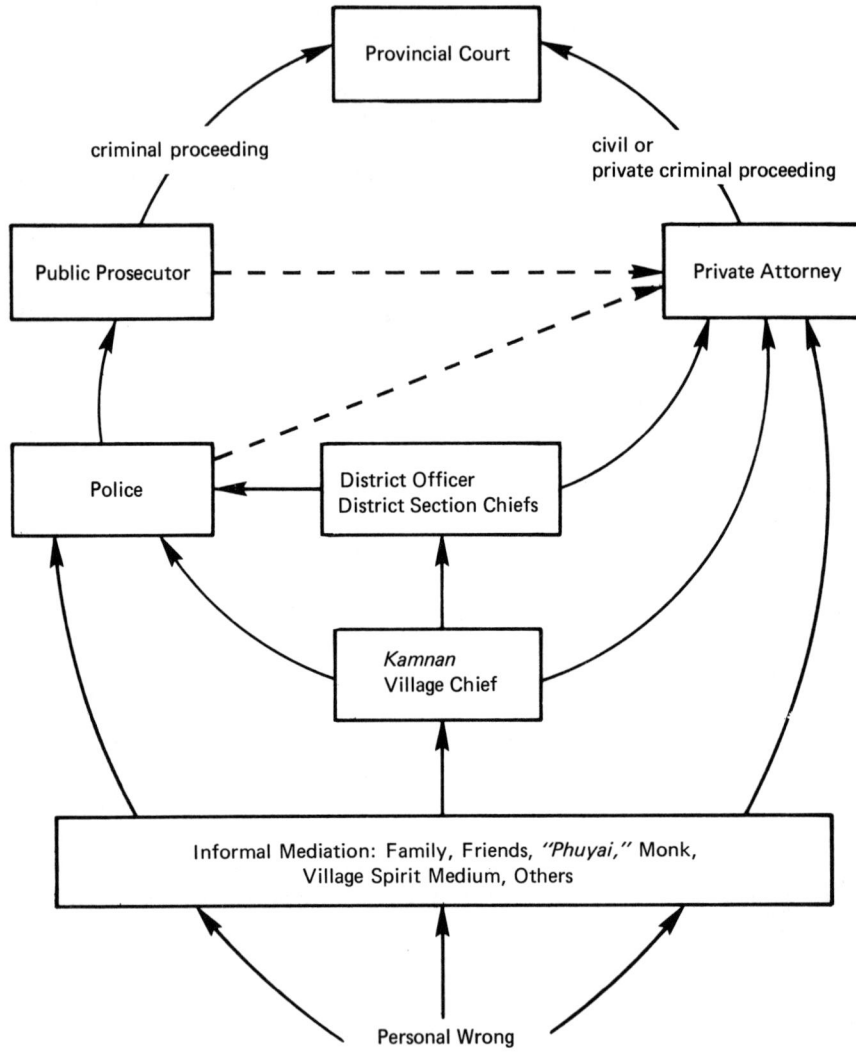

Alternatives to Mediation:

-absorb the injury
-verbal or symbolic expression of displeasure
-self-help, revenge

Figure 6. Levels of Mediation in Provincial Thailand

dispute might follow from one level to another. This is not to say that a dispute must rise sequentially from one level to the next, although in some cases this does in fact occur. Different mediators may be found appropriate for different kinds of disputes or disputants, and conflicts will tend to move directly to the forum considered appropriate by the complainant. Failure to resolve the dispute at a given level may cause the participants to abandon the matter, or to continue the quest for mediation at a different level. The levels of mediation delineated in this diagram will form the basis for discussion in the remainder of the chapter.

NON-OFFICIAL MEDIATION

We have seen that the ideal, and probably the most typical, response to a personal wrong is to absorb it, to continue on one's own path and to leave wrongdoers to their own fate. When victims find themselves unable to ignore the wrongs done them, they may resort to self-help in the form of verbal or symbolic expressions of their displeasure, the use of magic or direct physical revenge, or they may utilize the patron-client hierarchy as a channel for negotiations with the wrongdoer. It is not possible to identify all the authority figures in the traditional society who might act as mediators in such matters, because the patron-client hierarchies come in countless forms. Moreover, a position which in one village is occupied by a strong and respected figure may, in another village, be held by a weak individual who is never sought out as mediator. Nevertheless, by way of introduction, I shall try to identify some of the procedures for mediation most commonly found in village society throughout Thailand with particular attention to the northern region.

One figure who sometimes acts as mediator at the village level is the spirit medium. As we saw in chapter 4, when a dispute arises the guardian spirits of a village or household may be invoked to depersonalize the conflict and require that the wrongdoer make amends. This procedure puts the spirit medium in a position of mediation as he or she decides upon the identity of the wrongdoer and the appropriate penalty for the wrongful act.[2]

Other respected elders in northern village society also appear to have a semi-institutionalized role as mediators. Moerman mentions specifically the "group of elders" (*mu thao*) in the Thai-Lue village of Ban Ping. Within this group the "active elders," a sub-group of seven men, assist in the resolution of disputes and other quasi-legal matters:

---

2. Klausner suggests that such a role is played by the *câo khote*, the respected elder in northeast Thailand, who can interpret the wishes of the ancestral spirit that is offended by disputes among kinsmen (1974:57-58). Keyes adds that the *khao cam*, the intermediary between villagers and the village spirit in the northeast, may also perform an indirect mediating role (1975:196).

The active elders advise the headman on policy toward government directives, are used by him to influence village opinion, and help to adjudicate trouble cases even when they do not involve their immediate kinsmen. (1966a:163)

A second sub-group within the "group of elders" is the "group of old men" (*mu thao mu kae*). In a more informal manner, they may also be consulted by disputants:

[They] are consulted by the other elders and by the headman and also help to adjudicate trouble cases which involve the entire village or in which old people are disputants. They are, however, much less active than the active elders and, also unlike them, do not meet as a group. (*Ibid.:* 163)

Another village authority who might serve as mediator is the "irrigation headman." This individual has traditionally been elected by the villagers and is assisted in his work by a deputy and a clerk. His position, and the duties he is called upon to perform, point to the historical importance of the northern Thai irrigation system and the law and ritual which grew up around it. Moerman states that the irrigation headman traditionally "decided how much wood each farmer was to bring to the dam, directed the work of irrigation, and celebrated its completion with a sacrifice (a pig) to propitiate the 'spirit of the dam'" (1968:50). Wijeyewardene adds that, even in modern times,

The irrigation headman has complete authority over all matters concerning the system. He can call for labour as and when he feels it is necessary. He imposes obligations on the farmers to provide any materials that may be required and can fine anyone who does not fulfil his obligations. (1965:258)

It is reasonable, then, to conclude that many disputes concerning water rights, the use and misuse of canals and sluice gates, and damage to crops caused by negligently flooding or depriving fields of water, may well have been mediated by the irrigation headman.

The role of the clergy in mediating disputes is subject to wide variation, depending partly upon the individual priest and partly upon the nature of the dispute and the local traditions with regard to the monkhood. Kingshill writes that in the Chiangmai village of Ku Daeng, the priests did not play a strong leadership role of any kind. In that village, however, the *kamnan* was a dominant figure. In other settings, including two neighboring temples that Kingshill also visited, "the head-priests decidedly seemed to be the leaders in village life" (1960:112). When the latter situation prevails, the priests are more frequently consulted with regard to disputes among the laity. Such was clearly the case in the central Thai village of Bangkhuad observed by Kaufman, where "the abbot is undoubtedly the most influential, the most respected, and thus the most important individual in the community" (1960:118). In that temple, farmers would gather each day to discuss their problems with the abbot and to seek his advice (though two of the other monks are also sought out for advice from time to time). Matters pertaining to farming, loans, domestic troubles, and salvation are discussed. (113)[3]

Ingersoll found that the head priest at his research site in central Thailand was also consulted in such matters but that his role as mediator was limited by one important consideration: matters involving "violence or hostile conflict" were usually deemed unsuitable subjects for the clergy and were not discussed in their presence (1966:62). While a monk may be consulted about a marital conflict or a minor business dispute, it would be unseemly to involve him in a bitter feud or in a case of serious physical injury.[4]

Another factor limiting the effectiveness of northern priests as mediators may be their relative youthfulness and inexperience. Moerman notes that northern Thai clergy tend to be considerably younger than their counterparts in central Thailand. Of 183 priests in the entire district where he conducted his research, Moerman found that only about 25 were older than 40 years of age. In the village of Ban Ping itself, the abbot was only 22 years old, and among the ten villagers who had formerly been priests, none had remained in the priesthood past the age of 24 (1966a:139). The youthfulness of the northern clergy makes them less effective as community leaders and as mediators for disputes, since age is an important element in achieving the status that brings authority. Moerman observes that it is not the clergy, but the former clergy, who make up the effective leadership of the village: "In Ban Ping, honor and even power are the rewards less of being a cleric than of having been one" (ibid.: 155). Such persons after they leave the monastery are addressed with special honorific titles and, Moerman observes, are likely to be called upon when disputes arise (ibid.: 156).[5] It is not the wearing of the orange robe, then, as much as the learning and merit associated with an earlier stay in the temple, that qualifies these mature individuals to help resolve conflict at the village level.

Countless other persons at the local level may act as mediators, depending upon the particular circumstances within each village. Moreover, negotiation and mediation may take forms wholly different from those that have been described thus far: a thief may send an intermediary to his victim to negotiate the return of stolen property; an eloping couple may call upon the older brother of the bride's father, for he is in a special position to persuade the parents to accept the new union; an intra-family conflict may be resolved by a ceremony to ask forgiveness, complete with flowers, incense, and the prostra-

---

3. Kaufman adds, however, that "the bulk of advice sought pertains to auspicious days for business ventures and social functions" (1960:113).
4. Discussion of the priest as mediator in northeast Thailand appears in Klausner (1974:77-78) and Keyes (1975: 198).
5. In Moerman's words, they are asked to "speak on . . . behalf" of kinsmen who are involved in disputes (1966a: 156).

tion of the wrongdoer before the person wronged.⁶ There is no single institution in traditional Thai society through which mediation is conducted, but the process itself possesses certain regularities that we have already observed: face-to-face confrontation is avoided, blunt and direct assertions of rights are shunned, intermediaries are commonly utilized to act as spokesmen for the disputants, respected persons with power and authority are sought out as mediators, and the possibility of direct physical revenge always lurks in the background as a last resort for wrongdoers who are challenged too directly and for victims whose passions leave them no other recourse.⁷

MEDIATION BY VILLAGE CHIEF AND *KAMNAN*

The village chief and the *kamnan* are elected officials, paid by the government but residents of the village. They are a part of village life, natural authority figures who are also vested with important official powers and duties. Both the village chief and the *kamnan* are known to villagers in Chiangmai as *phǫ luang,* or "big father." The Law of Local Administration gives the village chief and the *kamnan* the kind of power in village affairs that makes them strong and effective mediators. The village chief, for example, must "preserve the peace and happiness and help protect against suffering and danger on the part of the villagers" (Section 27.1); he must "watch over the villagers to see that they perform the duties required of them by law or by governmental regulations" (Section 27.9); and he must "instruct or point out governmental rules to the citizenry" (Section 27.11). In criminal matters, the village chief has the responsibility to report suspicious activities or violations of the law to the *kamnan* (Section 28.1), to arrest persons violating the law or suspected of violating the law (Section 28.4), and to enforce arrest warrants for persons within his village (Section 28.5). The *kamnan* himself is granted all the duties and powers of the village chief (Section 34a). In addition, he must help to ensure that the citizens in his jurisdiction "behave according to the law"; he must protect against dangers and preserve the well-being of citizens in his *tambon;* and he must perform other official duties, with the assistance of the village chiefs and the *tambon* medical officer (Section 34). With regard to criminal matters, the *kamnan* possesses important investigative powers, as well as the power to arrest suspected lawbreakers, to enforce warrants for seizing persons and property, and to send suspects and evidence of wrongdoing to the district-level officials (Section 35).

---

6. The first of these three examples is described in Phillips (1965:186); the second is based upon conversation with Professors Jane and Lucien Hanks concerning their research in Bang Chan; the third is drawn from Keyes (1975:198).
7. Herbert Phillips has given some attention to aggression, face-to-face confrontation, and the expression of hostility in Thai village society. Some of his observations on these matters may be found in Phillips (1965:184-93).

Since the village chief and the *kamnan* are closely involved with situations where conflict occurs and with the suppression of illegal activities, it is natural that they should find themselves often in a position to mediate disputes.[8] Indeed, this role is expected of them by the official authorities as well as by the villagers. I was told by ministry officials as well as by village leaders that the authorities tend to blame the village chief and *kamnan* of a given locality when too many criminal or civil disputes rise beyond the village level to the district or provincial offices. This kind of situation is interpreted as a personal failure on the part of the village chief and the *kamnan* to preserve order and to assert their influence over disruptive forces within the village. Because of this attitude on the part of the authorities, the village chief and the *kamnan* have an added incentive to perform effectively the mediating role that their position naturally brings them.

The function of the village chief and the *kamnan* as mediators can be complicated by the dual role they must play. A former village chief told Moerman, "One is neither a villager nor an official. One is in the middle. It's hard and the money is small" (1969a:547). Two men who held the office before World War II commented, "In the old days, one was elder of the village. Now the headman is merely the hired messenger of the officials" (*ibid.:* 549). On many occasions, however, the skillful village chief and *kamnan* are able to use their dual role in a way that enhances their power and meets with the approval of both villagers and officials. By selective enforcement of the penal laws, for example, the headman can avoid aggravating the sensibilities of his villagers and can also gain leverage to assure their compliance with his recommendations for resolving disputes. A former village chief interviewed by Moerman had promised his villagers that he would protect them from "unfair" governmental regulations, but would invoke his official powers to suppress real evils, such as theft and violence:

> I will protect you if you merely butcher animals, gamble, and make whisky—for these harm no one and are only devices to take money away from the village in the forms of taxes, fines, bribes, and purchases from outsiders. But I will immediately report theft and violence to the police. (*ibid.:* 540)

The village chief and *kamnan* gain power and respect by their restraint, by their sense of the appropriate occasions on which to assert or ignore their official responsibilities. One village chief told me of a period when his village had experienced a rash of thefts. He realized that the time had come to insist upon his role as an official authority figure. Calling the villagers together, he

---

8. I shall consider the village chief and the *kamnan* together in this section. In some cases, however, disputes may first be mediated by the village chief and then move up to the *kamnan* for a second attempt at reconciliation. In other instances, including those cases where the village chief is himself a disputant, the *kamnan* alone may be consulted.

discussed the matter with them, reminded them that they were all "brothers and sisters," and warned them sternly not to steal from one another. Shortly after this meeting, approximately 500 planks of wood were stolen from *Nai* Sanit, who had prepared them to build a house. *Nai* Sanit notified the village chief, who spent two months quietly looking for the wood without informing the police. Finally he found the wood in the possession of *Nai* Khao, who lived in a different village and had purchased the planks in order to build his own house. At first *Nai* Khao refused to admit even that he had bought the wood, knowing that the low price he had paid would be clear evidence that the wood had been stolen. The village chief pressured *Nai* Khao by reminding him that he could be charged with receiving stolen property and that it would be far better for him to act as a witness for *Nai* Sanit. Finally *Nai* Khao decided to cooperate. He told the village chief that he had purchased the wood from *Nai* Intum, a young man 22 or 23 years of age. The village chief immediately forwarded the information to the district police. There was never any question of mediating this dispute. *Nai* Intum prepared himself to run away from the village before he could be arrested. His mother, however, came to see the village chief, and he advised her that her son should stay and endure a punishment that would ultimately catch up with him in any case. If he submitted to arrest at this time and confessed his crime, the punishment would not be great; but if he ran away he could get into far more serious trouble. *Nai* Intum followed the village chief's advice and was prosecuted and convicted for the crime of theft. His sentence was reduced from six months to three because of his confession. When *Nai* Intum was released he returned to the village without any feeling of resentment towards the village chief (according to the village chief's own account). After all, the villagers had been warned beforehand about the consequences of such actions. The village chief's strict enforcement of the government's penal code in this instance was accepted even by the wrongdoer himself.

The village chief may also use his police power simply to discipline a particular individual, to teach him to respect his authority and to stop disrupting the local peace. The headman of a large village not far from Chiangmai city told me a story of this kind concerning the local bully, who had frequently annoyed the villagers and displayed his lack of regard for the power and position of the headman. When a temple fair was held in this village, an ice and sweetmeats vendor arrived from the city to sell his goods to the crowds of people who came to celebrate. The bully, *Nai* Tim, saw that the man was doing an excellent business and for this reason provoked a quarrel with him. They began to fight, and the village chief was called to stop the brawl and seize both participants. *Nai* Tim had been involved in incidents like this many times before, and so the village chief decided to take both men to the police. At the police station, *Nai* Tim was given a stiff fine of 600 *baht*, about three times as large as would normally be assessed. Of this sum, 500 *baht* was given to the ice vendor to compensate for the wrong done him. The headman's motive in dealing strictly with this incident, he told me, was to teach *Nai* Tim a lesson, to "make him care." The police supported him fully in this respect.

The village chief and *kamnan* do not report all such criminal violations to the police, however. Frequently they will use the threat of arrest as a means to force the wrongdoer to come to terms and to reach a settlement with his victim. Why, after all, should money be paid to the police when it could remain in the pockets of the accused and the accuser? A typical occurrence of this kind was related to me by the same village chief, arising, as was frequently the case, out of a drunken fight. One morning *Nai* Thọng had a quarrel with his wife. Still angry, he went out of his house for a drink. At the restaurant he met *Nai* La, who was himself sitting and drinking whiskey. *Nai* La was a close friend with whom *Nai* Thọng usually drank, joked, and wrestled in fun. *Nai* La saw that *Nai* Thọng was upset, guessed the reason, and proceeded to tease *Nai* Thọng: "Did you just come from fighting with your wife? Don't you know it's not proper for a man to fight with his wife? " *Nai* Thọng became furious. As *Nai* La started to walk away, *Nai* Thọng grabbed a knife, chased after him, and gashed him on the head. At this point the dispute was taken over by the two wives. *Nai* La's wife went to the village chief and pleaded with him to notify the police. The village chief tried to cool her down. He asked if she was certain that she wanted this drunken quarrel to turn into a big lawsuit, especially since the men were ordinarily such good friends. *Nai* Thọng's wife was also called to the headman's house, and the two women, under pressure by the headman, finally agreed to forget the matter, provided that *Nai* Thọng would pay all the medical expenses. The same village chief who had dealt harshly with the village bully for a minor infraction, chose to mediate and pacify the participants in a serious criminal assault.

The village chief or *kamnan* is likely to go to the police, rather than to attempt mediation, when the wrongful act represents what he considers a threat to the orderly life of the village or to his own authority. He is less inclined to take such action if the wrongfulness of the act is not immediately apparent, if the act was a brief and isolated flare-up of bad temper, or if its prosecution would have some adverse effect upon the village as a whole. Kingshill, for example, tells of a fight between two brothers, in which one brother was cut on the head with a stick. Although the *kamnan* filled out all the proper legal documents describing the fight, including a signed confession by the brother who had caused the injury, he decided not to report the matter to the police because it was basically a family matter and "a jail sentence would make the father very sorry" (1960:84-85). In another case reported by Kingshill, the *kamnan* chose to mediate a dispute in which the proprietor of an illegal lottery failed to deliver a bicycle to the man who held a winning ticket. Threatening both parties with arrest for gambling, the *kamnan* forced the proprietor to pay 250 *baht* to the complainant in lieu of the bicycle. In this way the *kamnan* enforced standards of fair behavior even in matters considered illegal by the government (43-44). His authority as mediator was enhanced considerably by the knowledge of the disputants that he could just as easily have decided to arrest them and turn them over to the police.[9]

When the disputants agree to settle their grievances privately in cases involving criminal violations, they still run some risk of arrest and prosecution. Mediation of criminal infractions by the village chief or the *kamnan* has no official legal status, and in fact it could be deemed a violation of their duty to report all such matters to the authorities. When the police learn of such cases, therefore, they are likely to proceed against the wrongdoer without regard to the mediation effected by the village chief or *kamnan*. In one such case, I was told, an automobile driver struck a villager, causing a broken arm and multiple head wounds. The two men reached a private settlement, promoted by the village chief, with the driver paying 5,000 *baht* in exchange for a promise that the victim would not take any legal action against him. The police, however, learned of the accident and arrested the driver for reckless driving. He was prosecuted, convicted, and sentenced to 500 *baht* and six months in prison. As the village chief explained to me, the driver had mistakenly believed that by paying his victim he had put an end to the matter. Had he gone to "speak to the police or to treat them" he might have avoided the complications that ensued. In most cases, it should be noted, once a proper mediated settlement has been achieved, the victim will help to exculpate the wrongdoer in any formal criminal proceedings that might follow.

In disputes not involving criminal violations, mediation by the village chief or *kamnan* has none of these perils, although the capacity to manipulate the law may still be an important element of the mediator's authority. Moerman found that the village chief of Ban Ping was quite proud of his ability to manipulate and falsify documents he submitted to the government from his village, for he felt that he was advancing the interests of his villagers by doing so (1969a:541). With regard to the registration of land claims, in which the village chief is required to play an important role, Moerman found that

> Ban Ping's headman served his villagers well by sometimes failing to

---

9. Moerman (1969a:540-41) describes in similar terms the mediation of criminal offenses by the headman in the village of Ban Ping:

> During our fourteen months in Ban Ping, there were thirty occasions in which the headman met with litigants and interested elders over cases as diverse as the theft of a pomelo, desertion, divorce, armed assault, and rape. In these hearings the headman acts as an impartial examining magistrate determining facts, uncovering precedents, brandishing the written law (in which he is occasionally given elementary instruction at district meetings), and trying to reach the acceptable compromise which, whatever the relevant rules and precedents, constitutes the proper settlement of any case.

record the claimant's other holdings, by emphasizing the number of his dependents, or by exaggerating the amount of land he has worked to develop. (1968:110)

I was told by some village leaders that land disputes were quite common, especially those involving boundary controversies, but the role of the village chief and *kamnan* in mediating such disputes was limited by the laws and regulations associated with the Thai Land Code. They claimed that they usually had to refer these matters to the district officials who could lawfully resolve conflicting claims to the land. Moerman's observations during an extended stay in the village, however, suggest that there is a bit more leeway for mediation than these men admitted to me. It would not be surprising, therefore, to find that the village chief and the *kamnan* use their official powers under the land law as leverage to mediate disputes, much as they do with regard to criminal violations.

Among the disputes that come to the village chief and the *kamnan* for mediation perhaps the most common are marital conflicts. One former village chief, when asked for an example of this kind of dispute, told me that only a few days earlier a man had come to consult with him despite the fact that he had been retired from his village leadership position for several years. This man wanted to leave his wife and children because she spent all his money, because she was ill-tempered, argued constantly, and beat him. The former village chief advised this man not to act rashly. He was still young. If he left his wife he would eventually remarry. He would have more children, and this would create problems in the future. How would he divide his inheritance? His new wife would not want his first children to receive anything, but they, after all, were his natural offspring. Even if he registered his second marriage, the first wife would probably demand some sort of support money, and this would only cause the second wife to become angry. The complications caused by separating were more formidable than the discomfort of sharing a household with his present wife. The young man thought about this advice and finally agreed with the former village chief that it was better to leave things as they were. A separation, with all the secondary conflicts it would have engendered, was thus prevented.

The authority of the village chief and the *kamnan* as mediators arises in large part from their divided duties and responsibilities. If they are skillful they can play their two identities against one another, offering protection against the harsh workings of the laws and regulations which they enforce, and also threatening to use those laws and regulations against persons unwilling to negotiate disputes or persons disrespectful of their authority. In the area of criminal violations, the arrest and reporting powers of the village chief and *kamnan* give them a powerful club to wield over recalcitrant individuals. In land disputes, the power to manipulate official documents may induce disputants to stay in their good graces. In other matters, such as marital conflicts, the official powers of the village chief and *kamnan* merge with their good sense and their knowlege of administrative realities to induce villagers to heed their advice. One villager who did not follow the advice of a village chief, choosing instead to play out a run of good luck, ended up as the defendant in a lawsuit—precisely the kind of result most mediators would advise disputants to avoid at all costs. This man's story, which was recounted to me by his village chief, provides a fitting conclusion to this section on village-level mediation.

Nai Yang came from another village to marry a young woman in the community of the village chief. There he settled down. He used his mother's land certificate (*nǫ sǫ* 3) to secure a loan from a rich man in the village. With this money, he and a partner bought a mini-bus which he operated as a taxi, using the profits to redeem the land certificate. Later his partner found himself in need of cash, so *Nai* Yang bought out his interest in the enterprise. Suddenly, *Nai* Yang had a streak of good luck. He won approximately 20,000 *baht* in the national lottery and came to feel that his star was rising. All his undertakings at this point would surely meet with success. He bought some riceland for himself and also a lot on which he built a large two-story house. To crown his success, *Nai* Yang decided to acquire a second wife. At this point, his first wife became alarmed. She went to see the village chief, who called *Nai* Yang to his house and attempted to mediate. He warned *Nai* Yang of all the complications that would result from taking a second wife, but *Nai* Yang refused to listen. He went so far as to divorce his first wife at the district office and would not divide any of his property with her.

Nai Yang's wife refused to accept this situation. She took the unusual step of bringing a lawsuit against her former husband. Her suit was successful and the court held that the marital property had to be divided. *Nai* Yang paid his former wife as the court had ordered. In addition he paid a sizable fee to his attorney and to hers. He was also charged with the court costs for her civil suit against him. When it was all over, *Nai* Yang had nothing left. He was deep in debt and forced to leave his elegant new house for a more modest dwelling. Today he still lives with his second wife, but his money has all disappeared. Only by driving his mini-bus every day can he provide them both with food and clothing. *Nai* Yang's star rose and fell quickly. Had he listened to the good advice of the village chief instead of trusting to his own luck, he could have retained some of the fruits of his winning streak. Instead, he ignored the village-level mediator and was forced into the jurisdiction of the provincial court where he met with ruin.

DISTRICT LEVEL MEDIATION

A middle-aged government official told me that he recalled the days before World War II when the district officer (*nai amphoe*) and his assistants acted as investigators and magistrates in criminal and civil suits. Inquiry proceedings were held in the district headquarters, with the district officer presiding, an assistant seated on either side, and clerks busily handling the paper work. In those days, he told me, when people said, "I'm going to the court (san)," they meant that they were going to the district office in connection with a hearing of this kind. The police in those days were of lower rank and lesser importance than they are today. Law enforcement and quasi-judicial mediation was a primary function of the district officer and his staff.

The Law of Local Administration of 1914 originally granted district officers the power to mediate both criminal and civil disputes of a minor nature.[10] The criminal mediation power was withdrawn by royal edict in 1938, however, and was transferred to the inquiry officials (phanakngan sǫpsuan) of the police department where it resides at the present time. The district officer and his assistants, all appointees of the central government, have retained the power to mediate only in civil cases not exceeding 200 baht which arise in their district or in which the defendant is to be found in their district. These proceedings are held at the request of the complainant. The district officials can send a summons to the respondent in such cases and to witnesses stipulated by both parties. If an agreement results, it is signed by both parties and by the district officials. It is then enforceable in court and is granted the same legal status as a formal judicial decision (Section 108).

In modern times, the use of the district officer for purposes of mediation is not as common as it once appears to have been. Times have changed since the days when the district officer helped to catch the criminals and administer rough justice in courts where he himself presided. With the rise of the police as a separate and powerful force at the district level, the district officer's job has become more desk-bound. Still an extremely important figure on the local scene, his role as mediator tends now to center upon the particular legal matters administered in his offices. Since the district land office issues two of the most commonly held types of land certificates, for example, we find that disputes concerning rights in land are often mediated at the district level. Since marriages and divorces are registered at the district offices, disputes concerning these matters may also come before the district officer or his assistants.[11] The following case histories will illustrate how both of these matters may come to the district offices for mediation and will suggest that the results may sometimes be far from conclusive.

---

10. The technical legal term for "mediate" in this context is *priap thiap*—literally "to compare." The colloquial term for mediation or arbitration is *klai klia*—based upon the word *klia*, "to smooth off, level down" (Haas, 1964:39).

11. Land and marital disputes are discussed at length in chapters 10 and 11, respectively. The relationship between the litigation of such matters in court and prior attempts at mediation by persons such as district-level officials is discussed in chapter 9.

In 1969, *Nai* Čhuan purchased land from *Nangsao* Saeng on a contract with right of redemption. Within the one-year period stipulated by the contract, *Nai* Čhuan failed to pay the purchase price of 4,000 *baht* and the land reverted to *Nangsao* Saeng. She later maintained that she had allowed *Nai* Čhuan to continue living on the land in a house he had built there. *Nai* Čhuan, however, claimed that a second agreement had been made two years later according to which he would buy the land for 5,000 *baht*. He insisted that he had paid *Nangsao* Saeng 4,000 *baht* in January of 1970 with the final 1,000 *baht* to be paid on the day when she transferred title to him at the district office. No written documents, however, were executed as evidence of this agreement. *Nai* Čhuan claimed that *Nangsao* Saeng had constantly postponed the conclusion of this transaction, ultimately setting the date for transfer and final payment in January 1973. *Nangsao* Saeng, on the other hand, denied that a second agreement had ever taken place or that any money had ever been paid by *Nai* Čhuan.

In April 1970, the land suddenly became valuable. A survey team came to inspect the holding in connection with a new highway scheduled for construction by the government. *Nai* Čhuan, who was already on the land, informed the surveyors that he owned it and that he was therefore entitled to receive payment from the state for the portion that was to be purchased for construction purposes. *Nangsao* Saeng learned of his claim and brought the matter to the district officer, insisting that she was the rightful owner of the land and was entitled to any payments made by the state. Thus the district officer was called upon to mediate a dispute over conflicting claims to a piece of land, claims related to the function of the district office in registering interests in land and recording transactions of the kind *Nai* Čhuan alleged to have taken place.

Although the district officer had clear jurisdiction over the subject matter of the dispute, however, he did not have sufficient authority over the disputants themselves. *Nai* Čhuan simply ignored the district officer's attempts to mediate, refusing to meet with him and with *Nangsao* Saeng at various times suggested by the district officer. Clearly *Nai* Čhuan felt that the district officer had no hold over him, that he was not bound to respect or fear the district officer in the way that he might respect or fear his own village chief. *Nai* Čhuan instead brought the matter directly to the Chiangmai court, going over the head of the district officer and trying, perhaps, to bluff *Nangsao* Saeng into reaching a compromise. His strategy failed. In court, *Nai* Čhuan finally decided to acknowledge the truthfulness of all of *Nangsao* Saeng's claims. He was ordered to remove his house and other fixtures from the land, leaving *Nangsao* Saeng in sole possession. Her only concession to *Nai* Čhuan was an agreement to pay him 2,000 *baht* for moving expenses, a gesture commonly made by landowners who wish to evict squatters. The agreement that the district officer failed to achieve through mediation was quickly and decisively obtained in the provincial court.

On other occasions, the district officer can be more successful in mediating disputes and preventing them from reaching court. An assistant district officer told me, for example, that he frequently attempted to dissuade couples from obtaining divorces. The procedure for divorce by mutual consent is simple and can be concluded in a matter of minutes through an inexpensive registration process conducted at the district office. This official said that married couples would often appear in his office the morning after a heated argument and would take an action in haste that they later came to regret. He thought of himself as a counselor and mediator for spouses who were momentarily upset and needed to be reconciled by him rather than irrevocably separated by the law. He told me that he was often successful in this role. As we spoke, however, a young couple entered the office to register their divorce with a clerk. He interrupted our conversation to talk with them, asking why they wished to end their marriage. They laughed nervously and ignored him, continuing to fill out the required forms.

Mediation at the district level is not as common or broad-based a phenomenon as it is at the village or *tambon* level, despite its historical importance and its official enshrinement in the Law of Local Administration. District-level mediation occurs most frequently in connection with a particular subject matter that the district offices administer, such as land certification or the registration of marriage and divorce. Even in these cases, however, the district officer, despite his prominent political position, may lack the kind of personal authority over the disputants that is necessary to make his role as mediator an effective one. While the disputants may choose to place their case before him in the hope that he will be able to resolve it, they may just as well choose to ignore the district officer and search elsewhere for a more advantageous forum.

POLICE MEDIATION

The power to mediate minor criminal offenses has shifted over the years from the district officer to the inquiry officer of the police (Law of Local Administration, Section 105, as amended in 1938 and 1956). When such offenses occur, the police inquiry officer may try to promote a settlement in which the disputants will sign papers of compromise and the alleged wrongdoer will pay a fine or compensation at the police station.[12] The inquiry officer plays a double mediation role: determining the fine paid by the wrong-

---

12. A discussion of this procedure appears in Thailand's *Official Yearbook* (1964:279).

doer to the state and the compensation to be paid by the wrongdoer to the victim. Official forms are provided by the Department of Police for such settlements of minor criminal violations. The procedure is also sanctioned by Sections 37 and 38 of the Criminal Procedure Code of Thailand, and settlements of this type, according to Section 39 of the code, extinguish the right to institute a criminal prosecution for the same offense at a later time. The record of settlements achieved in this manner must be sent on the prosecutor's office for approval before they become final.[13]

The local police, according to this procedure, constitute yet another level within the province at which the mediation of conflict can take place. Mediation at this level occurs frequently, because the police have great power and can command the obedience of the disputants, and because they are involved by law in every criminal infraction that occurs within their jurisdiction. It is true that the village chief and other local mediators may in fact prevent certain criminal violations from coming to the attention of the police. In a great many cases this does not occur, however, and sometimes the village chief and *kamnan* will themselves bring disputes to the police after mediation has failed at the village level. Police units are located primarily at the district or provincial levels. Few are permanently assigned to individual villages.[14] Nevertheless, the police involve themselves in village affairs when they are called upon by the village chief or the *kamnan,* when special village functions require police supervision, or when they themselves undertake the investigation of unlawful behavior. In this way villagers become aware of the police, to a greater extent than they are aware of other district officials, and recognize them as potential mediators whose power cannot be lightly disregarded.

A typical instance of police mediation in a minor dispute was recounted to me by a village chief whom I interviewed. During the annual *songkran* festival that brings hundreds of tourists to Chiangmai each year, a minor bus accident occurred in his village, not far from the city of Chiangmai. One bus was parked on a narrow street and was scraped by the mirror of a second bus attempting to pass by. Normally the police would not be consulted in such matters. The drivers would decide themselves about the compensation to be paid, or perhaps would seek the counsel of the village chief. On this occasion, however, a policeman was already present to help control the crowds of people who had come to celebrate. He listened to the stories of the two drivers. The driver of the parked bus wanted 300 *baht* (approximately $15) to pay for body work to repair the scratch. The driver of the other bus refused

---

13. Regarding the police mediation procedure, see also Police Regulations Concerning Cases [*Rabiap kan tamruat kiao kap khadi*] (630-97) and Prakob Hutasingh's discussion in Thailand, The Supreme Court, *Record of the Third Asian Judicial Conference* (1969:378).

14. For a general description of the police in Thailand, see the chapter entitled "Public Order and Safety" in Frank J. Moore (1974:353-72).

to pay anything, arguing that his adversary had parked carelessly and was himself responsible for the accident. The policeman considered both arguments, probably decided that the financial resources of both parties were approximately equal, and told them they should simply split the difference. He suggested that the driver of the second bus pay the relatively small amount of 150 *baht,* that they fill out the necessary report form and go on their way. The dispute was resolved on the spot. Had one party appeared wealthier than the other, the policeman's decision would probably have been different. The outcome will vary from case to case, the policy of each policeman being slightly different, but will usually involve his estimate of the relative status, wealth, and degree of indignation displayed by the two disputants.

In the early stages of a dispute it is not always clear whether the conflict encompasses a criminal violation or is strictly civil in nature. Occasionally, therefore, the police will be called upon to mediate cases in which they have no legal authority, since no criminal cause of action is stated. In such cases the police may simply tell the disputants that it is a civil matter which they must resolve elsewhere, or they may try to use the authority of their position to achieve a settlement. While such settlements would have no official status by virtue of the policeman's position, they could bind the disputants contractually like any other "compromise agreement" of the type described in Book III, Title XVII of the Civil and Commercial Code. Thus in one case brought in the Chiangmai court for breach of contract, the plaintiff based his complaint upon a compromise agreement drafted by an inquiry official at the district police station. Plaintiff had contacted this policeman a year earlier when defendant failed to pay several thousand *baht* outstanding from the purchase of livestock belonging to plaintiff. The policeman had called in both parties and mediated an agreement whereby defendant would make monthly payments of 300 *baht* until the debt was extinguished. At the conclusion of the agreement, which the policeman had drafted and entered into the daily police register, he noted, "I, Police Sub-Lieutenant Prasit T———, inquiry officer, did receive this complaint. I have investigated and found that the case involves an agreement to buy and sell. The violation is a wrongful act under civil law. I have therefore advised the disputants that if this compromise agreement is violated, they should bring suit themselves." When defendant subsequently failed to perform, plaintiff did indeed bring a civil action in the provincial court and obtained the entire amount owed him by the defendant.

Not all the negotiations conducted by the police follow the strict letter of the law. In the course of my research I encountered allegations of misconduct on the part of some police officers. The mildest of these asserted that in settlements promoted by the police, one portion was set aside for their private benefit. Even in the case of minor traffic accidents, policemen sometimes seize the license of one of the drivers and refuse to return it without receiving some payment. When the wrongful act is of a more serious nature, some officers may require compensation for dropping the case, even after the complainant has already agreed with the respondent to settle. Factors such as these can deter individuals from asking the police to mediate disputes. Their legal authority and their constant involvement with injuries and unlawful behavior place the police in a natural position to act as mediators. Often they perform this role effectively. Most individuals, however, approach the police with hesitancy and fear. The very power that makes them effective as mediators also makes them hazardous and unpredictable in the eyes of many citizens. Rather than grant such individuals any power over their affairs, disputants who have a choice in the matter will often seek other more congenial methods of mediation.

MEDIATION BY PRIVATE ATTORNEYS

In the province of Chiangmai in 1975 there were thirty-seven private attorneys registered with the provincial court, approximately one attorney for every 29,400 people in the province.[15] Of these thirty-seven, only ten or twelve appeared with regularity in court, the others occupying themselves largely with other business enterprises. It is considered quite difficult to become a member of the Thai bar. Success in passing the bar examination on the first or even on subsequent attempts is by no means automatic for most law school graduates. Admission to the bar entitles "first class" attorneys to appear in any court in the country. For those who wish to become qualified as "second class" attorneys, however, it is possible to be admitted to the bar on the basis of a special examination set by the Thai Bar Association or on the basis of a degree or certificate in the study of law of a type specifically approved by the Bar Association. Second class attorneys may practice law in the courts of any ten designated provinces in the country. With special permission they may also appear in other provincial courts as well. On appeal, they may argue any case that was decided within their prescribed area.[16]

Private attorneys constitute a final level through which private disputes must pass before reaching the Chiangmai court. Disputes may come to them in several

---

15. This figure is based upon the rough approximation of Chiangmai's total population at the end of 1974 as 1,086,203. See note a, table 3, page 45. Nationwide figures for Thailand, including Bangkok, show a somewhat higher ratio of lawyers to population. In a study by the Committee on Legal Services to the Poor in the Developing Countries (1974:189), the size of Thailand's bar was given as 1,848 in the year 1964. Thailand's population in 1964 was roughly 29,700,000 (Thailand, National Statistical Office, 1964, table 1.2: "Estimated Population of Thailand by Sex: 1947-1964"), giving a national figure of roughly one lawyer for every 16,071 people. The figures for Chiangmai and for Thailand as a whole can be compared to the following estimates compiled by Marc Galanter (1968:77): United States in 1960, 728 persons per lawyer; Great Britain in 1959, 2,105 persons per lawyer; India in 1952, 4,920 persons per lawyer; Japan in 1960, 14,354 persons per lawyer; Indonesia in 1960, approximately 100,000 persons per lawyer.

16. See Royal Edict Concerning Attorneys, 1965 [*Phraratchabanyat thanaikhwam, B.E. 2508*], as amended in 1971.

different ways. First, when the police or public prosecutors decide not to pursue an alleged criminal wrong, complainants who still want to see the respondent prosecuted may take their complaint to a private attorney for further action. Second, disputes may come to the attorney as the result of a failure at some lower level of mediation: at the district, *tambon,* or village level. Finally, some disputes reach the attorney directly, without passing through any intermediate level of mediation. In any of these instances, the attorney may seek to mediate the dispute himself rather than proceed directly to litigation. Such a decision is less common, however, than one might expect. In cases involving private wrongs, attorneys seem to be viewed primarily as agents to represent their clients in court, and only secondarily as legal advisers or negotiators. The attorney is sometimes expected to assist with negotiations after the case reaches court. Before that time, however, he will not usually be sought out by mediation-minded disputants. They see little reason to pay a stranger to perform a function that their own patron or village leader could perform more effectively for free.[17]

One attorney told me that he felt limited in his ability to mediate private wrongs because, unlike the judge, he had no status above the two contending parties. Neither side owed him any special deference, nor did he have any particular power over them. The only leverage he could exert was the threat to wage a costly and perhaps successful lawsuit against his client's adversary. This was the only important incentive for submitting the dispute to his good offices. The attorney, therefore, was generally reluctant to play the role of mediator. He thought of himself primarily as a spokesman for his client. If he acted too aggressively to achieve a settlement, he feared that his client might grow dissatisfied with the results and put the blame on him. For this reason, he was inclined to be relatively passive, allowing his client to achieve mediation in other ways if possible, or else bringing the case to court and seeking the assistance of the judge to resolve the dispute.

Nevertheless, mediation does take place in the attorney's office, and I occasionally found lawsuits for breach of contract based upon a prior compromise agreement drafted by an attorney and signed by the disputants. When I asked this same attorney to describe a private settlement in which he had played a part, he told me of the following case. *Nai* Chum, the driver of a pedicab, was hit by a truck as he pedalled past a movie theater in Chiangmai city. He was taken to the hospital where it was determined that his leg was broken. After seven days in the hospital he was discharged with his leg in a cast and a bill for 400 *baht.* As long as the cast remained on his leg, he could not drive his pedicab. The driver of the truck, *Nai* Sakchai, paid *Nai* Chum's

---

17. This narrow view of the attorney as litigator appears to be less common, however, among urban people, particularly merchants, who are familiar with the variety of tasks the attorney can perform and may be more likely to consult with him on legal matters short of actual litigation.

medical expenses, but *Nai* Chum's relatives felt that he should receive at least 7,000 *baht* compensation in addition to the actual hospital costs. When *Nai* Sakchai came to the attorney's office to meet with *Nai* Chum and his relatives, he responded that he was poor and could pay only 2,000 *baht*. The attorney remained silent, knowing that *Nai* Chum could win at least 5,000 *baht* if he decided to litigate. *Nai* Chum, however, sympathized with *Nai* Sakchai and reduced his request from 7,000 *baht* to 2,500 *baht*. *Nai* Sakchai remained adamant, however, insisting that he was unable to pay more than 2,000 *baht*. Finally *Nai* Chum gave in and accepted the payment of 2,000 *baht*. The attorney drafted a compromise agreement, which was duly signed and witnessed. Later the attorney asked *Nai* Chum if he would have agreed to the payment of only 2,000 *baht* had he known that he could have won more than twice that amount in court. Yes, answered *Nai* Chum, he would have reached the same decision in any case. Going to court was, after all, just a waste of time.

CONCLUSION

The process of mediation at all levels of Thai society is reinforced by an almost universal wish to avoid one of its alternatives—litigation. In Chiangmai I was asked more than once if I had heard an expression invariably attributed to the Thai-Chinese: "It is better to eat dog shit than go to court." This attitude, as prevalent among the Thais, certainly, as among the Thai-Chinese, does not simply reflect a fear of the costs of litigation. Clearly some potential litigants are mindful of the potential for financial ruin of the kind suffered by *Nai* Yang, the minibus driver. Beyond the purely economic factor, however, the litigation of private wrongs implies to many Thai people certain characteristics that they strongly dislike: aggression, self-assertion, public and overt conflict, lack of subtlety in interpersonal relations, and the impersonal application of rules and forces which are removed from the traditional society and which are beyond the control of the very person who brings the suit. We shall see that this common perception of litigation does not always correspond to the manner in which lawsuits are actually handled once they reach the court. Nevertheless, the fact that this perception is so widespread in Thai society may help to explain why litigation is often avoided and why mediation is embraced as a preferred alternative.

In contrast to litigation, mediation is attractive for a number of reasons. It is economical and effective, for the mediator is usually an interested *phuyai,* an important person whose status and authority can help to ensure that the settlement will be accepted by both parties. The subtle and private nature of the procedure helps both disputants to avoid a public display of their grievances and an open insistence upon their legal rights. In this way their reputation is not greatly damaged, gossip is minimized, and they are not

Conclusion

forced to deviate too far from their ideal posture as cool and self-denying persons. Perhaps most importantly, mediation is utilized because the traditional organization of the society supports and nourishes it. I do not mean simply that mediation occurs because it is customary within the patron-client hierarchies that characterize Thai society. The influence of tradition is surely a strong factor, but Thai people are pragmatic and adaptable enough to abandon customs when they are no longer useful to them. Rather, I would suggest that the "entourage" system itself has survived in large part because of its usefulness in these very matters, because it has proven effective in resolving conflict without doing damage to the deeper concepts of justice and idealized behavior that are shared by so many Thai people. Among the reciprocal exchanges that occur between patrons and clients, expressive of the most profound kind of relationship that can exist between individuals, one of the most characteristic is the assistance of the patron in mediating disputes and resolving conflicts that trouble his client.

Mediation is therefore of the essence of the hierarchical relationships that pervade Thai society. Although it often occurs in an informal, unofficial setting, we have seen that the official administrative hierarchy may also offer disputants a forum in which mediation can take place. For disputes arising in the village, the village chief or the *kamnan* will usually be the first official who is consulted. This is because, of all the official mediators available, the village chief and *kamnan* are closest and most familar to the villagers. Their official rank most often corresponds directly to their unofficial status in the village hierarchy. When mediation close to home fails, however, persistent disputants can still avail themselves of several other mediators short of the provincial court itself, and some of these mediators are specifically empowered by law to perform such a function. Each of these figures—the district officer and his staff, the police official, the private attorney—has his advantages and disadvantages; but the likelihood of an effective settlement in each particular case may prove attractive enough to overcome the complainant's qualms about venturing among such distant and unpredictable persons.

Provincial Thai society is thus organized, in the official and unofficial sense, to mediate and resolve conflict rather than to foster litigation. In offering this description of the levels of mediation in Thai society, I have tried to suggest an answer to the earlier question: why do so few disputes concerning private wrongs reach the Chiangmai provincial court? The answer has involved a rather lengthy examination of the patterns a dispute can follow before it ever comes to the court itself. In the remainder of this study, I shall consider disputes involving private wrongs which do in fact reach the court, analyzing not only how they got there but also the ways in which traditional concepts of justice and procedures for mediation carry over into the more formal judicial setting.

Part Three
Private Wrongs in the Court: The Interaction of Traditional and Modern Elements

Some groups of devatā see that the other devatā are well off and have more prestige and splendor than they have; and they then become jealous and angry, there are quarrels among them, and they curse one another. If any of the devatā on either of the two sides can restrain themselves and are not angry, those devatā can still retain their life. What is the reason for this? The reason is that the hearts of the devatā who are angry become fires, whereas the hearts of the devatā who are not angry become water and put out the fires which are the hearts of the devatā who are angry; and for this reason they retain their lives. However, if the devatā on both sides each set themselves against the other in anger, do not restrain themselves, and continue to curse and quarrel with one another like that, each of the female devatā who are the attendants of those on both sides generally let their hair down and cry; the devatā on both sides each set themselves against one another like that, and the hearts of the devatā on both sides become fire and consume their bodies; those on both sides have their lives come to an end, and they die. When any group of devatā have their lives come to an end in this way, this is called expiration because of the force of anger.

from "The Realms of the Devatā"
in **The Three Worlds According to King Ruang**[1]

---

1. Mani and Frank Reynolds (1978). *"Devatā"* are gods or angels.

Chapter Seven
Civil and Private Criminal Suits

When a dispute based upon the allegation of a private wrong reaches an attorney's office and a decision is made to go to court, the dispute must then be characterized either as a private criminal suit or as a civil suit. In the private criminal suit, a private plaintiff prosecutes an alleged violation of the penal law with the theoretical goal of imposing state punishment upon the defendant for actions detrimental to the society as a whole. In the civil suit, the plaintiff's goal in theory is to recover damages for some wrongful act injurious to him personally or to obtain some form of mandatory decree. These, I would emphasize, are only theoretical goals. In fact, the choices and strategies of litigants in the Chiangmai court are seldom determined by the abstract purposes of these two kinds of proceedings. Uncomfortable in his strange new surroundings, subject to decisions by unknown court personnel, cut off from his environment of familiar social pressures and constraints, plaintiff's overall aim is usually to retain maximum control over the course and the outcome of his lawsuit. Plaintiff is acutely aware that he often stands to lose, in one way or another, more money than the sum he seeks to recover. Such a loss would not only be ruinous financially, but could represent a serious public humiliation. If plaintiff loosens his tight control over the course of the lawsuit, then it will be swept along by the requirements of the formal law codes and by the authority of the judge—controlled, that is, by rules and forces foreign to plaintiff's own social environment, which appear to him to be unpredictable, irrational, and even harmful. Because he senses this kind of uncertainty and potential danger in going to court, plaintiff's decision to sue is often a reluctant one, a calculated risk. After he has decided to bring his case to court, therefore, his subsequent decisions concerning the strategy of litigation will be designed primarily to get the case out again, on terms as advantageous as possible.

PRIVATE CRIMINAL SUITS AND JOINT PROSECUTIONS

Private criminal suits are not unique to the Thai judicial system. Although criminal acts are generally thought of as wrongful behavior injurious to the society as a whole, western legal systems have sometimes permitted the injured person rather than the representative of the state to act as his own prosecutor. This concept has usually been associated with the legal systems of England and some of her colonies,[2] but the private prosecution of certain crimes has also been permitted in European countries such as Austria and Spain (Esmein, 1913:596-97). Even France, during the revolutionary reforms of the late eighteenth century, experimented with private criminal prosecutions under the conscious influence of the English criminal law. The experiment was quickly abandoned, however, and the French public prosecutor was restored as the sole legitimate plaintiff in criminal suits. Only the state, it was argued, should have the capacity to prosecute acts injurious to itself:

> "Is not the government, as it is constituted in France, in itself the sole executive power? That being so, the execution of the laws belongs to the government alone, and to it belongs the duty of finding out and causing the prosecution of violations of these laws." (Esmein, 1913:441)[3]

The Thai decision to permit private individuals to prosecute criminal offenses did not, however, appear to be based upon a choice of English over French legal philosophy. Prince Damrong, explaining the decision in 1896, appeared to imply that the French approach was favored among all western nations:

> In foreign countries, even when an individual suffers some punishable offense, such as theft, it is considered an offense against the crown. This is because the king, as head of state, is responsible for the preservation of peace and order in the country. Thus the king will have his prosecutor litigate such offenses in all cases, and the injured person will appear only as a witness. (Sutčharit Thawǫnsuk, 1964:29)

Prince Damrong acknowledged that there were several important benefits to be derived from a criminal system in which the prosecutor alone could act as plaintiff for violations of the penal laws:

> First, [the public prosecution of crimes] prevents citizens from bringing falsified criminal suits in cases with heavy punishments. Second, it prevents agreements between wrongdoers and victims which result in the release of the wrongdoers and the avoidance of any criminal

---

2. See, for example, Holdsworth (1965-72: vol. 3, pp. 620-22 and vol. 15, p. 160) and Esmein (1913:598).

3. Esmein quotes Chabot de l'Allier during debate over the re-establishment of the public prosecutor in France in the year 1801.

punishment, or the imposition of a less severe punishment than is appropriate. Another advantage is that, if the victim is poor and unable to bring a lawsuit or to pursue it to a successful conclusion, then the state itself will help him to achieve his goals. (29)

Nevertheless, he continued, Thailand was not yet ready for a legal system in which the public prosecutor litigated all criminal violations to the exclusion of the injured person:

> If this system is seen as good, then we should adopt it here in Thailand. But at the present time, this would be impossible. Most Thai people are still unwilling to initiate litigation, and few indeed would place their trust in a public prosecutor. In addition, it is preferable to wait and see how much work our newly established prosecutors will be able to handle, rather than to risk failure by giving them at the outset more responsibilities than they can manage. For these reasons, the duty of the prosecutors with regard to people who bring criminal suits should be to proceed according to their wishes at first. In every case where a private person appears as plaintiff, the prosecutor should merely observe and prevent collusion between plaintiff and wrongdoer. Where the victim is indigent and cannot bring suit, or where the victim is satisfied to have the prosecutor bring suit in the name of the kingdom, then the prosecutor should accept the case for examination. If he finds the evidence is sufficient, then he should bring suit on behalf of the state.
>
> But in criminal cases without any plaintiff, or where the plaintiff does not proceed properly in some respect, it is then the duty of the prosecutor to conduct the litigation. (29-30)

Primarily because the office of the public prosecutor would be perceived as a new and somewhat suspicious institution in provincial Thailand, therefore, private individuals were allowed to prosecute alleged criminal violations from the very inception of the modern Thai judicial system.

Prince Damrong expressed some apprehension over the inevitable conflict between personal interests and state interests in the prosecution of private criminal suits. Some individuals, he believed, would reach out-of-court settlements with criminal defendants that might sacrifice the interests of society as a whole for their own individual compensation. In modern Thailand it is now felt, on the contrary, that the power to bring private criminal suits under Section 28 of the Criminal Procedure Code[4] is itself an important means to protect individual interests in dealings between criminal suspects and the prosecutors themselves. Should a prosecutor decide not to bring suit, the victim would nevertheless retain the right to bring the wrongdoer to justice. This right is specifically preserved by Section 34 of the Criminal Procedure Code, which

---

4. "Section 28. The following persons are entitled to institute criminal prosecutions in court: (1) the Public Prosecutor; (2) the injured person" (Criminal Procedure Code).

provides that "a non-prosecution order does not bar the right of the injured person himself to institute a prosecution."

The importance of the victim's right to bring private criminal actions was emphasized by its absence during periods of martial law over the past twenty years. A Thai lawyer told me of a case he handled during such a period in which a woman was murdered, but the prosecutor decided to drop the suit. The lawyer was barred by martial law from bringing a private criminal suit on behalf of the woman's family, as he would have done during normal times, but he believed the suspect to be guilty and was displeased with the decision not to prosecute. His only recourse, however, was to sue the suspected killer for defamation of the deceased, based upon remarks he had made to newspaper reporters concerning her inordinate sexual desires. In this way the family of the deceased was fortunate to recover some 15,000 *baht* in damages by an indirect route.

Occasionally, the injured person will encounter problems when the prosecutor *does* decide to prosecute, but fails to present a case which the complainant believes to be commensurate with the crime. When this occurs, the complainant will be barred by the Criminal Procedure Code from bringing a subsequent criminal suit alleging a more serious violation than the one the prosecutor stated:

> Section 39.—The right to institute a criminal prosecution is extinguished as follows:
> ... (4) by a final judgment in reference to the offense for which the prosecution has been initiated.

This clause has been interpreted by the Supreme Court of Thailand in the case of the Uthaithani Provincial Prosecutor v. *Nai* Sawai Kengket *et al.*, 2019/1949, to mean that future prosecutions will be prohibited if they are based upon the same alleged actions of the defendant that gave rise to the initial prosecution, even if a different crime is charged by the private plaintiff.[5] The prosecutor in that case had obtained a conviction for grievous bodily harm. When the victim subsequently died, his family sought to bring a private criminal suit against the same defendant for homicide. The Supreme Court held that Section 39(4) barred a second prosecution for the same alleged misconduct, even when a different charge was stated. Four years later, the Supreme Court held in a similar case—*Nang* Pao Nanti v. *Nai* Rüang Duangmala *et al.*, 1124/1953—that the right to bring a private criminal suit is extinguished as soon as judgment is entered in a prior prosecution based upon the same misconduct. This is true even when the private litigant brings his

---

5. The prosecutor's capacity to designate the particular criminal infraction arising from a given wrongful act is theoretically restricted by Section 90 of the Penal Code: "Whenever one and the same act violates several provisions of the law, the provision prescribing the most severe punishment shall be applied to the offender."

case *before* the public prosecution is instituted. The question is not who files first, but who obtains the first final judgment. Once that occurs, all further action is barred.

Thai law does offer the injured person a means to help determine the strategy of litigation when the public prosecutor decides to bring charges. The injured person is explicitly empowered by Section 30 of the Criminal Procedure Code to join as plaintiff in the criminal prosecution and to work with the prosecutor to obtain a conviction:

> Section 30.—In a criminal prosecution instituted by the Public Prosecutor, the injured person may apply by motion to associate himself as prosecutor at any stage of the proceedings before the pronouncement of judgment by the Court of First Instance.

As a joint prosecutor, the injured person can ensure that his interests are fully represented in the criminal proceedings. He can see that the complaint is drafted in a satisfactory manner, that the evidence is complete, that the site of the crime has been thoroughly inspected, and that most other aspects of the case are handled properly (Marut Bunnag, 1971:5). Some prosecutors, I was told, resent this intrusion upon their duties, for it indicates a certain lack of confidence in their work. On the other hand, the injured person and his attorney can offer the prosecutor a special form of assistance in the preparation of the case. For this reason, and because the law clearly entitles the injured person to participate in this way, the public prosecutor "should be satisfied" when joint prosecutions occur.[6]

I have suggested earlier in this study that the goals of private plaintiffs in criminal suits are often quite different from those of the state. Table 5 demonstrated that public prosecutions resulted in judgments completely favorable to plaintiff—that is, findings of guilt as charged—in 96.6 percent of the cases. Only 0.6 percent were withdrawn. For private criminal prosecutions, on the other hand, only 3.1 percent resulted in outcomes completely favorable to plaintiff, while 84.6 percent were withdrawn. The typical private criminal suit, unlike the typical public prosecution, is brought in order to force the defendant to come to terms with the plaintiff. The purpose is not usually to obtain a conviction, but to arrive at a settlement. Once a settlement is reached, the defendant will pay the plaintiff the amount agreed upon. The plaintiff will then withdraw his criminal suit. This pattern accounts for the fact that 84.6 percent of the private criminal suits were withdrawn before a verdict could be rendered. After the settlement was achieved, the determination of guilt or innocence by the court became unnecessary. Once the plaintiff received the compensation he sought, he was willing to relinquish his power over the

---

6. The quoted phrase, as well as the observation that prosecutors sometimes resent joint prosecutions, came from an interview with a former Chief Prosecutor of Chiangmai province.

defendant and extinguish the latter's liability under the criminal laws of the state. A private settlement with the injured person thus serves as a substitute for any obligations that the defendant may owe to society as a whole.

The plaintiff in a private criminal suit may, according to Section 35 of the Criminal Procedure Code, move to withdraw the suit at any time before the trial court enters a judgment, and the court may grant or deny such a motion "as it thinks fit." The permission of the accused to withdraw the suit is required, however, if he has already submitted his defense or at any time in the proceedings if the case involves a "compoundable" offense, so specified in the Penal Code. After the private plaintiff has withdrawn his suit, the public prosecutor may still institute proceedings if he chooses, unless the offense was a compoundable one (Criminal Procedure Code, Section 36(3)). Compoundable offenses generally are criminal infractions which do not involve serious bodily injury to the victim, serious threats of violence, or injury to the public as a whole. Defamation, cheating against creditors, and misappropriation, for example, are all "compoundable offenses" (Penal Code, Sections 333, 351, and 356). Mischief—the destruction of property—is a compoundable offense if the property is not "used or provided for the public" (Penal Code, Sections 361 and 360). Certain offenses against liberty may be compoundable if they do not cause death or serious bodily harm, and if they do not involve coercion or blackmail by arms or by criminal gangs or secret societies, and if they are not aimed at falsifying or tampering with documents of title. (Section 321). Trespass is a compoundable offense except when it is committed "(1) by using or threatening to use any act of violence; (2) by a person in possession of arms or by participation of two or more persons; (3) by night" (Sections 365 and 366). Rape and indecent sexual acts, despite their inherent violence, are compoundable offenses when they are not committed in public, when neither serious bodily harm nor death is inflicted upon the victim, when no torture of the victim is involved, when the victim is over thirteen years of age, and when the victim is not a descendant of the accused, a pupil under his care, a person under his control by virtue of his official authority, or a person under his tutorship, guardianship or curatorship (Section 281). It is also a compoundable offense to "take away any woman for indecent acts by any fraudulent or deceitful means, threat violence, (or) exercising undue influence or coercion..." (Section 284). For all of these compoundable offenses, then, a settlement between private plaintiff and defendant can extinguish criminal liability after the suit is withdrawn by the plaintiff.

As an example of the way in which private criminal suits are used to obtain an out-of-court settlement, I shall describe a typical criminal suit brought under the Royal Edict Concerning Violations Arising from the Use of Checks (1954). We have seen that such cases accounted for 56.3 percent of all private criminal suits listed in table 4. Although violations involving checks are not compoundable offenses, they are rarely brought by the public prosecutor, particularly after a private settlement has already been achieved. These cases are generally routine collection procedures in which money has been lent or credit given in exchange for a future-dated check. When the date for payment arrives, the bank informs the payee that there are insufficient funds on deposit. If a settlement cannot be arranged in any other way, the payee files a criminal complaint in the provincial court. In a suit brought in 1965, for example, plaintiff was a merchant who, on November 30, 1963, had sold certain goods to defendant. Rather than paying in cash, defendant gave plaintiff two checks. The first, for 268 *baht*, was dated December 31, 1963, and the second, for 1,690 *baht*, was dated January 8, 1964. Plaintiff presented both checks for payment on January 21, 1964, but was told by the bank that defendant had no funds in his account. Plaintiff notified the police on April 20, 1964, but the investigation, if any occurred at all, yielded no results. Therefore, on January 6, 1965, plaintiff himself filed a criminal action against the defendant.

A preliminary hearing was set by the court for February 9, 1965. Such hearings are held in every private criminal action in order to determine whether or not a *prima facie* case exists. Although such hearings may also be held in public prosecutions, this rarely occurs. As one judge explained to me, holding such a hearing would insult the police and prosecutors who are themselves responsible for determining that the evidence is sufficient to justify a trial. In many private criminal suits, the preliminary hearing is held before a settlement can be negotiated. In this particular case, however, plaintiff's lawyer appeared on February 9 to announce that defendant had already paid plaintiff 268 *baht* and that another payment had been agreed upon for April 8. Under the circumstances, plaintiff requested that the preliminary hearing be postponed until that time.

On April 8, plaintiff informed the court that a second payment had been made by defendant, this time in the amount of 690 *baht*. A postponement was again requested until the following month. On May 11, defendant appeared in order to request that proceedings be postponed until June 10, on which date he would be prepared to pay the amount still outstanding. Defendant made good on his promise, for a motion was filed by plaintiff on June 10 stating simply that "Plaintiff and defendant have reached an agreement. I ask to withdraw my suit."

Outright acquittals in check cases are extremely rare. Of the 330 check cases in table 4, only 8 resulted in a finding of innocent. This is only 2.4 percent of the total, an acquittal rate that is significantly lower than the figure of 23.2 percent for all other types of private criminal actions (58 of the remaining 250 cases, having excluded 6 in which the outcome was unknown). The difference appears to arise from the fact that check cases are essentially enforcement proceedings for clearly defined contractual obligations, which are clarified and safeguarded even further by the writing of the check. The only uncertain element in nearly all of these cases is how plaintiff will collect. Here the law has given the plaintiff an enormous advantage by making the writing of a bad check a criminal offense per se. Whenever defendant avoids plaintiff's efforts to negotiate payments on an informal level, plaintiff need only file a criminal action in court to subject defendant to the full power of the criminal law. Suddenly defendant must cope with court summonses, with the posting of bail, with the threat of fine and imprisonment—in addition to his original debt to plaintiff. Negotiations and settlement now become infinitely more attractive to the defendant. Although he may not actually have enough money to pay plaintiff, he will now liquidate his assets, borrow money from anyone who will lend to him, and take whatever measures are necessary to avoid criminal punishment. In short, the private criminal action serves as a strong stimulus to promote negotiations and payments which defendant would otherwise have avoided.

The private criminal suit is, however, a harsh and aggressive alternative for the complainant to choose, exposing defendant as it does to physical and economic hardship. The private criminal suit suggests that the plaintiff has a very hard-nosed business sense or else an unusually strong emotional involvement in the dispute. Otherwise he would not be expected to take such drastic steps to bring the defendant to terms. We have seen already that many cultural factors discourage potential plaintiffs from going this far. It should also be mentioned that there are certain legal factors that might inhibit plaintiff from bringing suit too rashly: the provisions of the Penal Code dealing with false evidence, false testimony, and the bringing of lawsuits based upon "false information" (Sections 167-99). Table 4 shows that such suits, grouped under the heading "offenses relating to justice," were more numerous than any other kind of private criminal action except check cases.[7] In many instances, they were brought by persons who were accused of crimes and prosecuted in private criminal suits. These persons responded to the accusations by bringing a criminal "countersuit," charging their prosecutors with perjury or falsification, exposing them as well to the hazards of criminal liability. This strategy puts pressure on both sides to reach a settlement, for both plaintiff and defendant now run the risk of criminal punishment. By distributing incentives for compromise to all the participants in a dispute, the private criminal action most clearly serves as a mechanism to promote negotiations, a harsh but effective means to resolve disputes once they reach the provincial court.

---

7. Technically, "offenses relating to justice" involve not only "offenses against judicial officials," such as those I have enumerated, but also "malfeasance in judicial office." No prosecutions under the latter heading, however, were brought in the Chiangmai court during the four years surveyed in table 4.

CIVIL SUITS FOR PRIVATE WRONGS

The civil suit represents a second alternative available to victims of private wrongs who have decided upon litigation. Since many private injuries constitute both crimes and civil wrongs, plaintiffs are often faced with a choice between the two types of proceedings. A number of factors may lead them to select one over the other. Although the civil action is quite drastic in comparison with informal mediation, it is much less harsh and coercive than the criminal action. Bail and the threat of criminal punishment are absent from civil proceedings. The defendant is liable only to the extent of the assets he or she owns. If the defendant fails to pay proper compensation, the plaintiff may request that the court seize certain of these assets, but the plaintiff's recovery will never exceed the value of the wealth owned by defendant. A defendant worth 10,000 *baht* will never be held liable for 20,000 *baht* in a civil suit, whereas he or she may sometimes be compelled to pay that amount privately to plaintiff under the coercion of a criminal suit.

On the other hand, from the plaintiff's point of view, it is more expensive to institute civil than criminal proceedings, because court costs are assessed in advance in an amount proportional to the amount in controversy. Criminal proceedings do not require the plaintiff to pay any court fees. Eventually the civil plaintiff may recover part or all of the fees he or she has deposited with the court. The court itself will refund portions of these fees if a settlement is reached before final adjudication is required. The defendant may also repay part or all of plaintiff's court costs in connection with a settlement or a judgment favorable to plaintiff. Nevertheless, the necessity of paying these fees in advance was often mentioned to me as a reason to choose criminal over civil litigation.[8]

The typical result of a civil action for a private wrong is, like the private criminal suit, a settlement between plaintiff and defendant. Whereas the criminal settlement is usually an informal, out-of-court payment by the defendant, however, the civil settlement is more likely to be a formal "compromise agreement" (*sanya prani pranǫm yǫm khwam*), which is filed with the court and enforceable by judicial officials.[9] The rule for private

---

8. Fees for civil cases were usually assessed in the Chiangmai court at the rate of 50 *baht* plus 2.5 percent of the amount in controversy up to a maximum fee of 50,000 *baht*. Thus a civil case in which 5,500 *baht* were at issue would require that the plaintiff deposit 187.50 *baht* (about $9.38) with the court in advance. The amount does not seem very large, but the expense nevertheless appeared to be a factor in plaintiffs' strategies. See Schedules I-V, Civil Procedure Code, for a detailed enumeration of the various court fees associated with civil litigation.

9. "Section 138. In a case where the parties come to an agreement or compromise as to the issues of the case without the plaint being withdrawn, and if such agreement or compromise is not contrary to law, the court shall write down in a detailed memorandum

criminal settlements is payment in advance, but for civil settlements the payments will usually occur in the future and will be spread over several installments. If defendant should default upon this agreement (assuming that defendant rather than plaintiff has the responsibility to pay compensation), plaintiff can request the court to order the attachment of defendant's assets and their sale at public auction (see Civil Procedure Code, Sections 271-323: "Execution of Judgments or Orders"). I read a number of cases in which this sort of enforcement action took place. I also heard, however, of cases in which plaintiff simply ignored defendant's default and forgot about the entire obligation. This is a belated version of the disputant's option to "absorb the wrong," and suggests that the criminal suit may offer a higher probability of ultimate compensation to plaintiff than does the civil suit.

The choice between civil and criminal litigation is not based solely upon a weighing of the various costs and benefits that I have described. More often, the choice will form a part of some larger strategy that may well involve both criminal and civil litigation. Generally speaking, civil litigation is undertaken only when the relative rights of plaintiff and defendant have already been established by some other means. Few civil suits for private wrongs are litigated when there is real doubt that defendant's wrongful act created an obligation to pay compensation to plaintiff. In most cases, this obligation will be clearly apparent, either as the result of a contractual agreement which forms the basis of plaintiff's claim (such as a tenant's failure to honor a lease, giving rise to landlord's suit for "wrongful act"—*lamoet*—and damages) or as the result of a prior criminal suit whose outcome defined the relative positions of plaintiff and defendant and stated a clear right of plaintiff to recover damages from defendant. Indeed, the most typical kind of civil litigation for "wrongful acts"—other than cases arising from breach of contract—are suits in which defendant has already been prosecuted, usually by the public prosecutor, and found guilty of criminal misconduct. The Code of Criminal Procedure stipulates that the findings of fact in the criminal suit shall be binding in related civil litigation (Section 46), although liability in a related civil suit must, of course, be determined according to the rules of the civil and not the criminal law (Section 47; Sanya Dharmasakti and Praphas Uaichai, 1975:271).

In a civil suit of 1965, to choose one example among many, plaintiff sought damages for lacerations and broken teeth resulting from a fight with defendant, who had already been convicted on a charge of bodily injury in the magistrates' court. Recovery for plaintiff was almost a foregone conclusion, the only question being the amount of the damages. In this case, defendant negotiated a rather favorable compromise agreement, paying only 700 *baht* of the 5,000 *baht* originally requested by plaintiff. It is difficult for

---

the terms of the agreement or compromise and give judgment accordingly..." (Civil Procedure Code).

defendants to escape entirely the liability established by a prior criminal conviction, especially since confessions are obtained in a vast majority of such convictions as a means for defendants to reduce their punishments. In one civil action for damages resulting from a motorcycle accident, the teenage defendant argued that his confession in the preceding criminal prosecution for bodily injury was not truthful. Since the criminal case had been tried during his high school examination period, he insisted, he had been forced to confess simply to give himself enough time to go home and study. This unusual argument was predictably unsuccessful, and defendant finally accepted financial responsibility for plaintiff's injuries.

The findings of fact in a prior criminal suit may serve as the basis for subsequent civil litigation even where defendant was acquitted. In one interesting case, plaintiff sued for damages that his son had suffered as the result of a prior prosecution based upon an erroneous accusation by defendant. Defendant, in the prior suit, had informed the authorities that plaintiff's son had stolen his bantam rooster. In the public prosecution that resulted from this accusation, it was established that the rooster in question was in fact different from the one that had been stolen from the defendant, and plaintiff's son was found innocent. Plaintiff was angered by defendant's readiness to call in the police without a more careful inspection of the disputed rooster, and he sued for damages. Perhaps because they were fellow villagers and because plaintiff realized that no malice had been involved, he chose to bring a civil action rather than a private criminal suit for false information. Using his son's prior acquittal as the basis for his civil suit, plaintiff succeeded in recovering 400 *baht* in damages.

Although many civil suits for private wrongs are based upon prior criminal prosecutions, it occasionally happens that the civil suit is litigated before defendant's criminal liability has been clearly established. In a civil proceeding in 1965, for example, plaintiff sued for damages arising from injuries sustained in a drunken fight with both defendants. At the same time, the prosecutor's office instituted a criminal action for bodily injury arising from the same incident. Both sides then agreed to stay the civil proceedings until liability was established in the criminal case. Nine months later, the civil action was resumed. The conviction in the criminal proceedings of one defendant made him liable to plaintiff, and an agreement was immediately reached between the parties. Situations of this kind are, however, relatively rare. Individuals are reluctant to litigate where liability is not already obvious, because any uncertainty regarding the ultimate outcome will remove the stimulus for negotiation and settlement. If the defendant has no incentive to reach a compromise agreement, the case may go to the judge for final decision, and the plaintiff will lose his close control over the lawsuit. This, as we have seen, is an uncomfortable situation and will be avoided by most litigants. The court is a useful forum in which to pursue negotiations when it provides plaintiff with leverage over defendant. In cases where plaintiff sees that such leverage does not exist, he will usually avoid litigation entirely rather than allowing the judge to decide a case in which the merits are evenly balanced.

THE JOINING OF CRIMINAL AND CIVIL LITIGATION

We have seen that civil litigation arising from a private wrong will often be related to criminal litigation based upon the same wrongful act. An option that some private plaintiffs select is to bring both the civil and the criminal action in a single lawsuit, without waiting for the criminal prosecution to reach its conclusion before instituting civil proceedings. The plaintiff may, for example, sue the defendant for theft under the criminal law and simultaneously demand under the civil law that the defendant return the article he has stolen or its cash equivalent. In addition, the plaintiff may sue the defendant for a criminal act such as bodily injury, while inserting a civil claim for damages (*kha sinmai thot thaen*) (Criminal Procedure Code, Section 40; Sanya Dharmasakti and Praphas Uaichai, 1975:260). The civil aspect of the lawsuit will be tried according to the rules of civil procedure. Findings of fact on the criminal side will, as usual, be binding in the civil dispute although the determination of liability may be different.[10] Court costs must be deposited in advance for these joint civil and criminal cases, just as they are for ordinary civil suits. For this reason, some litigants may avoid this form of action, preferring to bring a simple criminal suit in which no court costs are assessed, in the hope that defendant can be induced to settle. In joint civil and criminal suits, the court has the option to separate the civil case from the criminal case whenever it finds that the trial of the civil case will "delay or impede the criminal proceedings." If this occurs, the civil case may be tried separately, and the criminal case will be permitted to proceed to its conclusion (Criminal Procedure Code, Section 41).

A case brought in the Chiangmai court in 1970 illustrates clearly how a skillful litigant can manipulate the civil and criminal elements of a single lawsuit to achieve his goals. A merchant named *Nai* Di from a village outside Chiangmai city filed a lawsuit accusing the defendant, *Nai* Nǫm, of criminal misappropriation of property and also requested, in a joint civil action, that

---

10. "Section 46. In giving judgment in the civil case, the Court shall be bound by the facts as found by the judgment in the criminal case.

"Section 47. Judgment in the civil case shall be given in accordance with the provisions of law concerning civil liabilities, without regard to the conviction or nonconviction of the accused..." (Criminal Procedure Code).

Note also the following provision of the Civil and Commercial Code concerning "wrongful acts": "Section 424. The Court, when giving judgment as to the liability for wrongful act and the amount of compensation, shall not be bound by the provisions of the criminal law concerning liability to punishment or by the conviction or non-conviction of the wrongdoer for a criminal offense."

defendant repay partnership funds of 40,775 *baht* (approximately $2,040). The uncontested testimony of *Nai* Di and of *Nai* Nọm's older brother showed that *Nai* Di and *Nai* Nọm had formed a partnership in December 1969 to purchase cattle and buffalo for sale and to divide the profits. *Nai* Di was to provide the capital. *Nai* Nọm was to travel through the villages of Chiangdao district in Chiangmai to purchase livestock which *Nai* Di would take to the central region of Thailand for sale. After each sale, the profits were to be divided except when it was agreed to use them to purchase another group of animals. In mid-December 1969, and again in January 1970, livestock was purchased and sold according to the agreement between *Nai* Di and *Nai* Nọm. The enterprise was not a profitable one in its early stages, but the two men decided to try once again, and *Nai* Di agreed to invest an additional 30,000 *baht* for the purchase of more animals.

Nai Nọm used the new funds to purchase 59 water buffalo and 2 oxen, 24 of which were sold by *Nai* Di in February. The remaining 37 animals were left temporarily with *Nai* Nọm. In mid-March, *Nai* Di was to take these animals for sale as well. *Nai* Di hired a truck to transport the livestock, but when he brought it to the arranged meeting place, *Nai* Nọm was not there. *Nai* Di waited for him until April 5, when he learned that *Nai* Nọm had taken the animals himself, sold them to a local dealer, and absconded with the funds. *Nai* Nọm had received only 37,050 *baht* for the animals despite the fact that their value, if *Nai* Di had sold them according to the agreement, would have been at least 44,400 *baht*. *Nai* Di waited at the house of *Nai* Nọm's older brother until April 15, when *Nai* Nọm finally returned from hiding. *Nai* Di took *Nai* Nọm immediately to the police station where his complaint was recorded and *Nai* Nọm agreed to pay him his share of the partnership funds. *Nai* Nọm then disappeared permanently and the police refused to pursue the case for *Nai* Di. On May 20, *Nai* Di filed his lawsuit in the Chiangmai court.

Nai Di's problem was two-fold. First, he wanted the aid of the police in locating *Nai* Nọm and arresting him so that he could be forced to stand trial. Second, he wanted *Nai* Nọm not simply to go to jail for his misdeeds but to repay the money that was rightfully *Nai* Di's. Indeed, *Nai* Di had little interest in seeing *Nai* Nọm imprisoned. Rather, he wanted to use the threat of jail and the power of the criminal law to force *Nai* Nọm to make a fair settlement. *Nai* Di therefore added to his criminal charge of misappropriation the civil suit for repayment of partnership funds. *Nai* Di calculated his civil remedy as follows: *Nai* Nọm's sale of the livestock for 37,050 *baht* instead of 44,400 *baht* resulted in lost profits of 7,350 *baht*. Plaintiff's share of this sum, because of prior transactions between the two men, was 6,125 *baht*. Expenses incurred in hiring the truck to transport the animals amounted to 1,900 *baht*, and costs incurred while waiting for *Nai* Nọm to appear with the animals between March 20 and April 5 came to 1,600 *baht*. In addition, *Nai* Nọm owed *Nai* Di his outstanding investment of 30,875 *baht*. These figures added up to 40,500 *baht,* upon which *Nai* Di calculated interest of 275 *baht* accruing between the date when both men went to notify the police and the date when *Nai* Di brought suit in the Chiangmai court. In total, besides his criminal charge of misappropriation, *Nai* Di sought a civil remedy of 40,775 *baht.* The initial cost of filing the lawsuit came to 1,070 *baht.*

As the litigation proceeded, *Nai* Nǫm continued to avoid both *Nai* Di and the court officials who were sent to serve him with a summons to appear for preliminary proceedings. Despite *Nai* Nǫm's absence, a preliminary hearing related to the criminal charges was held on June 22, and *Nai* Di and *Nai* Nǫm's older brother both testified. The court held that a *prima facie* case existed and issued an order to proceed with the trial. On that same day, the court issued two summonses for *Nai* Nǫm, one criminal and one civil. Again the court officials were unable to find *Nai* Nǫm to serve him with either summons. On August 3, when *Nai* Nǫm was scheduled to appear in court in connection with the criminal case, *Nai* Di moved that his failure to appear constituted grounds for issuing an arrest warrant. The court agreed, and a warrant was issued on August 4, 1970. On August 6, *Nai* Di filed papers to the effect that *Nai* Nǫm had failed to file a timely answer in the civil case and was therefore in default. *Nai* Di applied for a court order declaring *Nai* Nǫm in default, as required by the Civil Procedure Code, Section 198. The application was approved and the order was issued. *Nai* Nǫm had now violated both criminal and civil procedural requirements by his failure to respond to summonses duly posted on his property. Proceedings were suspended until the police succeeded in arresting him.

On September 21, *Nai* Nǫm was located in the district of Maetaeng and was arrested and imprisoned. Finally *Nai* Di was in a position to exert pressure upon *Nai* Nǫm to reach a settlement. Until *Nai* Nǫm came to terms, *Nai* Di could be quite sure that he would remain in jail. On September 25, *Nai* Di filed a motion with the court to resume proceedings, and October 30 was set for the examination of plaintiff's witnesses. As it turned out, no further proceedings were necessary for *Nai* Di to achieve his purposes. While in jail, *Nai* Nǫm was persuaded to reach a settlement with *Nai* Di. *Nai* Di was willing to arrange this settlement in the form of a civil "compromise agreement," which meant that *Nai* Nǫm agreed to make payment at a future date, subject to enforcement proceedings by the court in the event of a default. The agreement filed with the court on October 30 provided that *Nai* Nǫm would pay, within one month, the full amount of 40,775 *baht* and 7½ percent interest on the original 40,500 *baht* accruing from May 20, the date when *Nai* Di first filed suit. In addition, *Nai* Nǫm would pay all court costs, which ultimately amounted to 290 *baht* after the court refunded the unused portions to plaintiff. Finally, *Nai* Nǫm agreed to pay 2,000 *baht* in attorney's fees for *Nai* Di. In return for these payments, which represented a total victory for plaintiff, *Nai* Di agreed to withdraw his criminal suit against *Nai* Nǫm and to end further civil proceedings.

The Joining of Criminal and Civil Litigation 117

By manipulating the civil and criminal elements of his claim against *Nai Nǫm*, *Nai* Di was able to force his former partner to negotiate with him. The criminal law was used to locate, arrest, and imprison *Nai* Nǫm. *Nai* Di was then able not only to communicate with his adversary, but to threaten him with continued imprisonment unless he agreed to pay the money he owed. The civil law then provided the form for the "compromise agreement" (*sanya prani pranǫm yǫm khwam*) that the two men finally arranged. In addition, civil enforcement proceedings could now be invoked if, at the end of the month agreed upon for payment, *Nai* Nǫm again defaulted or went into hiding. Should that occur, *Nai* Di could now ask the court to seize *Nai* Nǫm's property and, if necessary, sell it at public auction in order to satisfy *Nai* Nǫm's obligation. In short, *Nai* Di achieved exactly what he wanted: an enforceable agreement to repay funds that had wrongfully been taken from him. While he might have achieved the same results by bringing a simple criminal action against *Nai* Nǫm, *Nai* Di probably realized that *Nai* Nǫm would require some time to locate sufficient funds to pay *Nai* Di what he demanded. As long as *Nai* Nǫm was in jail, he would be unable to raise the sizable amount of money he owed *Nai* Di. If, on the other hand, *Nai* Di dropped the criminal charges and *Nai* Nǫm were released from jail without some form of binding agreement between the two of them, *Nai* Nǫm would simply disappear again. The civil element of his case thus provided *Nai* Di with the ingredient he needed—a binding agreement enforceable even after *Nai* Nǫm was released from prison. In this way the goals of the plaintiff, if not those of the state, were satisfied by the skillful blending of criminal and civil elements in a single lawsuit, and maximum control was retained by the plaintiff throughout the proceedings.

Chapter Eight
The Interaction of Code and Custom in the Court

We have seen that there are often significant differences between the goals of private litigants who bring actions for private wrongs and the goals of the state in making such actions possible under the modern legal codes. In this chapter I would like to pursue the subject further, to explore specific areas in which code and custom diverge during the course of litigation. My purpose is not simply to show that there are discrepancies between the norms of the legal codes and the norms of the individuals who become involved in disputes. It would be surprising and unusual if this were not the case. Rather, my purpose is to show how these discrepancies are incorporated into the strategies of the litigants and are made a dynamic part of the process which, in most cases, resolves the dispute. In order to illustrate this theme, I shall discuss three separate areas in which I found a particularly interesting interaction between code norms and customary norms: (a) the concepts of standing and liability for injury; (b) the concepts of a remedy; and (c) the effect of prior settlements on litigation in the court. My treatment of these three topics is intended to be suggestive rather than exhaustive. I shall not attempt to describe all the intricacies of the law regarding standing, scope of liability, remedies for wrongful acts, assessment of damages, and the effect of prior settlements. Instead, I shall present specific cases in which these concepts proved important and in which they interacted with customary concepts to produce distinctive results.

STANDING AND LIABILITY FOR INJURY

The first topic involves a two-fold question basic to any legal system in the world: who shall be held liable for injuries resulting from wrongful acts, and who shall be entitled to a remedy for such injuries? The range of possible answers is wide indeed, from the individual victim and wrongdoer, to the groups of which they are members, to the society of which they are part, to the supernatural beings that control the society. The description of the entourage in chapter 5 touched upon certain aspects of this subject in discussing the voluntary assumption of liability that can take place between patron and client. If we compare the codified law of agency with the customary liability of the patron for wrongful acts by his client, for example, then we have a clear illustration of the divergence between code and custom. We have seen that the patron will come to the aid of a client who injures a third party if the intensity of the relationship between patron and client is such that this sort of protection is seen as appropriate. The patron will aid his client by intervening with the authorities, by paying compensation to the injured party, or by lending money to the client himself. Since the patron-client relationship involves the whole life of the participants, it is not necessary that the client incur the liability while on the business of the patron. The reciprocal obligations between patron and client exist at all times and in all spheres of activity.

The Thai law of agency, on the other hand, defines liability of the principal to third parties injured by the agent with reference to the classical western concept of scope of authority:

> The principal is bound to third persons by the acts which the agent or the subagent has done within the scope of his authority by virtue of his agency. (Civil and Commercial Code, Section 820)

Stated negatively, the principal is never liable to third persons for wrongful acts by his agent that are done outside the scope of his authority, unless the principal specifically ratifies such acts once they are performed:

> If an agent does an act without authority or beyond the scope of his authority, such act does not bind the principal unless he ratifies it.
>
> If the principal does not ratify, the agent is personally liable to third persons, unless he proves that such third persons knew that he was acting without authority or beyond the scope of the authority. (Civil and Commercial Code, Section 823)

The liability of the principal is thus limited strictly by the contractual relationship existing between himself and the agent. Any acts performed by the agent outside this contractual relationship will not create liability in the principal unless he subsequently ratifies them. If, for example, an employee commits a wrongful act injurious to a third person, and the act is done within the scope of the employment contract, then his employer can be held liable for damages:

> An employer is jointly liable with his employee for the consequences of a wrongful act committed by such employee in the course of his employment. (Section 425)

In short, the law of agency bases liability of the principal upon the concept of *scope of authority,* while the customary rules of the entourage base liability of the patron primarily upon the *depth of relationship* between patron and client. Under the rules of the code, the principal may be held completely liable for injuries inflicted pursuant to the specific contractual duties of the agent. This is, as one Thai commentator explains, because the employee is likely to be poor, whereas the employer is likely to have money. Since the injury occurred only because the employee was performing the business of the employer, it is appropriate that the latter should pay all the monetary compensation: "otherwise the injured person would not know how he could collect damages from a poor man" (*Phra* Wǫraphakphibun, 1970:45).[1] In the context of the entourage, on the other hand, liability is distributed with greater flexibility. Not only does the patron have the choice of accepting or denying responsibility for his client's actions, he also has various options as to the nature and extent of his financial commitment. His decision will be based primarily upon the nature of the relationship, and only secondarily upon the wealth of his client (not all agents are poor). His financial contribution may take the form of a gift or a loan, and loans, as we have seen, may be strictly or loosely enforced. In addition, the amount of interest paid by the client may depend upon the depth of relationship between the two individuals, and in some cases may not be required at all.

The concept of scope of liability is significant in relationships other than that of employee and employer. Under certain circumstances, for example, parents may be held responsible for injuries caused by the wrongful acts of their children. One interesting lawsuit in the Chiangmai court illustrates the concept of parental liability according to the different rules of code and custom, at the same time that it raises another interesting problem: how to identify the "injured person" (*phu siahai*) who has standing to call for restitution from the wrongdoer. The lawsuit really consists of two separate cases, for a remedy was first obtained under customary law and then a suit was brought for the same injury in the Chiangmai court. By comparing the two procedures and the two outcomes, we can contrast the legal norms at work and draw some preliminary conclusions concerning the concepts of liability and standing in the parent-child relationship.

Early one morning, a sixteen-year-old girl named *Nangsao* Pan went to pick corn in a field near her home in the *Müang* district of Chiangmai. By 7:30 a.m. she had finished picking, and she and her younger brothers loaded the corn into an ox cart which she drove back towards her home. As she passed through a market area, a funeral was taking place and the people were beating on drums and gongs. The oxen became confused by the sound and stopped. *Nangsao* Pan

---

1. There are, of course, other reasons for holding the principal liable under the classical theory of agency, such as the principal's ability to foresee and prevent many injuries arising during the course of his business or to insure against them or to pass on the cost of liability in smaller units to his customers.

Standing and Liability for Injury

shook their ropes and, according to plaintiff, beat the oxen with a stick to make them move on. The oxen panicked and bolted ahead through the market place. The wheels of the cart struck and instantly killed a seven-year-old boy, Somphong, who was with a group of children in the market. Somphong's father, *Nai* Bun, notified the police of the accident on the day it occurred, but they took no action. *Nai* Bun also contacted *Nangsao* Pan's father, *Nai* Tha, who agreed to pay all the funeral expenses for the dead boy. These expenses, which included the cost of food, drink, and religious rites conducted over a period of two days, came to 1,773.75 *baht*.

Perhaps *Nai* Bun felt that the payment of funeral expenses was not a sufficient remedy, for he brought a private criminal suit two months after the accident, charging *Nangsao* Pan with negligence resulting in death. After the preliminary hearing and the presentation of evidence by both sides, the case went to the judge for a verdict. During the course of the litigation, the parties had been unable to reach an out-of-court compromise. The judge held that the dead boy's father, *Nai* Bun, had no standing to bring a criminal action against *Nangsao* Pan on behalf of the deceased, because his marriage to the boy's mother had never been lawfully registered. *Nai* Bun was therefore not an "injured person" and had no right to prosecute *Nangsao* Pan for her allegedly wrongful act. On these grounds, *Nangsao* Pan was acquitted.

The relationships among the various individuals in this case are illustrated in figure 7.

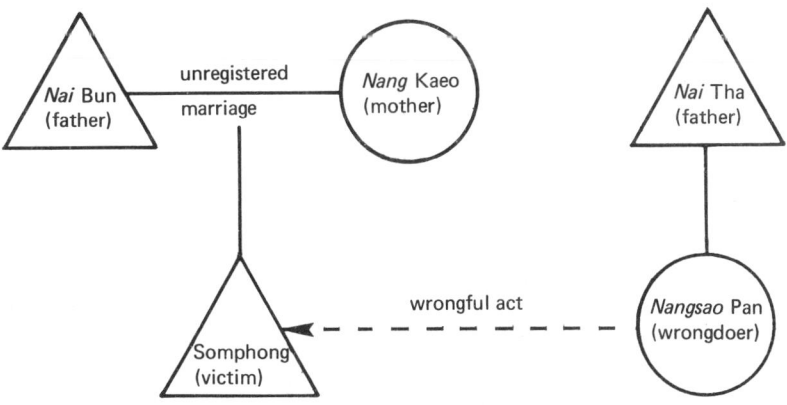

Figure 7. Relationships Among Participants in Ox Cart Dispute

In the first phase of the dispute, *Nai* Tha in effect admitted that he was liable for his daughter's acts and that *Nai* Bun was the person to whom this liability was owed. Liability was defined with reference to the actual cost of Somphong's funeral rather than with reference to some other legal concept such as pain and suffering, lost income, or punitive damages. The procedure that was followed in this phase of the dispute is illustrated in figure 8.

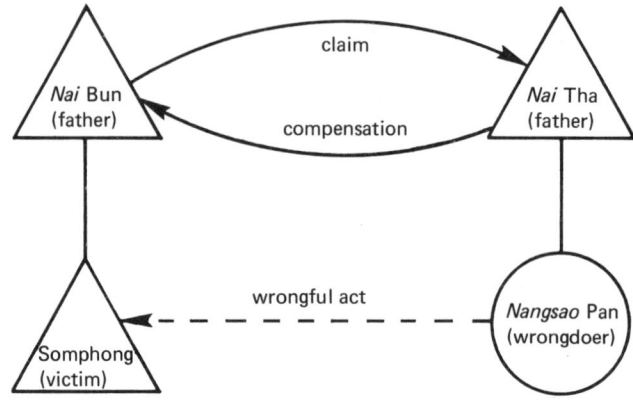

Figure 8. Customary Compensation Procedure in Ox Cart Dispute

After receiving customary compensation in the form of funeral expenses, *Nai* Bun apparently decided that he was also entitled to a cash payment for the death of his son. This decision was probably the reason he brought a private criminal suit, hoping to pressure *Nai* Tha into paying more money rather than seeing his daughter, *Nangsao* Pan, sent to prison. Under the Penal Code, however, *Nai* Tha was no longer the person liable for the wrongful act. On the contrary, *Nangsao* Pan herself was liable for her own negligence, and she was therefore made the defendant in *Nai* Bun's suit. Undoubtedly, *Nai* Bun was perfectly satisfied to sue *Nangsao* Pan rather than her father, because this merely added to the pressure on *Nai* Tha to reach a settlement and prevent his sixteen-year-old daughter from being sent to jail. In place of *Nai* Tha, therefore, the Penal Code substituted *Nangsao* Pan as the person liable for the wrongful act. The real problem, however, was to decide who had standing to enforce this liability and to vindicate *Nangsao* Pan's victim. In the customary procedure, there was no question that the dead boy's father was the secondarily "injured person," and it was he who negotiated the payment of funeral expenses. In the court of law, a different result obtained, however, a result dictated by the Code of Criminal Procedure:

> Section 5. The following persons may act on behalf of the injured person:
> (1) the legal representative or custodian, where the offense was committed against a minor or incompetent person under his or her charge....[2]

---

2. For purposes of clarity, I have reworded the translation of this provision.

Standing and Liability for Injury

Nai Bun and his wife, *Nang* Kaeo, had been married for twelve years, but their marriage had never been registered according to Thai law. Therefore, *Nai* Bun was not a "legal representative" of his natural son, Somphong.[3] Only the mother in such cases had the right to bring suit. In contrast, then, to the customary procedure illustrated in figure 8, the correct code procedure is illustrated by figure 9.

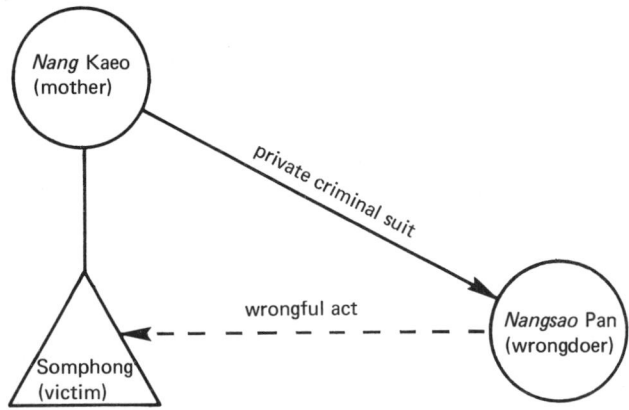

Figure 9. Proper Legal Procedure in Ox Cart Dispute

The code procedure appears on the face of it to have changed the dispute entirely. Instead of being a conflict between *Nai* Bun and *Nai* Tha, the code transforms the dispute into a lawsuit involving *Nang* Kaeo and *Nangsao* Pan. Except for the formalistic changes, however, the procedural requirements of the law codes do not really alter the goals of the disputants at all. The ultimate purpose of the plaintiff is still to receive compensation from *Nai* Tha, just as it was from the beginning. *Nang* Kaeo, if she had brought such a suit, would presumably be acting on *Nai* Bun's behalf, for he had emerged as the more active disputant of the two. Similarly, *Nangsao* Pan would play the role of defendant in name only, for she herself would not be expected to pay compensation to the dead boy's family. Everyone would understand that such compensation, if a settlement were achieved, would come from her father and not from her, despite the fact that she would be the one threatened with criminal punishment. In short, the law codes change the form but not the substance of the dispute. The traditional goal of compensation is pursued by manipulation of the Penal Code. The traditional concepts of standing and

---

3. "Section 1541. A person exercising parental power is the legal representative of the child. . . .
"Section 1538. The parental power is exercised by the mother in any of the following cases if: . . . (5) the child was born out of wedlock and has not been legitimated by the father. . ." (Civil and Commercial Code).

liability are also retained implicitly, despite the fact that figurehead plaintiffs and defendants must be substituted for their traditional counterparts in the process of litigation.

The liability of parents for wrongful acts by their children is a concept with strong roots in Thai history and in customary practice. Nevertheless, there is a voluntary component even in the parent-child relationship, as we have seen, and there is some indication that historically a parent could avoid liability by deciding to sever that relationship. The Thai commentator *Khun Wičhitmattra* writes that parents were able to avoid liability for future violations by their children if they voluntarily informed the authorities of an infraction already committed. The expression, "to inform the authorities" *(bǫk sala)* became an idiom that implied not only an avoidance of liability by the parents but a dissolution of their relationship with the child (1970:552-53). Its idiomatic use suggests that the concept has been a familiar one in Thai society. In actual practice, parents who choose to preserve the parent-child relationship will, as a matter of course, accept the responsibility to pay customary compensation to third persons injured by the wrongful acts of their children. The modern law codes do not necessarily support this concept of parental liability, however. As we saw in the ox cart case, a minor such as *Nangsao* Pan can be the sole defendant in a criminal suit for her wrongful act, without any legal liability attributed to her parents. In civil actions, both child and parent are held jointly liable for wrongful acts, *unless* the parent can affirmatively show that he or she exercised proper care in supervising the child. If such proof can be made, then the child alone will be held liable to the limits of his or her own worth:

> Section 429. A person, even though incapacitated on account of minority or unsoundness of mind, is liable for the consequences of his wrongful act. The parents of such person are, or his guardian is, jointly liable with him, unless they or he can prove that proper care in performing their or his duty of supervision has been exercised. (Civil and Commercial Code)

Attempts by parents to absolve themselves of liability under the Civil and Commercial Code and to place sole responsibility upon their own child can sometimes be rather extreme. In one civil suit brought in the Chiangmai court, the parents of a teenage boy were sued together with their son for damages resulting from his negligent motorcycle driving. The parents clearly wanted to have their son alone held liable, because he had few assets and their own property would thereby be placed beyond plaintiff's reach. In their answer to plaintiff's allegations, therefore, they did not try very hard to deny that their son had been negligent. Rather, they implied that he had always been a terrible driver who loved to borrow other people's motorcycles and drive them recklessly. The parents, according to their reply, had frequently scolded their son and even whipped him to try to break this bad habit. They had prohibited him from riding any motorcycle, and had sold their own motorcycle to remove it from his temptation. They had even spoken to his teachers at school to ask them to prevent their son from riding motorcycles. In this case, they had no knowledge that their son had borrowed a motorcycle and driven it in such a way as to injure plaintiff. Because of their strenuous efforts to prevent just such an accident, they argued, they were in no way liable for his wrongful act. The parents' argument, although ingenious, was not notably successful. In the end they paid a small sum to the plaintiff in addition to compensation they had previously rendered in a prelitigation settlement.

The concepts of standing and the "injured person" raise some important questions in a third kind of litigation, wholly unrelated to employer-employee or parent-child relationships—namely, lawsuits brought by persons who have paid bribes to government officials. The problem that Thai courts have faced is whether or not to consider the briber an "injured person" with the right to sue by virtue of his illegal payment. The Chiangmai court confronted this issue in a 1968 criminal suit for malfeasance brought by the payer of a bribe against the government officials who allegedly received it. The plaintiff, *Nai* Narong, was arrested by the defendant police officers for gambling. According to *Nai* Narong's complaint, defendants demanded the payment of 1,000 *baht*, in exchange for which they would drop the charges against him. When the money was provided, *Nai* Narong was freed. A month after these events were alleged to have taken place, *Nai* Narong brought a criminal suit against the policemen for accepting the bribe money. The court heard plaintiff's evidence and held that a *prima facie* case existed, but later reversed itself and found, without further testimony, that plaintiff's case must be dismissed because plaintiff was not an "injured person" as defined by Section 2(4) of the Criminal Procedure Code: " 'Injured Person' means a person who has received injury through the commission of any offense . . . ." The court reasoned that *Nai* Narong had admitted violating the law and should properly have been arrested, imprisoned, and charged for his criminal wrongdoing. Instead, by allegedly paying money to the defendants, *Nai* Narong had escaped prosecution entirely. Far from receiving any injury, *Nai* Narong had received a benefit to which he was not entitled under law. Therefore, he had no standing to sue defendants for their alleged misdeeds.

Nai Narong appealed this decision of the Chiangmai court, arguing that even if he had violated the law, defendants had also been guilty of criminal misconduct and their wrongful act had resulted in their enrichment at his expense. Plaintiff's attorney went on to argue that, as a matter of policy, standing must be given to persons such as *Nai* Narong, for otherwise official corruption would go unchecked. The public prosecutor, he argued, would seldom bring a criminal action against his fellow officials, particularly when they were policemen with whom he must maintain a good working relationship. What would happen, plaintiff asked rhetorically, if the prosecutor himself were to take money from a criminal suspect in return for an order not to bring charges? When the state's own plaintiff is the recipient of a bribe, who then will be allowed to prosecute? Will the court simply hold that the malfeasance laws do not apply in such cases, or will they follow the better policy of granting standing to the briber himself? The Appeals Court, however, was unimpressed with plaintiff's arguments, noting curtly that his hypothetical example was meaningless since no such case was now presented to the court for decision. Instead, the court held that plaintiff had acted voluntarily, not under coercion, when he made the illegal payment to defendant. Had *Nai Narong* been coerced, he would have been an "injured person" with standing to sue. Since he was found to have acted voluntarily, however, he had no right to do so.

The court did not explain why it found *Nai* Narong's actions to have been voluntary rather than the product of coercion, but we may infer that *Nai* Narong's own admission of criminal misconduct prior to the bribe was influential in this respect. An innocent person who pays the police a bribe may be presumed to have done so under duress, for he has no other reason to avoid a judicial hearing. An admitted criminal, on the other hand, gains a tangible benefit from his payment of a bribe—his undeserved freedom—and may therefore be presumed by the court to have acted voluntarily. This type of reasoning appears to underlie the decision of the trial court and the appellate court, as well as the Supreme Court decisions cited in their support.

The concept of an "injured person" thus raises questions both as to *who* such a person shall be considered to be and *what* precisely shall be said to constitute an injury. The process of definition is important in determining the extent to which codified legal norms will be integrated with customary legal norms and also in determining matters of significance with regard to public administration. The broader the definition of injury, the greater the number of people entitled to prosecute the wrongful acts of public officials and others. When the definition is narrowed, as it has been with regard to persons who bribe policemen in order to escape prosecution, then the litigation of unlawful conduct is taken from the hands of private individuals and given solely to the public prosecutor. The choice of a broad or a narrow definition of the term "injured person" will therefore have a decisive effect upon the way in which the formal legal system is used and the extent to which it will be seen as sustaining or destroying customary concepts of standing and liability. Insofar as the formal legal system provides an answer that conforms to popular concepts of justice, it will offer the public a forum in which customary remedies may confidently be pursued.

PROVIDING A REMEDY

We have seen that the concepts of "injured person" and liability for injury will determine the identity of the parties who appear in the provincial court. In this section, we will explore the different concepts of remedies that the litigants may pursue. Once again, the interplay between customary concepts and the concepts articulated by the law codes will be of central interest. The attitudes of potential litigants towards the court will depend largely on the capacity of the formal law codes to provide them with a remedy they view as appropriate to the wrong that has occurred. We shall find three important ways in which code and custom interact in this regard: (1) the new codified rules divert the dispute into new legal issues and "technicalities" and make the achievement of customary remedies impossible; (2) the codified rules are manipulated by the litigants—sometimes in a manner irrelevant or contrary to the norms suggested by the codes themselves—in order to achieve customary remedies; (3) persons formerly immune to pressures by the complainant are made susceptible to lawsuits brought under the legal codes and are forced to provide the injured person with a customary type of remedy that they could have avoided but for the existence of the codes.

When the courts are called upon to handle disputes under a codified regime of law, the application of technical rules to resolve the disputes may create an impression that the law works in an arbitrary or inequitable way. The technical rules appear to bear no relationship to the customary concepts of justice or fairness: they are relevant only to the internal logic of the court's own rational functioning (Abel, 1973a:264-65). Occasionally, we find such outcomes in the case records of the Chiangmai court. In a criminal trespass suit, for example, a tenant sued her new landlord for destroying her fence and roof in an attempt to force her to vacate. Rather than ruling on the property rights of the holdover tenant as against the claims of the new property owner, however, the court dismissed the suit on the grounds that the plaintiff had not signed her own complaint. Her lawyer had carelessly signed the complaint on her behalf, confusing the requirements of a private criminal action with those of a civil suit in this regard. The court, citing the requirement of the Criminal Procedure Code, Section 158(7), refused to rule on the merits and dismissed solely on the basis of the attorney's technical error.[4]

A far more sophisticated decision in a different case also found the codified law in conflict with customary norms and left the plaintiff without a remedy to which she might have been entitled in traditional Thai society. Plaintiff in this civil suit was a 25-year-old village woman I shall call *Nangsao* Lai, who claimed to have fallen in love with a young man, *Nai* Mun. *Nangsao* Lai stated that she had been deceived by *Nai* Mun, who had

---

4. Criminal Procedure Code, Section 158: "A charge must be made in writing and contain: ... (7) the signature of the prosecutor, the drafter and the writer or typer of the charge."
  In this case the court, for reasons that are not disclosed, chose not to allow the plaintiff simply to correct her technical error, as it could have done under Section 161: "Where a charge does not conform with the law, the Court shall order the prosecutor to correct the charge, or dismiss or refuse to accept the charge."

promised to ask her parents for permission to marry her and had sworn his love for her many times. As a result, she had had sexual relations with him and was now pregnant. *Nai* Mun, however, had begun to avoid her and became involved with another woman, refusing to marry her as he had once promised. In his reply, *Nai* Mun denied ever having been *Nangsao* Lai's lover or exchanging any promises with her. The court tried to mediate the dispute, but the two sides were unable to reach an agreement. Without hearing any evidence, the court then rendered its verdict on the basis of the legal questions presented.

The court held that, even if the facts were found most favorable to plaintiff, she would still lose her suit. The decision was divided into two parts, the first dealing with the question of "wrongful act" and the second with the question of breach of contract. In the first part, the court found that *Nangsao* Lai had voluntarily agreed to have sexual relations with *Nai* Mun and therefore no "wrongful act" could be said to have taken place, as defined by Section 420 of the Civil and Commercial Code.[5] This interpretation of "wrongful act" followed the Supreme Court decision in the case of *Nang* Khiao Sitthimongkhon v. *Nai* Kham Sisung, 576/1945, in which it was held that no "wrongful act" occurs when a woman agrees to have sexual relations with a man, even if she does so as a result of the man's false promise to marry her. The second part of the Chiangmai court's decision concerned itself with *Nangsao* Lai's argument that *Nai* Mun had broken an oral betrothal contract, and that *Nai* Mun was therefore bound to pay compensation:

> Section 1438. After the betrothal has taken place, if either party commits a breach of the betrothal agreement, such party shall be liable to make compensation. (Civil and Commercial Code)

The court observed that, although *Nangsao* Lai was 25 years old, she still lived with her mother and father. The Civil and Commercial Code stipulates that no betrothal agreement can be formed under those circumstances without the consent of the parents with whom the individual lives.[6] Since *Nai* Mun had never asked for the consent of *Nangsao* Lai's parents, as he allegedly promised to do, no betrothal agreement was created, and *Nai* Mun could not be required to pay compensation to *Nangsao* Lai.

As a matter of law, *Nangsao* Lai was denied her right to compensation either on the basis of a "wrongful act" or a contract. The court's decision was a legally proper one, carefully adhering to the requirements of the Civil and Commercial Code and the guidelines laid down by the Supreme Court. Never-

---

5. Civil and Commercial Code, Section 420: "A person who, willfully or negligently, unlawfully injures the life, body, health, liberty, property, or any right of another person, is said to commit a wrongful act and is bound to make compensation therefor."

6. Civil and Commercial Code, Section 1435: "... If the man or woman lives with the father or mother, the consent of such father or mother is required [for betrothal]."

theless, one senses that the result of this lawsuit would have been much different had it been resolved according to the customary rules of the traditional society. If the facts were as *Nangsao* Lai alleged, then *Nai* Mun would normally have been required to compensate *Nangsao* Lai, her parents, or the spirits who were offended by the premarital sexual activities. The technical requirements concerning the formation of a contract would not have obscured the primary fact of *Nai* Mun's responsibility for *Nangsao* Lai's pregnancy. The fact that *Nangsao* Lai voluntarily brought this lawsuit in the Chiangmai court, risking gossip and embarrassment to obtain compensation, tends to suggest that her claim had a basis in fact. It is not clear why *Nangsao* Lai was unable to enforce this claim against her former lover at the local level. When she subsequently brought her claim to the provincial court, however, her attempt to recover a customary remedy did not even win her the right to a hearing on the merits. Her traditional claim was translated into the legal terminology of "wrongful act" and "betrothal contract." Stated in those terms, her case was untenable, as the judge properly found. Regardless of the traditional remedy to which she might have been entitled, the norms of the civil code required as a matter of law that her case be dismissed.

Although the legal codes may sometimes conflict with traditional concepts of justice and deny remedies that appear fair and appropriate, it is perhaps more common for the rules and procedures of the legal codes to be used by litigants to enforce customary norms. Very often the goals and purposes of the codes themselves are obscured by the strategies of private litigants, who manipulate the law in order to obtain their customary remedies. In private criminal actions, for example, we find some outrageous criminal offenses settled out of court, freeing the alleged offender in exchange for his payment of traditional compensation to the victim. In a criminal action brought in 1965, for example, the mother of a six-year-old girl accused her next-door neighbor of raping the child and infecting her with venereal disease. After the presentation of plaintiff's evidence and the finding of a *prima facie* case by the court, defendant agreed to pay damages to plaintiff in exchange for withdrawal of the lawsuit. The remedy sought by the mother was money, not the imprisonment of her neighbor, and she obtained it by invoking the appropriate provisions of the Criminal Procedure Code. It is possible that the complainant settled for money damages instead of criminal punishment in this case for reasons other than mere tradition. Plaintiffs in private criminal suits are keenly aware that a defendant who feels victimized by an unreasonable adversary will harbor his grudge in prison and be likely to seek revenge when he is released. The customary remedy of compensation is thus a two-edged sword, creating certain expectations in the defendant as well as the plaintiff. Neither side can easily abandon these expectations in favor of the procedures suggested by the criminal codes.

A final point to be made about remedies is that the codified procedures now enable many plaintiffs to obtain customary remedies in situations where defendants could not otherwise be induced to pay. This is because the court provides a plaintiff with leverage and a source of coercive power that he would not otherwise possess. Where certain defendants could simply ignore plaintiff's informal requests for compensation at the local level, they can no longer do so when the plaintiff arms himself with the appropriate provisions of the civil or criminal law. This point can be illustrated by a criminal suit brought by a merchant I shall call *Nai* Soem against a post office official, *Nai* Anan, whom he accused of taking away his daughter for indecent purposes and of rape. *Nai* Soem admitted quarrelling with his 18-year-old daughter, *Nangsao* Prani. Following this quarrel, *Nangsao* Prani left *Nai* Soem's house and went to live with *Nai* Anan. Although *Nai* Anan was already married, he apparently persuaded *Nangsao* Prani to become his second wife and offered protection against her father's temper. Plaintiff became angry when he found that his daughter had left him, and he notified the police that *Nai* Anan had taken her away. The police went with him to *Nai* Anan's house near the post office, where they met *Nangsao* Prani. She flatly refused to return home, and *Nai* Soem brought a criminal suit against *Nai* Anan within a week.

Nai Anan was a man of status, a government official, and such men sometimes take second wives in the locality where they work. It is not unheard of, moreover, for young women to become unhappy with their parents and elope with a lover. In most cases, the parent can tolerate such an elopement if the couple later seeks the approval of the parent and shows some willingness to pay the brideprice expected in traditional society. In this case, however, no such reconciliation appears to have been attempted and no brideprice offered. *Nai* Soem was only a merchant with no influence over the government official, *Nai* Anan. What he wanted, I would suggest, is not revenge or punishment, but simply the brideprice to which he as a parent was entitled. Under normal circumstances, it would have been very difficult for him to obtain such a remedy as long as *Nai* Anan was unwilling to pay. Within two months after bringing this criminal suit, however, *Nai* Soem notified the court that *Nai* Anan had paid him "damages" (*kha siahai*) and that he was now satisfied. He accordingly withdrew his criminal charges. We do not know whether a reconciliation between *Nangsao* Prani and *Nai* Soem was ever achieved. What is clearly suggested, however, is that *Nai* Soem obtained the traditional remedy of the brideprice by bringing a criminal action against a man who would not otherwise have been obliged to pay him anything at all. Not only were the punitive provisions of the criminal code manipulated so as to provide *Nai* Soem with a traditional remedy, but they were used against an individual who might well have avoided paying that remedy if it were not for the existence of the modern judicial system.[7]

---

7. Information regarding this case was obtained from plaintiff's pleadings and testimony and from the police report.

EFFECT OF PRIOR SETTLEMENTS

We have seen some of the ways in which code and custom interact as traditional ends are pursued by codified means in the Chiangmai court. What happens, however, when the traditional remedy has already been obtained, and the same dispute subsequently arrives in the court for adjudiciation according to the formal law codes? In fact, a number of these cases have already been discussed in other contexts. In the ox cart case, for example, *Nai Tha*'s payment of funeral expenses was a traditional remedy followed by *Nai Bun*'s criminal suit in the provincial court. In that case, the court dismissed *Nai Bun*'s case on the grounds that he lacked standing to sue on behalf of his natural child. In the civil suit brought against the reckless teenage motorcycle driver and his parents (pp. 124 and 125 above), a settlement of 2,400 *baht* had been negotiated by the police before plaintiff decided to bring suit in court. As a result of that lawsuit, defendants paid a nominal sum (500 *baht*, or about $25) in return for plaintiff's withdrawal of the litigation.

A clear pattern emerges from these and other cases and from my discussion of this question with local judges and lawyers. When the disputants have already made an informal settlement according to customary procedures, the court will take notice of this fact and will usually reduce the liability of the defendant under the formal rules of law. If defendant has already compensated plaintiff, and if the compensation was appropriate to the injury suffered, the judge will be reluctant to hold defendant liable to any substantial degree when the same dispute appears in court. This attitude applies as well to criminal cases brought by the public prosecutor, where the defendant has already paid private compensation to his victim. In such cases, the court may be required by law to render a verdict, but the treatment of defendant will be as lenient as possible. Similarly, insofar as the judge can influence the terms of private settlements between litigants in the civil and criminal suits that appear in court, he will urge plaintiff to settle for only nominal compensation if he feels that the prior informal settlement was an adequate one. If the plaintiff acts too harshly, the judge will interpret the law strictly and narrowly to dismiss his suit if possible, or else to take any proper steps to limit defendant's liability.

Prior payments by the defendant are not always regarded so favorably by American courts, where they can be construed as admissions of wrongdoing, more helpful to plaintiff's case than to defendant's. I heard a story concerning an American official in Chiangmai, who was unaware of the attitudes of Thai judges in this regard. He was involved in an automobile accident with a local resident, who insisted that he was entitled to compensation despite the American's belief that he himself had been entirely in the right. Nevertheless, his adversary was tenacious, and the American was more than willing to pay whatever it would take to be rid of him. He was convinced, however, that as soon as he made any payment, he would immediately be sued for civil damages in a court where his prior payment would be used against him as an admission that he had been at fault. Reluctant to be drawn into a situation where the payment of a few thousand *baht* could make him liable for hundred of thousands of *baht* in court, the American considered his alternatives. His solution was eminently sensible by American standards but unnecessary in Chiangmai: a written declaration that he, by the payment of a certain sum of money to this individual, in no way admitted any wrongdoing in the automobile accident that had taken place and denied all legal liability for injuries that had resulted from the accident. The statement was witnessed and signed and held by the American as a protection against any future litigation by his adversary. In fact, the American was now protected, but it was the payment itself, rather than the written document denying responsibility, that would limit his liability in any lawsuit that the other individual might decide to bring.

Where a settlement has already taken place in accordance with customary practices, the court finds itself in the position of adjudicating two cases at once. First, it must decide in essence whether the prior settlement was appropriate according to traditional norms. Then it must decide the merits of the formal lawsuit according to the requirements of the legal codes. Its second decision, as we have seen, is likely to be influenced by its first decision, and the provisions of the codes will be manipulated by the judge—as they have been by the litigants—to reflect this influence. The process is largely an unconscious one, particularly because so many private wrongs are resolved in court by mediation rather than by an explicit rationalized decision of the judge. In the negotiating process, the judge and the litigants can implicitly allow both code and custom to play their part—the one interacting with the other and shaping the strategies and decisions of all the participants.

Chapter Nine
Court as Mediator

The mediation of private wrongs in Thailand has strong roots in Thai history and culture. Marc Galanter has noted that a society's ideology or belief systems concerning conflict do not necessarily reflect the actual patterns of litigation to be found in that society. In India, for example, he observes that "litigation flourishes alongside an avowed preference for compromise and reconcilation" (1975:365). In Thailand, however, this is not the case. The values of Thai society are strongly non-litigious, and they are directly reflected in the procedures by which private wrongs are handled in and out of court. It is not clear why this should be true in Thailand but not in India. It is perhaps inadequate to say simply that cultural continuities are significant in most facets of Thai life, that the Thais have throughout their history displayed a special genius for adapting foreign models to conform with Thai values and purposes. Certainly Thailand's avoidance of colonization helps to explain why Thai cultural institutions have remained largely intact despite the influx of western legal and political models over the past century. A centralized legal system administered primarily by Thai bureaucrats was far more likely to permit and encourage the persistence of customary legal behavior than was a system administered by English or French officials. Such explanations, however, point to the deeper and perhaps unanswerable question of why Thai culture has displayed such resilience and independence in the face of external pressures, bending and adapting when necessary, yet retaining for the most part the basic values and patterns of behavior that have traditionally given meaning to life.

Despite the creation of a national judicial system with its adversary process and adjudicative procedures, the traditional practice of mediating private wrongs has remained strong in Thailand. There has been a continuity with the past, even within the very institution that would appear to destroy customary juridical practices. The procedural codes themselves, while creating a process by which the court can adjudicate legal matters brought before it, also provide the mechanisms by which mediation can be achieved. They permit the settlement and withdrawal of private criminal suits; they allow the judge to promote settlements in civil suits; they provide for the refunding of fees in civil suits which are settled without adjudication; they spread individual trials out into a series of monthly hearings and presentations that provide a maximum opportunity for negotiation. In short, the process of mediation is supported both by tradition and by specific provisions in the procedural codes themselves.

Yet I found that the judges were not strongly conscious of their role as mediators or their place in the structure of mediation that typifies Thai society. They tended to conceive of their function in idealized terms as legal specialists who presided over the presentation of evidence, who evaluated that evidence and applied the rules of law to it. The role of mediator, however, is natural to Thai judges and is expected of them by the other participants, if for no other reason than to save them all from the inconvenience and risks of the judicial process in which they have become enmeshed. The situation is similar in this respect to Hahm's description of mediation in the Korean judicial system:

> Whether a lone policeman in the rural police box or a judge in Seoul, the role of a mediator comes to him naturally. In many cases these official decision-makers do not hesitate to exert pressure on the parties to settle their disputes non-juridically. It is interesting to note that these decision-makers are somewhat furtive about their mediational role. They feel that they are being unfaithful to their official duties by indulging in their "feudal" propensities.... It is ironic that the best argument that can be made by the official decision-makers to persuade the disputants is to convince them of the "horrors" of judicial process. (1969:43)

THE PROCESS OF MEDIATION

The primary participants in the process of judicial mediation are the litigants, their attorneys, and the judge. Other court officials, particularly the registrar, may also be involved in some instances, as may the friends or relatives of the litigants. For purposes of this discussion, however, I shall ignore these secondary figures in the mediation process and shall consider each of the three primary participants in turn.

When I was trying to understand what sort of person would bring a lawsuit in the provincial court, I asked a Thai judge to describe the litigants who appeared before him. He told me that most Thai people, whether rural or urban, preferred not to make an issue out of their conflicts with others. If a dispute arose over a matter of a thousand *baht* or even more, most Thai people would simply say, "forget it" (*chang thoe*), and would never think of bringing the case to court. On the other hand, he continued, there would always be some people who are stubborn (*dü*), who are unwilling to let anyone get the better of them (*mai yọm sia priap*), or who are quick to anger (*čhai rọn*). These are the kinds of people, he concluded, who bring their disputes to court. His comments are not necessarily an accurate depiction of the typical litigant in the Chiangmai court, but they do indicate a common perception of people who are inclined to litigate. Judges and attorneys often feel that the litigants are less than admirable individuals and should be restrained from their rash impulse to do legal battle with their adversaries.

Interestingly, several of the litigants whom I interviewed shared this negative attitude towards the decision to litigate. Although they were generally shy and non-assertive people who appeared to have suffered serious legal injury, they were embarrassed and reluctant about bringing their dispute to court. They were not proud of their decision to assert their rights in a public forum and appeared to feel that by doing so they had behaved in a way that would be viewed as overly aggressive. It is significant that all the participants in the process of mediation, including the plaintiff and defendant themselves, tend to view the litigants with some ambivalence. Although the court is known on an abstract level to be a forum where justice is dispensed, the decision to bring a dispute to this forum is nevertheless seen in many cases as misguided. In light of this attitude towards those who participate in lawsuits, it is not surprising that so many litigants are extremely receptive to the process of mediation that usually takes place in the provincial court.

The attorneys, as I have suggested earlier, tend to be relatively passive, their role limited both by law and by custom. The tradition of public oral advocacy is not strong in Thailand. Opening and closing arguments are rarely presented at trial, and even on appeal most attorneys will decline to give an oral presentation.[1] Procedural objections were rarely raised by local lawyers with regard to the conduct of their adversaries in judicial hearings. The Thai law of evidence is not lengthy or rigorous, but it does prohibit the use of leading questions in the direct examination of witnesses. Nevertheless, I often observed such questions asked as a matter of course without any objection by opposing counsel. The reluctance of attorneys to play an overly aggressive role, however, results only in part from their lack of orientation towards oral advocacy. A more important factor, I believe, is the dominant role of the

---

1. See Marut Bunnag (1971:113-14). In his manual for lawyers, he urges them to give oral arguments on appeal even when they are inclined not to do so, because only one of the appellate judges deciding their case will normally have read the entire case file.

W.A.R. Wood writes that the first time he sat as a judge in the old International Court, he put the opposing attorneys to the unfamiliar task of delivering closing arguments. Although one of them acquitted himself well, "the other advocate, with tears in his eyes, explained that he had never made a speech in his life, and was too old to begin. However, he added, producing a document, he had written down all he had to say, and begged the Court to read it carefully" (1965:51-52).

judge, who is a figure of such great authority that the attorneys hesitate to assert themselves too strongly in his presence. Such behavior might be resented by the judge as a sign of disrespect for his own status. In addition, an attorney who plays too active a role in the process of mediation exposes himself unnecessarily to the recriminations of his client if the agreement later breaks down. It is wiser and more appropriate to allow the judge, whose status is clearly superior to that of the other participants, to play the most important role in the mediation process and to accept responsibility for its outcome.

The judges in the Chiangmai court tend to be very active in conducting the business of the court, wielding their authority with great confidence and dominating the proceedings. They often take part in the interrogation of witnesses, not merely to facilitate their own transcription of the testimony, but to clarify important points, to bring order to a disorganized presentation, and to catch the witnesses in apparent contradictions. In one case, when plaintiff's lawyer failed to appear at a scheduled hearing, the judge denied plaintiff's request for a postponement and acted himself as the interrogator of plaintiff's witnesses. The judges are, for the most part, outsiders to the local community, rotated frequently to avoid the kind of local "entanglements" that were formerly the essence of personalized justice. Nevertheless, because of their institutional function as dispute resolvers, they are often expected by the other participants to play a more traditional role, to abandon their impersonal posture and to mediate disputes with regard to factors of personality and favoritism which they are required by law to ignore. As one judge complained to me, "Even though I have come to a place as far away as Chiangmai, people still call upon me to ask for favors." Litigants described the judges to me in strongly favorable terms. Even when they had been strict in conducting the proceedings, the litigants would later say that they had been "kind" and "good." Although the litigants may have felt inhibited about expressing negative feelings to me, it is nevertheless apparent that the status and the professional expertise of the judges make them figures inherently worthy of great respect according to traditional values.

The actual process of mediation can take place in the courtroom itself or in a more informal setting. The judge may even talk with a litigant in the corridors of the courthouse, urging greater flexibility in a bargaining position or the reconsideration of a suit that the judge considers frivolous. Mediation in the courtroom itself will usually entail direct discussion between the judge and each of the litigants. The judge may ask plaintiff how much he or she would settle for, or the judge himself may suggest a figure. The judge will then ask defendant if he or she will agree to plaintiff's proposal. The judge may express his own opinion as to the equities of the case. He may urge an unreasonable individual to modify his or her position, or he may reassure the plaintiff that if he or she has really suffered a wrongful injury, then some compensation will certainly be obtained. Sometimes the judge warns the parties that litigation will not bring them satisfaction, that their case may have to pass through more than one appellate level. It is in the interests of the litigants and the judge himself to avoid a full-length trial. Therefore, the judge will typically use his influence to promote a settlement if this accords with the interests and desires of the parties as he perceives them. Because of the judge's status and power, the litigants are strongly inclined to accept his efforts at mediation and in many cases a settlement will indeed be achieved.

The Chiangmai court possesses all the trappings of an adversary system of justice, and in certain types of lawsuits that is precisely the pattern that litigation follows. With regard to the litigation of private wrongs, however, the pattern is more typically conciliatory than adversary. When mediation proves to be feasible, the role of the judge becomes dominant and the attorneys play a secondary role. The judge, because of his authority and prestige, is well-equipped to act as a traditional mediator, and the other participants willingly defer to him in this process. The litigants do so because of their respect for the judge and their own ambivalent feelings about being involved in a lawsuit at all. The attorneys defer to the judge because of their subordinate position to him, their desire to remain on good terms with him, and their reluctance to assume responsibility—and possibly blame—for the outcome of the negotiations. The courtroom established for adversary proceedings thus converts itself readily into a forum for mediation, and the strong and active judge is well prepared to play the traditional role of mediator in the modern court of justice.

THE "MISSING *PHUYAI*"

In this section, I shall discuss the general proposition that most lawsuits involving private wrongs in the Chiangmai court share a single characteristic: at some stage in the development of the dispute, a *phuyai* (a "big person") fails to play his expected role as mediator. The "missing *phuyai*," like the dog in the Sherlock Holmes story conspicuous for its failure to bark, is the most important feature of these disputes in their pre-judicial stages. For various reasons, the person who would normally mediate the dispute fails to do so, the disputants are unwilling to abandon their claims, and the conflict transforms itself into a lawsuit. In short, the vacuum created by the missing *phuyai* is filled by the judge, and mediation in its traditional setting is, in most cases, replaced by mediation in the setting of a modern court of law.

This general proposition assumes certain facts about disputes in Thai society. It assumes, for one thing, that mediation is the normal procedure for handling disputes which the participants do not abandon—mediation conducted by a third person with status and authority sufficient to resolve the matter. It assumes, in addition, that the litigation of private wrongs is generally an aberrant pattern, a pathological development in the traditional setting, and that the appearance of such cases in court therefore indicates the breakdown of normal procedures at some earlier point. I feel these assumptions are justified not only by the materials presented up to this point but also by the data contained in case after case pointing to the significant absence or ineffectiveness of an authority figure whom we would normally expect to intervene. The failure of the *phuyai* to resolve the dispute may occur for many reasons: he may be too closely tied to one side or the other to command the respect of both disputants; he may himself be a participant in the dispute and thus unable to act at the same time as mediator; his influence may be nullified by the participation in the dispute of another strong authority figure; the disputants may come from such distinct or distant social groups that no single intermediary is available. Each of the following cases illustrates the missing *phuyai* phenomenon in a slightly different context:

Case One. Plaintiffs brought a civil suit alleging that a wrongful act by defendant caused damage to their property. The plaintiffs were joint owners of a tobacco field bordering to the south on defendant's onion field. An irrigation canal flowed from south to north along the western boundaries of both fields. A sluice gate on plaintiffs' land (gate #1) permitted water to flow from the canal into their field. A second sluice gate (gate #2) connected defendant's field to that of the plaintiffs and channelled part of the water flowing through gate #1 away from plaintiffs' field and into defendant's (see figure 10). Plaintiffs alleged that defendant negligently left open the first gate after watering his own crops and allowed the water from the irrigation canal to flood plaintiffs' field, destroying 3,600 *baht* worth of tobacco plants.

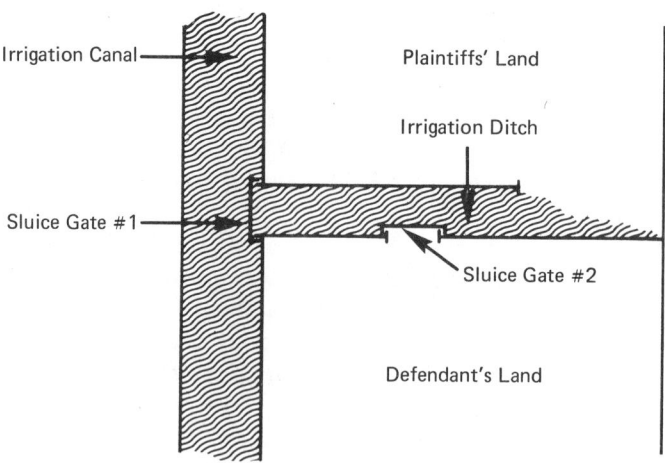

Figure 10. Schematic Map of Irrigation System in Tobacco Field Case

Defendant replied that he closed the gate properly after using it. Both parties were from the same village, but the village headman was unable to resolve the dispute. Plaintiffs brought the complaint to the deputy district officer, who was then the acting district officer. Even at the district level, the two sides were unable to reach an agreement, and the case was brought to the provincial court. Plaintiffs listed as their primary corroborating witness the village chief of their village, while defendant listed the local *kamnan*. The judge mediated the dispute and defendant agreed to pay plaintiffs 1,500 *baht* in three monthly installments.

The failure of prior mediation in this case involved a split between the village chief and the *kamnan*, each of whom apparently supported a different side in the dispute. Had the district officer been there, he might have resolved this split among his subordinates, but his deputy lacked the authority to do so. Three potential mediators were therefore unable to perform their traditional roles, and the provincial judge had to act in their place.

Case Two. Plaintiff, the former village chief, brought a criminal suit for bodily injury against the present village chief and his three underlings. Plaintiff alleged that he was attacked without cause by the four defendants, who kicked him and beat him with brass knuckles, causing serious injuries. Plaintiff notified the *kamnan*, who attempted to mediate the dispute. Three of the defendants offered to pay 800 *baht* in compensation to plaintiff, but the incumbent village chief refused. The *kamnan* took the matter to the police. The result of the police investigation was that all the participants, including the plaintiff but not including the village chief, were prosecuted on a misdemeanor charge in the Chiangmai court. All confessed except plaintiff, whose case was still pending when he brought these charges. When plaintiff brought his private criminal suit, the judge held a preliminary hearing and then tried to mediate the dispute. Finally, the village chief agreed to an unspecified settlement with plaintiff, stating that, after all, it was simply a matter of having drunk too much. He also agreed to pay any fine that might be imposed upon plaintiff in the pending misdemeanor prosecution.

The failure of early mediation in this case appears to have resulted from a political struggle between plaintiff and the incumbent village chief. Six months before the incident, plaintiff had been forced out of office because of accusations of wrongdoing. Bad feelings undoubtedly existed between himself and defendant. The village chief was eliminated as a possible mediator since he was a direct participant in the dispute. The *kamnan* proved an ineffective mediator because he could not persuade the village chief to agree to the settlement which was acceptable to all the other participants. Because both sides boasted individuals of some status and power, a mediator of unusual authority was required. The judge proved to be such a mediator.

Case Three. Plaintiff, a schoolteacher, brought a criminal suit for fraud against the widow of a former colleague. Defendant's husband had died six years before this lawsuit, but she had continued to live in a house provided by the school for its teachers. The school had later assigned this house to plaintiff, but defendant would not vacate. The two parties finally signed a contract according to which plaintiff would pay 3,000 *baht* for improvements made by defendant, and defendant would leave the house within two and one-half months. Plaintiff paid 1,500 *baht* at the time the contract was signed and was to pay the remaining 1,500 *baht* within three days after taking possession of the house. Defendant, however, did not move out of the house on the date agreed, despite being reminded by plaintiff and by an official in charge of school property. She claimed that she had been unable to find a new house. She also refused to refund plaintiff's first payment of 1,500 *baht*, because she claimed to have spent it all. After negotiations with defendant failed, plaintiff filed this action in the Chiangmai court. A *prima facie* case was found, and then a series of postponements ensued. Nine months after the suit was filed, an unspecified agreement was reached and plaintiff withdrew his prosecution.

In this case, the "missing *phuyai*" was the headmaster of the school. Normally a powerful figure with regard to all matters concerning the school, its property, and its teachers, the headmaster was, for some reason, uninvolved with this dispute. Although his absence may have occurred for a number of reasons, we may guess that an important factor was the defendant herself. Being the widow of a former teacher in the school, she was a figure who inspired sympathy. She had no real right to remain in the school's house for six years after her husband's death, but the headmaster may have avoided evicting her because he felt *krengčhai* towards her (see page 64, above). When the headmaster failed to act, plaintiff was required to search for a *phuyai* who would recognize his valid legal claim to the house. The Chiangmai court provided him with the forum he needed.

Case Four. Plaintiff, a 32-year-old farmer, brought a criminal suit for the destruction of his beans and garlic crop by defendant's water buffalo and cattle. With this criminal suit, he joined a civil suit for 1,696 *baht* in damages. Defendant was a 62-year-old farmer, quite elderly by village standards, and no longer active. The animals had been in the care of his son, who denied that any of them had wandered into plaintiff's fields. They had all been securely tied. When plaintiff discovered the damage, he went to inform the *kamnan* who lived in his village. The *kamnan* ordered his assistant to inspect the damage. The assistant inspected the field, spoke with both parties, and drafted a brief memorandum listing the damages and attributing them to the animals owned by defendant. The memorandum was allegedly read aloud to defendant, who was illiterate. Plaintiff signed the memorandum, and defendant recorded his thumbprint. The disputants were then taken to the *kamnan* himself, where mediation was attempted. Defendant at that point refused to pay anything for the damages, and the *kamnan* took both parties to the police station. Once again defendant refused to pay compensation. Plaintiff was obliged to bring his case to court. The court found that a *prima facie* case existed, and defendant was required to post a bond of 34,000 *baht*. In the meantime, defendant had filed a countersuit for false prosecution, which is also a criminal offense, and the court found that a *prima facie* case had been established in that case as well. Plaintiff was required to post bond in the amount of 25,000 *baht*. Before further proceedings could take place, the disputants reached a settlement out of court and both withdrew their lawsuits. Unfortunately, the details of the settlement are not included in the case records.

There are two missing *phuyai* in this case: the *kamnan* and the police inquiry officer. Their failure to mediate this dispute can be explained in at least two ways, one favorable to plaintiff and the other to defendant. The first explanation is that defendant was simply a stubborn old man. Because of his age, he was unimpressed with the status and power of the *kamnan* and was unintimidated by the police. Because he did not recognize the power of the customary mediators, he could not be induced to settle until confronted with the authority of the Chiangmai court. The second explanation is that defendant was the victim of a conspiracy. He was tricked into recording his thumbprint on a document without knowing its real contents and was thus made liable for damages which he himself could not possibly have caused. The *kamnan*, working together with the plaintiff, tried to make defendant accept responsibility for these damages. When the defendant rightly refused to do so, the *kamnan* brought a false accusation to the police. Again, defendant refused to negotiate. Only when the matter reached the Chiangmai court was defendant forced to pay compensation to plaintiff (or, as an alternative hypothesis, only when the matter reached the court was defendant able to convince the judge that he had been tricked). In any case, whatever the true facts behind this lawsuit, its most significant feature for our purposes is the failure of the two *phuyai* to promote a settlement in the early stages of the dispute, and the necessity of bringing the dispute to court before such a settlement could be achieved.

These case studies illustrate the phenomenon of the missing *phuyai* in four different settings. In each case, the mediator who might have intervened to resolve the dispute was unable to do so. I do not wish to suggest, however, that whenever a mediator is himself involved in a dispute, then mediation will be impossible. On the contrary, the involvement of the mediator will often facilitate a settlement. One village chief told me that his daughter had been seriously injured when a truck backed up and struck her while in the market place. The driver had behaved well. He did not run away, but stayed to help the girl and took her to the hospital. The village chief notified the police of the accident, but this precaution proved unnecessary. The owner of the truck came promptly to discuss the matter and offered to pay all hospital costs and an additional "payment for the *khwan*" of 5,000 *baht* (approximately $250).

Hospital costs, which included expenses for a major operation in which the girl nearly died, came to another 5,000 *baht*. In addition, the village chief told me, the truck owner had to pay the police in order to have them drop charges against his driver. He did not know how large a payment was required for this purpose. The fact that the girl's father was the village chief, a figure of some authority and credibility, undoubtedly influenced the owner of the truck to reach a proper settlement rather than become involved in a dispute that might lead to litigation. If the case had ever reached court, the village chief would have made a very persuasive plaintiff, and the truck owner would certainly have paid far more than he did in fact.

It is not always possible to discern why the *phuyai* is absent from the disputes that reach the court. In the case involving the schoolteacher, for example, we can only guess that compassion and the feeling of *krengčhai* towards the widow somehow dissuaded the headmaster from playing his expected role as mediator. Nevertheless, we normally find two distinct situations in which the "missing *phuyai*" problem occurs. In the first situation, the mediator exists but is, for various reasons, prevented from playing his expected part in the dispute. In the second situation, no mediator exists at all because the disputants have no common social links, no channels of communication through which negotiations can be conducted. This second situation is perhaps the more vivid illustration of the missing *phuyai* phenomenon. The type of negotiation depicted earlier in figures 4 and 5 (page 77, above) cannot take place because there is no common authoritative figure, no crossover point between the two patron-client hierarchies. The second situation, the total absence of any effective mediator, can result from a number of factors that work to create "gaps" between the two disputants: significant age or status differences, differences involving political power, language barriers, and others. Two such factors—geographical distance and ethnicity—proved easier to isolate than the others, and I would like to discuss each of them in turn.

It is possible to suggest quantitatively the impact of geographical distance upon the disputes that actually reach the Chiangmai court in the form of lawsuits for private wrongs. By "geographical distance" I do not mean necessarily the number of kilometers that separate the homes of the disputants, but rather the size of the smallest common administrative unit in which both disputants live. The smaller the common unit, the more readily the two would have access to a mutually acknowledged authority figure, and the closer the "distance" between them. We must assume, in this regard, that frequency of litigation should be measured in terms of the number of "interactions" that occur within the society. All other things being equal, we would expect a greater number of lawsuits where interaction is most frequent, and a lesser number where interaction is rare. Since the residents of a given village interact far more frequently with each other than with residents of other villages, *tambon*, districts, or provinces—perhaps by a factor of hundreds or thousands—we would expect to find far more lawsuits among disputants who live in the same village than among disputants from different villages, far more lawsuits among disputants from the same *tambon* than those from different *tambon*, and so on. In short, if other factors were not at work, common sense would lead us to expect an inverse relationship between geographical distance, in the sense in which I have defined it, and frequency of litigation.

In fact, however, geographical distance does not appear to be inversely related to frequency of litigation. Indeed, the opposite appears to be the case. At distances where interaction may be presumed most frequent, the rates of litigation are the same as—or even lower than--the rates of litigation at distances where interaction is relatively rare. In table 6, I have analyzed a sample of 123 lawsuits involving private wrongs. These lawsuits were selected from the court logs of 1965 to 1974 to approximate the proportions in which the various causes of action, both civil and criminal, appeared in the Chiangmai court during that ten-year period.[2] The results suggest that litigation occurs less frequently between residents of the same village and *tambon* than between residents of the same district or province but different villages and *tambon*. If we consider the figures in relation to the number of interactions that must take place between neighbors as opposed to distant strangers, then we can conclude that lawsuits are far more likely to occur among the latter group than the former. The likelihood that interaction will result in litigation increases greatly with the distance between the disputants (table 6).

TABLE 6
Frequency of Litigation and Geographical Relationship of Litigants in Lawsuits Involving Private Wrongs

Geographical Relationship of Litigants	No. of Lawsuits ($N = 123$)
Same village	24
Different villages—same *tambon*	16
Different *tambon*—same district	38
Different districts	39
Unknown	6

---

2. The sample for table 6 was drawn from the 222 cases whose files I originally had selected from the court registers to read in their entirety. Since these 222 cases do not in themselves constitute a scientific sample, the findings in table 6 should be interpreted accordingly. The cases were, however, selected from the court registers of 1965-74 primarily on the basis of their subject matter, without regard to any factor that would bear directly upon the geographical relationship of the litigants. For purposes of the analysis in table 6, 53 of the original 222 cases were eliminated, because they did not involve the litigation of private wrongs. Of the 169 cases that remained, 46 more were eliminated by the drawing of lots in order to make the various categories of lawsuits in the sample roughly proportional to the frequency with which they appeared in the court registers (see table 4, page 48). As a result, the ratio of criminal cases (78) to civil cases

At least two factors are probably at work in producing these surprising figures. First, it is possible that interaction among strangers is more often characterized by conflict than is interaction among neighbors. The likelihood of litigation is therefore greater among strangers partly because the ratio of conflict to interaction is higher. It is probably true that Thai people feel less *krengčhai*, less hesitant to press claims against strangers than they feel with regard to members of their own community. A sense of familiarity, of community solidarity, may deter conflict and litigation with neighbors. Also, there may exist a justifiable fear that the nearby adversary or his group could retaliate more effectively than could a distant adversary. Second, and perhaps more important, is the fact that the administrative units listed in table 6—village, *tambon*, and district—each provide their own mediators. The most effective are those who are part of the local community: the village chief and the *kamnan* of the *tambon*. The greater the distance, the less likely the adversaries are to have an effective "middle-man" (*khon klang*) to assist in resolving the dispute. Conflicts that arise between persons living far apart, according to this hypothesis, are much more likely to end up in court because of the absence of effective mediation. As the frequency of interaction and conflict among strangers increases in Thailand, with technological improvements in roads, in vehicles, and in communication media such as newspapers, radio, and television, then we may expect a proportionate increase in the number of private wrongs litigated in the Chiangmai court.

Ethnicity is a second factor that, like geographical distance, can produce unbridgeable gaps between disputants. When disputants belong to different ethnic groups, there is often no common *phuyai* for them to consult, even if they live in the same village or *tambon*. More specifically, we find a great many cases in the Chiangmai court brought by "ethnic outsiders" against ethnic Thais.[3] These ethnic outsiders typically lack the leverage necessary to persuade their adversaries to negotiate and come to terms. Moreover, in many cases they are unfettered by the cultural inhibitions concerning litigation that

---

(45) in the sample is comparable to the ratio indicated in table 4 (586 criminal cases to 357 civil cases involving private wrongs). Also, the numbers of cases listed under each cause of action are roughly comparable to the proportions indicated in table 4, with the exception of check cases, which are slightly underrepresented in the sample. The sample for table 6 is made up of the following types of cases: violations involving checks (22), offenses relating to justice (12), cheating and fraud (7), defamation (4), misappropriation (4), homicide (4), trespass (4), bodily harm (3), theft (2), malfeasance in public office (2), other private criminal suits (14), civil wrongful acts (35), divorce and related marital matters (10).

3. Properly, "ethnic Tais." See chapter 2, note 1. The great number of cases brought by ethnic outsiders against ethnic Thais is apparent from the surnames of litigants in the court registers and from data contained in the case files. It is impossible to provide precise figures, however, since some surnames are ambiguous with regard to ethnicity and since many ethnic outsiders have adopted Thai surnames. Some even assert in court that they are ethnic Thais despite clear evidence to the contrary elsewhere in the court records.

deter so many ethnic Thai people from going to court. The result is perhaps the ultimate irony of the centralized Thai judiciary: the Chiangmai court, symbol of the advent of Thai political power, is shunned by many ethnic Thai people but is used skillfully and effectively by other ethnic groups to sue the non-litigious Thais for private wrongs, to invoke rights articulated in the Thai legal codes, and to force their adversaries to negotiate a settlement that could have been avoided under the traditional system of justice.[4]

A majority of the criminal suits for bad checks are brought by persons identifiable ethnically as Indians or Pakistanis. Indeed, one man alone, residing in Chiangmai but holding Indian citizenship, accounted for more than 160 such lawsuits from 1965 to 1974. Litigation has been far more readily accepted in Indian culture than in Thai culture. This particular individual followed the practices of his own society in the Thai setting and brought criminal prosecutions for bad checks just as often as was necessary to collect debts. When his loans fell due, he simply filed in court the check that his debtor had deposited with him and presented the debtor with the alternatives of payment or imprisonment. This form of behavior was considered odious by most Thai people, not only because of its brutality but because an illegal amount of interest was often concealed in such transactions by overstating the "principle" in the loan agreement. I do not wish, however, to portray such lawsuits entirely in negative terms. Indian merchants in Thailand face their own difficulties, both financial and cultural. Those who lend money are often people without substantial economic or political resources, lacking any effective means to collect their debts except through legal channels. Since litigation for them carries little of the stigma that it does for ethnic Thais, it is natural that they should turn to the courts for the enforcement of their legal rights.

Besides the check cases, I encountered a number of other suits for private wrongs brought by ethnic outsiders against ethnic Thais. Not all plaintiffs in such cases came from litigious cultures, but all of them appeared to lack access to an effective mediator in the Thai community who could intercede on their behalf. In one case, for example, a Vietnamese sausage-maker brought a civil suit against a Thai merchant for a motorcycle accident in which plaintiff lost two toes. The circumstances of the case seemed to state a clear obligation to pay compensation, especially since defendant had been found guilty of careless driving in a criminal prosecution arising from the same accident. Nevertheless, plaintiff was unable to persuade defendant to make payment to him until he brought his case to court. Once the case came to

---

4. This is not to imply that in its other "modes of justice" the court does not function with precisely the opposite effect. For example, the court acts as an effective agent of Thai political power against ethnic outsiders when it convicts hill tribesmen of criminal violations under statutes protecting the forests from slash and burn agricultural practices, or when it enforces the government's licensing and certification requirements against non-Thai merchants.

court, the negotiations were fast and effective. Within one month, defendant agreed to settle the case for 2,000 *baht*.

In another case, a private criminal prosecution for malfeasance by a public official, the plaintiff was a Burmese trader whose goods had allegedly been confiscated by the Thai border police. The defendants were accused of seizing plaintiff's eight jade stones, a tiger skin, and a collection of tiger bones, altogether worth nearly 120,000 *baht* (approximately $6,000). They had demanded the payment of 5,000 *baht* in tariffs, but when plaintiff presented this sum to them, they had returned only three of the jade stones and nothing else. Plaintiff was a foreigner, not even a resident of Thailand, and presumably lacked connections that would enable him to negotiate with the defendants for the return of his goods. His only hope was to bring a private criminal action that would force the defendants to come to terms. Formal allegations of malfeasance are taken seriously by government officials whose careers can thereby be placed in jeopardy. Within one month after filing this lawsuit, plaintiff announced to the court that an understanding had been reached and that he wished to withdraw his suit.

We have seen that the Chiangmai court can effectively fill the role of the missing *phuyai* when ethnic outsiders sue ethnic Thais because they lack other channels for negotiation. I would like to conclude this section with a further extension of the same principle: an unusual suit between two fringe groups in Thai society mediated by the judges of the centralized Thai judicial system. In 1967, a lawsuit for murder was brought by the mother of a Karen hill tribesman against a Meo tribesman living nearby. It was extremely rare to find a lawsuit in which a hill person appeared as plaintiff, for the "tribes" are separated from the life of the towns and valleys by geography, culture, and language. I read the case with special interest and was later fortunate to find a brief discussion of its background in a master's thesis entitled "Blue Meo Religion" by Nusit Chindarsi, a Thai student of hill tribe culture. *Ajaan* Nusit writes that the Meo people in the vicinity of the dispute were suffering from a shortage of land. The populations of the Chiangmai hill tribes were rapidly increasing, and insufficient mountain lands were available for the slash and burn agriculture which most of them practiced. Competition and hostility among the tribes was on the rise. This particular group of Meos had already begun to splinter because of the land shortage, some of them moving to other provinces in search of new cultivation areas. Others who remained were forced to work lands that had already been claimed by the neighboring Karen tribes. The Karen were fearful of the Meo because of their skill in using modern guns, and they resented the intrusion of the Meo upon Karen lands:

> In 1967, as I have said, there was no forest left for the Miao [alternative spelling of Meo] to clear for new fields, but some of them cleared the secondary-growth fields which belonged to the Karen. The Karen became very angry with the Miao, because they were afraid of

The "Missing *Phuyai*" 147

them taking more land again and they wanted the Miao to move away, so they tried to force them away by stealing crops in the field and sometimes letting their animals in to eat the crops. (1970:17)

This, then, was the setting in which the killing took place. In April 1967, a 22-year-old Karen man was found shot to death in the forest about 100 yards from one of the Meo fields. The Meo owner of the field was arrested by the police, but the public prosecutor ordered that no prosecution be brought in connection with the shooting. The Karen were dissatisfied with this result. As *Ajaan* Nusit describes it, the incident served to mobilize the Karen community against the Meo encroachers. Not only did they believe that the Meo man should be punished for the killing, but they felt that a victory in this matter would drive the Meo away and solve all their difficulties concerning claims to the land:

> The Karen headman collected the money from every Karen household to fight the Miao in court. The Karen believed that if they won the case then the Miao would be afraid of them, and would move their village away from [the area]. The Karen would then have enough land for their people and nobody would bother their land any more. (17)

As it turned out, the lawsuit was resolved not by any clear-cut adjudication of the facts but by the more familiar process of mediating the conflicting claims. Defendant was arrested and held without bail after he failed to appear for a scheduled hearing. His absence was later attributed to the breakdown of a bus and to the great distances between his home and the court, but the judge rejected his excuse and held him in prison for the latter part of the proceedings. Plaintiff produced an eyewitness to a quarrel that had allegedly taken place between defendant and the deceased shortly before the killing. The witness claimed, through an interpreter, that the two had argued in northern Thai dialect (which he could not understand), that he had observed them through some bushes without being seen, that he had walked away and then heard a gunshot fired in the area where they had been quarreling. At the time he did not imagine that the gunshot had any connection with the argument he had just observed. Only later did he realize that defendant must have shot the deceased with the rifle he had been holding.

The proceedings ended anti-climactically eight months after they had been initiated. At that time, plaintiff filed a motion asking to withdraw the lawsuit, stating that defendant had agreed to pay "damages" and "funeral costs" (only a figure of speech here, since the body had long before been cremated at the spot where it was discovered). The Karen had not achieved the dramatic victory they had envisioned. Perhaps they had been worn down by the distances involved, the inconvenience and expense of waging a lawsuit in the provincial court far from their home in the mountains. Perhaps, too, they had come to realize that their case was not a strong one, that the defendant was ably represented by one of Chiangmai's leading attorneys and had the support of certain prestigious figures at Chiangmai University whom he had assisted in their research on the hill tribes. A solution to the underlying conflict over land was not achieved in the Chiangmai court, but the murder case itself was effectively mediated and resolved. The lawsuit thus provides a striking illustration of the "missing *phuyai*" principle, in which a court of the national Thai judicial system opened a channel for negotiations between two distant ethnic groups locked in conflict on the farthest fringes of Thai society.[5]

Although I have concentrated in this chapter upon the court as mediator, I do not wish to leave the impression that judges never adjudicate lawsuits concerning private wrongs. In a small percentage of the cases, the disputants do fail to reach compromise agreements during the course of the litigation, and the final disposition is left to the court. When this occurs, the judges render verdicts in written form, explaining their findings of fact and of law. While decisions sometimes turn upon interpretations of legal issues (see, for example, the case of *Nangsao* Lai and *Nai* Mun, page 127), more typically the court will search through the witness testimony for contradictions in fact which are taken as evidence of non-credibility. A finding for plaintiff or defendant will frequently be justified with reference to such factual discrepancies rather than with reference to the broader legal or equitable issues presented. One feels, in many instances, that rendering such decisions and reducing them to written form is not a comfortable process for the judge any more than it is for the litigants. The necessity of converting a living dispute into abstract legal norms, of reducing all the complexities into simple findings of right and wrong, of depersonalizing the conflict and deciding it without reference to the status or character of the litigants—these requirements often weigh heavily on all the participants in the process of adjudication. The search for factual contradictions in the record is therefore a convenient way to rationalize decisions that were reached on broader grounds, a short-hand expression for a complex process of evaluation that may have incorporated both traditional and modern legal considerations.

---

5. This conflict between the two hill tribes vividly illustrates the discussion by Sally F. Moore (1972:76-79) of social conflict seen both in macrocosm and in microcosm. Moore suggests that we look not merely at the legal wrong itself but at the corporate groups to which the disputants belong, asking "when and under what circumstances do they mobilize as units against each other? What kinds of events may be used (*or not*) as the occasion for confrontations? How are confrontations rationalized?" The group decision to mobilize over a specific legal wrong depends in part on timing: "Many considerations are involved in the question of timing, of when and where and against whom to turn a quiescent competitive position into active hostile competition. The most fundamental of these presumably have to do with the degree of underlying pressure on power and resources, and the degree of encroachment of one's competitors and the opportunities for bettering one's own position." When the time is ripe, as it was in the case of the two competing hill tribes, then "certain legal disputes can be used to rationalize active structural conflict and bring it to a head at a particular moment."

One is reminded in this context of observations by J. D. M. Derrett on the royal administration of justice in India before the Muhammadan conquests:

> ... the value of a judicial decision would be appraised less from its approximation to abstract justice than from its aptness to please (or displease) both parties, to compromise their conflicting claims, and to prevent their reopening the matter upon some pretext later.... The mental image of two angry litigants, whose rights are unclear, being forced to come to an agreement or compromise by a king hammering them like a smith hammering red-hot iron is certainly forceful. When the irons cool they cannot again be separated provided they have been hit hard enough. What was wanted was not only a compromise, but one that stayed binding upon those who were brought to agree to it. (1968:219)[6]

A consideration of justice in Thailand, a different country in a different historical epoch, suggests that the litigation of private wrongs still tends toward the kind of resolution that Derrett describes. What is sought on all sides is less an "approximation to abstract justice"—as denoted by the legal codes—than a forceful hammering together of the heated disputants. The metaphor of heat is particularly apt in Thailand, where the complainant is "boiling hot" and unable to maintain his "cool heart." When the dispute cannot be resolved at some earlier stage, it will be brought before the judge— the "smith" whose power extends by law over all persons and all ethnic communities within his territorial jurisdiction. If no other individual had the capacity to hammer out a lasting compromise, the judge of the provincial court usually will. Whether his influence is applied directly or indirectly to the disputants, it will nearly always prove sufficient to induce them to come to terms, to negotiate and settle their quarrel rather than risk the unpleasant alternatives that now face them. By this blending of modern legal power and traditional attitudes toward conflict, the provincial court acts as the mediator of last resort and bridges the gaps of age, distance, ethnicity, and status that can prevent the resolution of disputes in traditional Thai society.

---

6. The image of king as smith is suggested in this passage by a quote from Bṛhaspati, III, 46, which I have deleted.

Part Four
Areas of Conflict: New Laws in the Traditional Society

Every right is thus a source of power of which even a hitherto entirely powerless person may become possessed. In this way he becomes the source of completely novel situations within the community.

Max Weber
The Sociology of Law[1]

---

1. Weber (1968:667).

In the preceding chapters, I have emphasized the traditional procedures for handling disputes and their impact upon the formal system of litigation established in Thailand at the beginning of the twentieth century. We have seen that a general preference for mediation exists among most active disputants. When the disputants are separated by certain unbridgeable gaps—such as geographical distance or differences in age, status, and ethnicity—then the Chiangmai court may be called upon to bridge the gaps and act as a mediator of last resort. Until now we have focused upon the characteristics and relationships of the disputants rather than the subject matter of their dispute, and upon the persistence of tradition in the legal system rather than the changes that have accompanied the new rules of law.

The quotation from Weber's *Sociology of Law* that begins this final section suggests a different set of concerns. In the next three chapters, we shall examine disputes in which the assertion of new legal rights tends to impede the traditional system of mediation, just as the existence of various "gaps" between the disputants was seen to obstruct mediation in the preceding chapters. In the cases that follow, the disputants are separated, not merely by differences related to their personal attributes, but by discrepancies between the traditional and the modern legal norms upon which they rely. I shall try to demonstrate a relationship between the transformation of Thai law and the growth of certain "novel situations within the community" and to show how the resort to litigation can reveal—and in some instances can cause—significant changes in Thai society. As new rights are asserted in the traditional setting, local mediators find themselves unable to handle the subject matter of the dispute, and the participants are forced to go to the provincial court for an interpretation of the law and a resolution of their differences. The court, through mediation and through adjudication, dispenses bits of power to one side or the other and, as a result, helps to reshape relationships within the community where the disputes arose.

While retaining our focus upon the litigation of private wrongs, we shall, in the final three chapters, examine three areas of law in which new rights are commonly asserted in the Chiangmai court against old claims and privileges: conflicts concerning claims to the land, conflicts over the relative rights and status of women and men, and conflicts between government officials and ordinary citizens.

Chapter Ten
Rights in Land

REGISTRATION AND RENTAL OF REAL PROPERTY

By tradition and by law, the ownership of land in Thailand was long defined in terms of occupation and productive use.[2] During the reign of King Chulalongkorn and afterwards, modern Thai law introduced a competing consideration in the determination of ownership, namely, registration and the certification of rights in land by provincial and district-level officials. Attempts were made to conform the modern laws to traditional practices in certain respects, but inevitably discrepancies arose.

In the first section of this chapter, I shall describe two kinds of conflict over land, both of which place modern law in opposition to traditional concepts of ownership. The first kind of conflict involves rival claims by purported owners of land. Such disputes are now controlled primarily by the Thai Land Code of 1954 (and the related regulations issued by the Ministry of Interior) and by Book IV ("Property") of the Thai Civil and Commercial

---

2. The traditional concept of land ownership established through occupation and productive use is illustrated by the following passage from an early Chiangmai palm-leaf legal text. The date of the manuscript is unknown, although it appeared to the compiler to be "very old." The text itself purports to restate the traditional law passed on by King Mangrai in the thirteenth century:

> If a peasant has claimed riceland, has cleared the fields and built homes and orchards on the land, after he has used the land for three years it is right to collect taxes from him.
> If one man has worked on the land until it is a decent piece of land and there is another man who comes to snatch it away by offering a price for it, this is not proper, so do not remove the man. No matter how much he seeks to impress you with his wealth or status, you should not be persuaded because of those things. If you give in, then the peasant will truly be discouraged from creating and producing in the future.

(Mangrai Custom Law; Transliteration Series 1 [*Mangraisat; phak pariwat lamdap thi 1*], 1975:3-4). I am grateful to *Ajaan* Mani B. Reynolds for helping to translate these two provisions from the old northern Thai dialect.

Code. The second kind of conflict involves competing claims by landlords and tenants in disputes regulated by the Thai law of contracts and by statutory enactments dealing with the rental of the land. Both of these topics, it should be noted, concern the impact of modern law upon traditional concepts of land ownership: how ownership is established, how it is retained or transferred, and how its powers can be limited by the voluntary creation of leasehold interests. The first of these topics, together with the historical background of land registration in Thailand, can be introduced by a case study involving an attempt to manipulate the new land registration requirements in order to acquire real property by fraud.

Nai Wong, a widower living in Sanpatong District, died in 1943. In accordance with traditional practices, his farmland was divided more or less equally among his five surviving children: *Nai* Im, *Nai* Am, *Nang* Pik, *Nai* Bai, and *Nai* Nuan. When *Nang* Pik died in 1953, her portion was divided among her three children, *Nai* Khao, *Nai* Kham, and *Nai* Som. After her death, the five plots of land were distributed among seven of *Nai* Wong's descendants (figure 11).

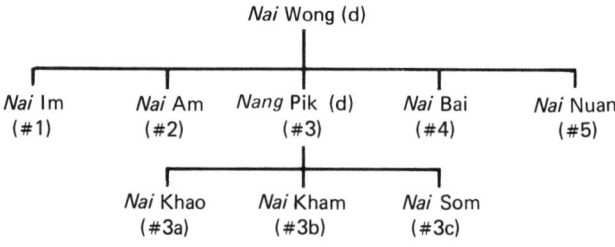

Figure 11. Distribution of *Nai* Wong's Land Among His Descendants

In 1954 the modern Thai Land Code was enacted, and all persons who occupied and used land without legal certification were required to register their holdings within 180 days from the date of promulgation (November 6, 1954). Learning of this new regulation, *Nai* Im offered to register the land of *Nai* Khao, *Nai* Kham, *Nai* Som, and *Nai* Bai at the same time that he registered his own. They all accepted his offer, and *Nai* Im went alone to the district office where he obtained the new documents. None of the recipients of *Nai* Im's generosity ever saw the certificates that he received. When they asked about the matter, he replied that he had lost them.

In 1955, *Nai* Am sold his holding to *Nai* Im who then sold it to a third person (X). Later, *Nai* Im purchased the holdings of *Nai* Kham and *Nai* Som. In 1959 he sold these holdings to *Nai* Bai for 2,000 *baht*. *Nai* Bai also bought *Nai* Khao's land, for 1,500 *baht*, and thereby acquired all of *Nang* Pik's original share of the estate. The distribution of the land after these transactions is illustrated in figure 12.

These plots of land were held and farmed without incident for many years. Once, in 1962, *Nai* Bai asked *Nai* Im to procure certification of his holdings for him from the district offices, but *Nai* Bai did not follow up the matter

Nai Im (defendant):	#1
Nai Bai (plaintiff):	#3a, 3b, 3c, 4
Nai Nuan:	#5
X:	#2

Figure 12. Distribution of *Nai* Wong's Land at Time of Dispute

and everything remained as before. Suddenly, in May 1973, *Nai* Im had a tractor plow all the land held by *Nai* Bai and planted soybeans in the fields. *Nai* Bai protested and brought the matter to the village chief, but *Nai* Im replied that he was now the owner of all the land, that he had long before registered his own name at the district office, and that *Nai* Bai was welcome to bring the matter to court if he wished. *Nai* Im refused to listen to the counsel of the village chief, apparently because he felt that he, as holder of the proper documentation, had an indisputable legal claim to the land. In June 1973, *Nai* Bai brought a civil suit in the Chiangmai court for 2,475 *baht* in damages resulting from *Nai* Im's interference with the cultivation of rice on the disputed land.

Nai Im did not fare as well in court as he had anticipated, but the reason appears to have been the intervention of his wife rather than the action of the law. *Nai* Im never accepted the summons served by the court, and he never hired a lawyer to defend himself. Instead, he granted legal authority to his wife to settle the case on his behalf, and within a month she negotiated a compromise agreement with *Nai* Bai and his lawyer. According to this agreement, defendant paid plaintiff in advance the sum of 2,500 *baht,* promised not to interfere further in the land, agreed to transfer the land immediately to plaintiff, and promised to give plaintiff the entire crop of soybeans that defendant had planted in the disputed fields. *Nai* Im's total capitulation, we may guess, could well have resulted from his wife's shame at her husband's deceptive dealings with his own brother. Her sense of honor may have short-circuited *Nai* Im's ambitious plans, producing an informal resolution of a dispute in which legal forms were pitted squarely against traditional claims to the land and in which the failure of local mediators to reconcile the disputants had led to formal litigation.[3]

Conflicting claims to the land, and to the water that irrigates the land, have always presented difficult problems in Thai society.[4] King Chulalongkorn

---

3. The facts of this case are based upon plaintiff's uncontested evidence. I have here departed from my normal practice of rejecting such one-sided material, unless there is a stipulation of the facts by the opposing party, because defendant's total capitulation in this case made plaintiff's story appear unusually credible.

4. See, for example, the discussion of early northern Thai irrigation laws in Kraisri Nimmanahaeminda (1965a).

tried to resolve some of these problems by issuing new forms of documentation to persons who, for the most part, had justified their claims of ownership with reference to the traditional concepts of occupancy and beneficial use. On the one hand, new forms were made available to occupants of unsurveyed land who wished to reserve a formal claim of ownership on the basis of their beneficial use (*chanot tra čhǫng*). On the other hand, a cadastral survey of certain portions of the country was undertaken, which led to the issuance of full title deeds (*chanot thi din*) to the rightful owners of the land surveyed (Hooker, 1975:377 and 383-84; Michai Rüchuphan, 1970:4). The concept of absolute ownership implicit in these two documents, however, gave rise to new problems when traditional claims to the land were asserted by occupants who, for one reason or another, had failed to obtain either the reserve license or the title deed. Some adjustments were made in 1936 when an amendment to the earlier legislation of King Chulalongkorn created a procedure by which new occupants of unclaimed land could register their interests and obtain documents of ownership (*tra čhǫng*).

The Land Code of 1954 attempted even greater flexibility by formally certifying claims to the land short of the actual title deed or other document indicating uncontestable ownership. Among the forms used under the Land Code to certify legal interests in land, the most common are the "form for reporting land occupation," known by its Thai abbreviation as *sǫ khǫ* 1, and the "certificate of beneficial use," abbreviated as *nǫ sǫ* 3. The *sǫ khǫ* 1 form consists only of a brief verbal description of the boundaries of the land by the applicant, a rough map, and the signatures of the claimant, the village chief or *kamnan*, and two witnesses. It is issued by the district offices without any formal inspection of the land and is therefore questionable with regard to the precise boundaries and the existence of other claimants to the same property. Its formal function is not to vest the holder with a claim of ownership, nor with the right to dispose of the land (except by will), but rather to establish his prior claim of occupancy and to give him a chance to pay taxes upon the land and to put the land to productive use. If after three years he has not done so, then his interest in the land is extinguished.

The *nǫ sǫ* 3 form, unlike the *sǫ khǫ* 1, is granted by the district offices only upon an official "investigation" of the site by an agent of the district offices. The *nǫ sǫ* 3 document certifies that the holder has occupied the land and has put it to productive use "appropriate to the condition of the land in that locality and to the business of the claimant" (Michai Rüchuphan, 1970:26). The holder thereby acquires the right to transfer the land or to retain it indefinitely and perhaps ultimately to apply for the title deed, which will give him an absolute claim to the land. For the *nǫ sǫ* 3 form, unlike the title deed, however, no formal survey is conducted nor is the complete history of ownership necessarily determined, so there is still ample opportunity for conflicting claims to arise. Many farmers, moreover, do not take the trouble to certify their claims in any way, partly because they do not like to deal with the bureaucracy and partly to avoid taxation. The village chief may act in the interests of his villagers in these matters, manipulating evidence regarding the size and nature of their holdings to their best advantage (Moerman, 1969a:541). The system, in short, is far from precise, is not clearly understood by many farmers, and, even when it is understood, is often adjusted to reflect the customs of the community rather than the interests of the government.[5]

The requirement of registration, intended to bring greater certainty to the occupancy and use of land, has had the effect in many cases of removing the question of ownership from the traditional setting and introducing the central government into the process of resolving local land disputes. As we saw in the dispute between *Nai* Im and *Nai* Bai, local mediators may be unable to promote settlements when rival claims to the land are asserted. While they can occasionally manipulate the forms that underlie such claims, their authority in land questions is negligible in comparison to the authority of the central government, which can be invoked by the person who holds the proper certification. Moreover, the conflicting claims are now resolved according to the relatively clearcut rules of the Land Code, for which the government bureaucrats are the spokesmen, rather than the more flexible customary rules involving the actual acquisition, occupation and use of the land, which the local mediators would follow. As I have mentioned earlier, two village leaders told me flatly that disputes concerning land were beyond their jurisdiction and could be resolved only by the government land officials. While these individuals probably exaggerated the extent to which they had been disabled as mediators in land disputes, their statements indicate an awareness that the subject matter has been taken over largely by the government.

Land changes hands rather freely in rural Thailand, as we saw in the case study that began this chapter. It is treated, as Wijeyewardene has phrased it, "as a commodity, not as a traditional heritage nor as a symbol of membership and status in a local community" (1967:75). When the head of a family dies, the land is usually divided more or less equally among his or her children. The fractional shares may then be reconsolidated by gift or sale among the siblings or else sold to outsiders. The common use of land as security for indebtedness also accounts for many of the transfers that take place. One piece of land may therefore have a number of different owners in a relatively short period of time. When registration requirements of the central government are not observed promptly or precisely, then the discrepancy between formal law and customary practice becomes significant. Fraud and deceit may be used to

---

5. This discussion of land registration is based primarily upon Michai Rüchuphan (1970); The Thai Land Code of 1954 and related regulations and edicts; Yano (1968); Hooker (1975).

obtain the official document—the symbol of legitimacy—despite the fact that the person who gains the document may have no claim to the land recognizable under customary practices. The struggle for the document can thus give rise to behavior that falls within our classification of "private wrongs." Disputes of this kind prove particularly resistant to mediation at the local level and appear frequently in the Chiangmai court in the form of suits for fraud, trespass, theft, destruction of property, and wrongful acts.

In one particularly complex and unpleasant land dispute, an elderly, illiterate woman and her feebleminded brother were forced to sue her own son and other close relatives. Plaintiffs, the victims of a scheme to obtain their land by fraud, had unwittingly transferred their $n\varrho$ $s\varrho$ 3 certificate to defendants, thinking that they were merely guaranteeing a loan. Having obtained plaintiffs' thumbprints on the necessary documents, one document at a time over a period of six years, defendants finally revealed to plaintiffs that the land had officially changed hands. They warned plaintiffs not to harvest their own crop of rice, which by then had ripened in the fields. This bitter intra-family dispute gave rise to several lawsuits for fraud, trespass, falsification of documents, and false information to an official. Most of the claims were decided favorably to defendants on proper legal grounds (statute of limitations, plaintiffs' admitted awareness that certain forms could in fact be used to transfer title to the land even though they had not imagined that the land would actually leave their possession). The case represented a triumph of legal forms over traditional equities, as official documents were executed and manipulated to alter rights and obligations in a drastic manner, suddenly vesting one group with a power of ownership that had never been contemplated by their unsophisticated adversaries.

Suits for private wrongs may involve the competing claims of landlords and tenants, as well as purported owners of the land, and such disputes form a second general topic for discussion in this section. In the Chiangmai area, the leasing of real property typically takes the form of sharecropping agreements between farmers and landowners, although contracts for the rental of living quarters are also found throughout the province. In the municipal area of the city itself, approximately 29.5 percent of the households in 1970 were occupied by renters, and an additional 5.5 percent were provided for employees as payment in kind for their services. Outside the municipal area the figures were 3.7 and 0.6 percent respectively.[6] Conflicts resulting from leasehold agreements raise issues that are regulated by the Thai law of contracts rather than the Land Code. In most cases the disputants are concerned with the effect of temporary agreements between private individuals regarding the occupation and use of the land, and not the rights and obligations created

---

6. *1970 Population and Housing Census; Changwat Chiangmai,* "Table 3: Private Households by Type of Tenure of Living Quarters," p. 115. Figures are an estimate based upon "a percent sample enumeration."

by the government's own certification procedures. Insofar as the formal law codes articulate a new set of norms concerning contractual dealings of this kind, we find, therefore, another illustration of the discrepancies that can arise between modern legal requirements and traditional patterns of behavior and obligation.

One example of the discrepancy between code and custom in the rental of land is provided by a private criminal prosecution for trespass brought by a tenant against the owner of her land. *Nang* Lamai occupied a house and lot recently acquired by *Nang* Nit. *Nang* Lamai had negotiated a ten-month lease with the former owner, and the term of the lease had begun before ownership had been transferred. When *Nang* Nit discovered that *Nang* Lamai was a tenant in the house she had just purchased, she told her to leave. *Nang* Lamai refused, citing the lease as a basis for her right to remain. *Nang* Nit decided to take direct action to enforce what she thought of as her rights of ownership. She showed her documents of title to a policeman and asked him to accompany her to the disputed household. The policeman stood by and observed as *Nang* Nit ordered her workmen to destroy the fence, clotheslines and electrical lines on two sides of the property in order to open it into the neighboring lot which she also owned. She then brought a civil suit to evict *Nang* Lamai. In response, *Nang* Lamai brought a criminal action for trespass against *Nang* Nit, alleging 800 *baht* in damages. The court, faced with a situation in which the owner of a house and lot was accused of trespass upon her own property, found that no *prima facie* case was presented and dismissed *Nang* Lamai's suit. The court held that the crime of trespass could be committed only against the property of another person. Since *Nang* Nit owned the property, she could not have been guilty of trespassing upon it. In short, the court assumed that the owner's interest in her own land was paramount, even when that land had been leased to another person. The tenant did not, by virtue of her contract, "own" the land in the sense that she could prevent the landlord from entering upon and even destroying the property that she had rented.

The decision of the trial court was promptly reversed by the Court of Appeals, which cited prior decisions of the Supreme Court establishing the rights of tenants against interference with their leasehold estate. Despite the fact that *Nang* Nit had purchased the land and the documents of ownership, *Nang* Lamai was a lawful occupant. By virtue of her contract she held certain rights that even *Nang* Nit was bound to respect. The Court of Appeals had rejected the traditional concept of ownership as a monolithic and absolute right and had asserted instead one of the primary values of the modern legal system: the enforceability of contracts, even contracts made with a prior owner.[7] If land is a mere commodity, then it is subject to contractual agree-

---

7. "Section 569. A contract of hire of immovable property is not extinguished by the transfer of the ownership of the property hired. *(cont.)*

ments that convey specified interests over fixed periods of time. The holder of such contractual rights can assert them against third persons, and even against the lessor, as long as the contract is still in effect. Just as the Land Code had vested a dramatic new power in mere holders of land certificates as against persons with a more traditional claim to the land, so the codified law of contracts was interpreted to vest a significant power in lessees as against their landlords.[8]

This tendency of the modern law to alter the nature of leasehold relationships was taken one step further in the Edict to Control the Rental of Riceland, a controversial piece of social legislation enacted in 1974 to protect tenant farmers against oppressive practices of certain landowners. Under this statute a formula was provided to fix the maximum rent that could be charged, based upon the expenditures of the tenant farmer and the actual value of the crop he obtained. No lease, moreover, could run for less than six years, regardless of the period of time that the parties might actually have specified in their leasehold agreement.[9] By enacting this edict, the government injected itself directly into the contractual relationships between landlords and tenants. In order to protect the tenants from unfair leasehold arrangements, the government proclaimed certain contractual provisions void and changed the terms of others. Through legislative intervention in the process of contract formation, a "hitherto entirely powerless" segment of the population was vested with a legal power that could be asserted against the very owners of their land. Many tenant farmers in Chiangmai and elsewhere in Thailand responded by bringing lawsuits against their landowners under this new edict, indicating a growing desire during the recent period of parliamentary democracy to readjust a customary pattern of relationship in the local community and thereby stimulate a significant form of social change in provincial Thailand.

RESOLUTION OF PRIVATE WRONGS INVOLVING LAND

The enactment of new legal norms concerning ownership and control of the land has, as we have seen, given rise to disputes that local mediators find difficult to resolve. The holder of a land certificate may resist local efforts to negotiate his interest in the land, even when the adversary is a sibling or a parent, for his claim no longer derives its authority from any local consensus

---

"The transferee is entitled to the rights and is subject to the duties of the transferor towards the hirer" (Thai Civil and Commercial Code).

8. Ultimately this case was decided for defendant on the grounds that she lacked *intent* to have committed the crime of trespass.

9. Although the exact amount of rent would vary from place to place, depending upon the decisions of committees established under the edict in each district, it was provided that the tenant farmer would subtract from the value of his crop not less than one-third of the total to recover his own investment and expenses. Of the amount remaining, not more than one-half could be collected by the landlord as rent (Section 11).

Resolution of Private Wrongs Involving Land 161

but from the formal laws of the central government. Although local mediators, such as the village chief or *kamnan,* can play a significant role in the land registration procedures, once certification is obtained they may feel powerless to challenge the holder of official documentation. The disputants are forced, therefore, to move up the hierarchy of potential mediators and to seek out those officials who can exercise legal authority over the forms themselves. In practice, this will usually mean the district officers, the provincial land officials, or the courts.

An example of the mediation of a land dispute at the district level is provided by a civil suit brought in the Chiangmai court in 1965 for violation of a compromise agreement. In this case the deputy district officer had acted as mediator, with the participation of the disputants, their village chief, and their *kamnan,* and had achieved a compromise agreement which later became the subject of formal litigation. The facts presented by plaintiff and ultimately admitted by defendants were as follows: *Nang* Sai was a 64-year-old widow without children, who lived alone. Because she needed someone to care for her, she asked her sister's daughter, *Nang* Riam, and her husband, to come and stay with her. In exchange she transferred to them in 1964 three pieces of land and a house. This transfer was officially registered at the district office. The younger couple did not get along well with *Nang* Sai during the next year, and she felt that they were not caring for her properly. Finally her dissatisfaction at their ingratitude became so great that she demanded that they return the land to her and leave. The ensuing quarrel led finally to mediation at the district office. There it was agreed that *Nang* Riam and her husband would retain one piece of land in order to repay a debt which they had contracted with a third party. A second piece of land would revert to *Nang* Sai. The third piece would be divided between the disputants, with *Nang* Sai receiving the portion on which the house stood. This agreement was recorded by the deputy district officer and read back to all the participants in the negotiations. *Nang* Riam and her husband initially alleged in court that the agreement had not been read to them and that they had never agreed to the terms, but the court ruled against them on this point on the basis of the deputy district officer's testimony to the contrary.

The mediation session provides a classic illustration of disputants who were forced to seek a higher level of authority because of the subject matter of their dispute. The presence of the village chief and *kamnan* in the negotiations suggests that they had been involved before that point but had lacked sufficient legal authority to promote a settlement. Since the registration of certified land transfers was a function of the district office, the adversaries were forced to take their dispute to the district level in order to reach an agreement. As it turned out, however, even the authority of the district office proved insufficient to produce a lasting settlement. *Nang* Riam and her husband simply refused to transfer the land back to *Nang* Sai according to the terms of the agreement. *Nang* Sai was forced to move up one more level—to the provincial court—where her rights as specified in the compromise agreement were recognized by the judges and enforced by a formal court order.

In the case of *Nang* Sai and *Nang* Riam, the dispute first went to the district office and then, for enforcement purposes, was taken to the provincial court. In a variation upon that pattern, we shall examine a second case involving a boundary dispute, which went first to the provincial court and there was referred to the provincial land office for an official determination of the rights of the disputants. It is interesting to note, too, that the first dispute involved only the *nǫ sǫ* 3 forms, the "certificates of beneficial use," which are issued by the district office. In the second dispute, a title deed was involved—a document issued under the authority of the provincial government—and therefore it was the provincial land office, rather than the district office, that the court asked to assist in the resolution of the dispute.

The facts of the second case show that *Nai* Ma and *Nai* Inta both owned plots of land that had originally been part of a single holding bordering on a highway. When the original owner divided this holding into ten parts and sold them to separate purchasers, each purchaser acquired a joint interest in a minor connecting road running down the middle of the land to the highway. All purchasers and their subsequent assignees held *nǫ sǫ* 3 certification of their rights in the land and the connecting road. Later *Nai* Inta applied to the provincial land for a title deed for his plot. An official survey was made of his land, unlike the rough map made by the district officials for the *nǫ sǫ* 3 certificate. When this survey was completed, *Nai* Inta built a fence around his land. *Nai* Ma examined *Nai* Inta's fence and found that it encroached upon the common roadway and upon the land of two adjoining residents. He complained to *Nai* Inta, but the latter refused to move his fence, maintaining that his rights had been established by the survey officials. *Nai* Ma was forced to take the matter to the provincial court. Unlike the plaintiff in the preceding case, he did not first consult with the provincial officials responsible for documentation of interests in land. Perhaps he was afraid that they would regard his complaint as an allegation of incompetence on their part. Whatever the reason, *Nai* Ma's suit brought to the court the issue of the precise boundaries of *Nai* Inta's land, and the court needed the help of the provincial land office to decide this issue. The court therefore had the two parties stipulate that the case would be referred to the provincial land office for a new survey of the entire area, and that this survey would serve as a conclusive determination of their claims. The survey took place one month later and proved that *Nai* Ma's contentions were partially justified. A final compromise agreement was signed in the provincial court less than two weeks after the survey. This case and the preceding case are illustrated schematically in figure 13.

There are, of course, many cases in which the court does not depend upon compromise agreements or findings of fact by the district or provincial

Resolution of Private Wrongs Involving Land 163

authorities concerning competing claims to the land. In a 1966 lawsuit for wrongful acts, for example, the court itself cut through the complexities and contradictions of prior certification and brought about an unusual resolution to the dispute. The dispute was actually a battle of conflicting legal forms.

1. District-level agreement is enforced by court (*nǫ sǫ* 3 forms)

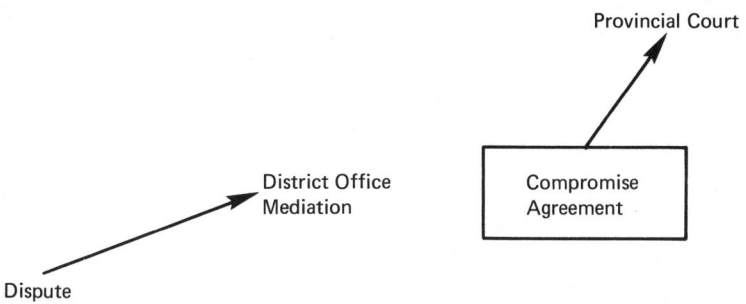

2. Province-level survey produces compromise in court (title deed)

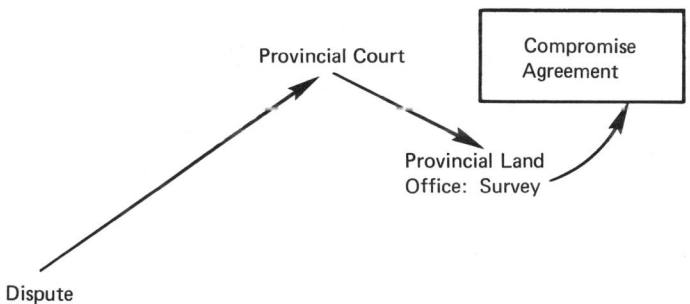

Figure 13. Role of Court and Administrative Officials in Obtaining Compromise Agreements in Two Land Disputes

Nai Mi held land that he claimed to have purchased from *Nai* Som by the transfer of a *sǫ khǫ* 1 document.[10] This land had been the property of the deceased wife of *Nai* Som. When she died, there had been a disagreement as to who acquired the land: *Nai* Som or her four children by a previous marriage. Before the disagreement was resolved, *Nai* Som surreptitiously sold the relevant *sǫ khǫ* 1 document to *Nai* Mi for 1,000 *baht*. Apparently

---

10. Theoretically, the *sǫ khǫ* 1 form does not give its holder legal power to sell the land (see p. 156).

unaware that *Nai* Mi now occupied the land, district officials finally arranged a compromise agreement between *Nai* Som and the children. It was agreed that they all held equal interests in the land but that *Nai* Som would relinquish his interest in exchange for other property of the deceased. Accordingly, a *nǫ sǫ* 3 certificate was issued in the names of the four children. This document was, of course, in conflict with the *sǫ khǫ* 1 form, which *Nai* Som had already "transferred" to *Nai* Mi. When *Nai* Mi discovered that his *sǫ khǫ* 1 form had been superseded by the more authoritative and more recently issued *nǫ sǫ* 3, he sued *Nai* Som and the four children in the provincial court to force them to relinquish their claims to the land. *Nai* Som replied that he had been tricked and made drunk by *Nai* Mi so that he had not known what he was doing when he had recorded his thumbprint on the documents that purported to transfer the land to *Nai* Mi. In any case, he maintained, the land was now in the lawful possession of the four children, by action of the district officials.

The court's solution to this thorny problem was unique. Rather than deciding the merits of the case, the court approved a compromise agreement which stipulated that the land be held for a private auction among all the disputants. The highest bidder would obtain an undisputed right to the land. The proceeds of the auction would then be distributed between plaintiff and defendants in a ratio of 6 to 4. If this auction failed to conclude the matter, then a public auction of the land would be held with the proceeds to be distributed among the disputants in the same manner. Through this novel technique, the lawsuit was resolved in the court itself, without involving the administrative authorities at all. Indeed, the court may have felt that the district office had already acted incompetently in the matter by issuing a *sǫ khǫ* 1 form to an individual who was in open and peaceful possession of the land, and then issuing a *nǫ sǫ* 3 document for the same land to a rival group of claimants without regard to the prior inconsistent claim. In any case, the court had the authority and the inclination to resolve the competing claims to the land by its own independent action, and it proceeded to do so in a speedy and unusual manner.

When the provincial court acts to resolve private wrongs arising from conflicting claims to the land, it does not often promote settlements of the type illustrated by the preceding case. Normally the judge will simply take testimony, examine the relevant documents, and draw his conclusions as to the worthier claimant. Occasionally the judge may visit the disputed land to aid in the determination of rights. While the judge himself cannot award the proper certification to the side presenting the stronger case, he can issue an order that such certification take place or he can approve an enforceable compromise agreement in which both parties agree that a certain registration procedure shall be followed. The judge is thus an effective mediator for private wrongs involving the land, because his settlements are backed directly by the enforcement power of the state. While the district or provincial officials could also mediate these disputes effectively, and indeed must do so frequently in the course of issuing land documents, they lack the enforcement power that the court provides. Settlements mediated by administrative officials may ultimately require the additional step of formal litigation if one party breaches the agreement and the other party wants to enforce it. The role of the court in disputes involving land is thus enhanced by two factors: the court is one of the few effective mediators with legal authority to handle the subject matter of land disputes, and the court, unlike the other potential mediators, offers the possibility of direct enforcement once a compromise agreement is reached under its auspices. For these reasons the court is frequently called upon to bridge the gaps between claimants that the formal laws create and to bring its competence and authority to bear upon private wrongs arising from claims to the land.

Chapter Eleven
Women and Men

This chapter is concerned with the litigation of private wrongs arising from conflicts between men and women, conflicts predicated specifically upon differences in the social or legal status of the sexes. As in the preceding chapter concerning conflicts over land, we shall find in this chapter that the rights and obligations of the disputants are in a state of flux. In part, this situation has resulted from the influence of western social norms concerning relationships between the sexes. In part, too, the influence of the law has been exerted, both deliberately and inadvertently, to reshape the traditional patterns of behavior involving men and women. As the law has become involved in this area, the courts have been called upon to mediate disputes that arise in the traditional society, pitting new legal claims against customary social norms and "hitherto entirely powerless" persons against adversaries formerly immune from their demands.

There has always been some ambiguity in the relative status of women and men in Thai society, particularly when seen from a western viewpoint. On the one hand Thai women, especially in the north, appear strong and even dominant in many areas of life. In managing the household affairs and finances, northern women are equal to men and often superior to them in their authority (Davis, 1974:25 and 64; Kingshill, 1960:51 and 73). Northern Thai women have historically played important roles in public administration (Prisna Sirinam, 1973:53) and in the legal system as well.[1] The prominence of women in Thai society was even noted by Chinese visitors to Thailand during the Ming dynasty, who observed that "When there are affairs to be settled, they are settled by women. In determination and judgment, the women really

---

1. Prani Sirithǫn Na Phatthalung, for example, tells of a princess from the northern province of Lamphun, known for her legal skills and courtroom prowess. Born during the reign of King Rama III, *Cḃaoying* Khampǫ was an active and widely respected representative for disputants in the traditional courts of the north (1963: vol. 2, 50-52).

surpass the men."[2] In modern times, one source of social influence for women has been a strong tendency, especially in the north, towards uxorilocal residence.[3] This practice emphasizes the importance of the wife's family and her community over that of the husband and also results in what Davis calls a "*de facto* tendency towards female ultimogeniture in the transmission of the house and yard." Although all siblings usually have equal rights in the estate of the last deceased parent, competing claims to the residence itself are commonly relinquished in favor of the "married sibling living in the parental home at the time of the last parent's death"—normally a woman (Davis, 1974:63-64).

On the other hand, the woman's role in Thai society is subordinate to that of the man in many important respects. It is the prerogative of the successful man, acknowledged by custom if not by law, to take more than one wife, while a woman may have only one husband at a time. The Buddhist religion as practiced in Thailand is centered around the men, who are generally expected to become monks at some point in their lives. Although women may be ordained as nuns, the practice is often understood to be a reaction to some special misfortune or sadness and is not a normal part of the quest by most women for spiritual improvement.[4] Education, which is now provided for both sexes equally, was traditionally offered in the temples primarily to boys, with monks acting as their teachers. The low literacy rates among older women in Chiangmai, as compared to their younger counterparts and to men of the same age group, illustrates the fact that education was for many years a male prerogative (table 7).

TABLE 7
Comparison of Female and Male Literacy by Age Group in Chiangmai Province, 1970[a]

Age Group	Population		Number Literate		Percent Literate	
	Female	Male	Female	Male	Female	Male
70 & over	14,638	11,166	648	3,928	4.4	35.2
60-69	22,316	21,512	1,397	8,201	6.3	38.1
50-59	26,745	28,015	4,216	14,858	15.8	53.0
40-49	50,819	54,748	23,891	39,765	47.0	72.6
30-39	65,478	68,696	44,409	53,076	67.8	77.3
20-29	61,713	63,941	48,825	54,500	79.1	85.2
10-19	131,214	132,943	115,182	118,772	87.8	89.3
Unknown	681	687	124	176	18.2	25.6

Source: Derived from 1970 Population and Housing Census; Changwat Chiangmai (table 12).

[a]Literacy defined as the ability "to read and write simple statements in any language. If a person can read but cannot write, then he was classified as illiterate." (XVI).

---

2. Quoted in Benedict (1952:3) from Ming Shih chapter 324, pp. 19b-20a.
3. Kingshill (1960:47) estimates that more than half of the newly married couples in Ku Daeng "live initially with their maternal parents-in-law." Davis goes further and states

Historically, while women may in fact have occupied authoritative social positions, the laws were nevertheless designed to render them the "property" of the household head—their parents or their husband (Lingat, 1935:98-99):

> Under ancient law, a woman was at all times under someone's protection. If single, no matter how old, she was under the care and protection of her parents; when married, she was under her husband's protection. Parental power was converted into conjugal power and transferred to her husband. (Adul Wichiencharoen and Luang Chamroon Netisastra, 1968:91)

Despite some real areas of social and political power, therefore, women in Thai society have traditionally suffered certain serious disadvantages. Many of the ambiguities in the relative status of men and women continue to be important legal and social issues and are themselves responsible for some of the disputes that will be examined in this chapter.

The effect of modern law has been, on the one hand, to emphasize the standard of universal legal equality, while on the other hand it has deprived women of certain rights and protections that had been guaranteed by traditional laws and customs. When it was decided that the modern Thai family law should mandate greater sexual equality by prohibiting the widespread practice of polygyny, for example, one unfortunate result was to deprive the traditional "minor wife" of her legal claim to a share in her husband's estate. The children of the minor wife, moreover, were now considered "illegitimate" without a formal act of acknowledgment by their father.[5] The twentieth-

---

that the rule of uxorilocal residence is *mandatory* in northern Thailand, unlike central Thailand where the rule is not always followed (1974:61-62).

4. Wijeyewardene suggests that a structural symmetry exists in northern Thailand in which the "maleness" of the Buddhist religion and the Buddhist shrines are opposed by a "femaleness" associated with the spirit shrines of the house, village and province. Whereas the former are associated with "celibacy, detachment and spiritual well-being," the latter are associated with "territory, political dominance, sexuality . . . and material well-being" (1970:254).

5. King Vajiravudh, for one, foresaw this unfortunate effect of the proposed monogamous marriage law when he wrote in a memorandum in 1913 that,

> when we have *no illegitimate children in our Laws, it is not desirable to provide for their coming into being.* It is true that at present there are already many cases of children who are not acknowledged by their fathers, but there are no laws to strengthen the position of such unnatural fathers. Should, however, the monogamous system be adopted as the principle of our Marriage Law, a father who does not wish to acknowledge the children of a minor wife would simply take refuge behind the Law. (Adul Wichiencharoen and Luang Chamroon Netisastra, 1968:94).

The Marriage Law, as finally enacted, did provide a procedure for legitimizing children born out of wedlock, with the consent or at the request of the father (Civil and Commercial Code, Sections 1529-1530) or by a unilateral legal action brought by the mother if there was an "open cohabitation" with the alleged father at the probable time of conception (Section 1529(4)). The latter procedure is not invoked very often, however, and in modern times there has developed a real stigma concerning the term "unmarried mother" (Adul Wichiencharoen and Luang Chamroon Netisastra, 1968:106).

century laws governing matrimonial property also deprived women of important rights that had previously been theirs. Before enactment of the modern Civil and Commercial Code, a married woman

> was subjected to no legal disabilities in dealing with the community property known as *Sin Borikon*.... The wife had equal rights with her husband to hold and enjoy the *Sin Borikon,* to sue and be sued in the courts, and to make contracts. (Sanya Dharmasakti and Wimolsiri Jamnarnwej, 1972:3)[6]

Now, however, a married woman "cannot, without the permission of her husband, do any act binding the common property *(Sin Borikhon)*" unless it is uncertain whether her husband is living or dead, unless he has deserted her, has been adjudged incompetent or quasi-incompetent, has been placed in a hospital because of unsoundness of mind, or is imprisoned under a sentence of one year or more (Civil and Commercial Code, Sections 38-39). Generally speaking, the married woman has lost her independent legal control over most marital property which she has not specifically segregated by an ante-nuptial agreement, a document rarely drafted by engaged couples in Thai society.[7] Without her husband's permission the wife cannot enter into any contract involving the community property nor can she bring a case in court. In short, while Thai law no longer considers married women to be the property of their husbands, it has imposed severe disabilities upon married women which often fail to reflect the actual authority and independence that they exercise in Thai society.

To some extent, the modern legal disabilities of women correspond to or may have contributed to—a trend in modern Thai society to differentiate the sexes more explicitly than was done in traditional society and to place the woman in a more dependent and subordinate role relative to the man. Kingshill, for one, observes that western influence in the mid-twentieth century began to disrupt the traditional northern Thai equality of the sexes, bringing beauty contests and western fashions to villagers and a new image of the woman in Thai

---

6. Community property, or *sin bǫrikhon* consists of (a) *sin doem*—basically, property belonging to either spouse before marriage and not specifically designated as separate property at the time of marriage, together with property acquired during marriage through will or gift and declared by such will or gift to be *sin doem* [Thai Civil and Commercial Code, Section 1463]—and (b) *sin somrot*—all property acquired by either spouse during marriage which is not otherwise identified as *sin doem* or some form of separate property [*ibid.,* Section 1466]. Separate property, on the other hand, known as *sin suan tua,* consists of property so designated by an ante-nuptial agreement, "property for personal use according to station in life, or tools necessary for carrying on the profession of either spouse," property acquired during marriage through will or gift and declared by such will or gift to be *sin suan tua,* fruits of *sin suan tua,* and property given by the man to the woman before marriage "as evidence and security that the marriage shall take place" (known as *khǫngman*) [Section 1464].

7. One important exception to this general rule is the *khǫngman*—or engagement gift—which belongs separately to the wife even in the absence of an ante-nuptial agreement. See generally, Virada Somswasdi (1974).

village society (1960:76). In urban society, Thai women sometimes compete professionally with men on equal terms, yet there are certain professions that have been reserved primarily for males. There are few women attorneys in Thailand, for example—none practices law in Chiangmai—although several Thai women are distinguished and highly respected in the legal field. Until very recently women could not become judges in any but the juvenile courts, could not be elected village chief or *kamnan*, and were chosen as members of parliament only in very small numbers.

Nevertheless, the revolution of 1973 brought to fruition many changes in the legal status of women which had long been advocated by a small but articulate women's movement in Thailand. Indeed, the Constitution of 1974 went further than most proposals put forward by any group up to that time, by providing flatly in Section 28 that men and women should have equal rights under law. The equal rights guarantee was limited only by a proviso that a two-year grace period should be provided during which all sexually discriminatory laws could be revised without legal challenge (Section 236). The impact of the equal rights provision was soon felt, as traditional prohibitions were eliminated and women became eligible for many positions from which they had previously been barred, including judgeships and leadership roles in the local administration. When the Constitution was abolished in 1976, however, this area of the law—like many others—was thrown into confusion. It remains to be seen whether there will be further legislative efforts to reconcile some of the discrepancies between code and custom that resulted from the legal reforms of the early twentieth century.

As for the role of men and women as litigants in the Chiangmai court, we have already noted that no married woman could bring suit without the written permission of her husband.[8] In addition, it is possible that social as well as legal constraints make men more likely than women to appear in court, both as plaintiffs and as defendants. Table 8 shows that men are far more frequently involved than women in the litigation of private wrongs in Chiangmai.

In this chapter I shall examine in detail two specific areas in which men and women have confronted one another in the Chiangmai court: marital disputes and sexual offenses. By discussing the litigation of private wrongs under these two headings, I hope to clarify some of the ways in which the law and the legal process interact with changing local customs to determine the relationships and relative positions of the sexes in Chiangmai society. As in the preceding chapter, it may be possible to discern how new regulations and new distributions of power in the traditional society render the customary mediators ineffective and require the provincial court to exert its power over the disputants and resolve their conflicts with reference to the codified rules of law.

---

8. This rule remained in effect through the time of my research in Thailand.

TABLE 8
Frequency of Litigation of Private Wrongs by Sex of Litigant in Provincial and Magistrates' Courts of Chiangmai Province in 1965, 1968, 1971, and 1974

	Private Criminal Suits				Civil "Wrongful Acts"[a]			
	Plaintiff		Defendant		Plaintiff		Defendant	
	No.	%	No.	%	No.	%	No.	%
Male	447	76.3	430	73.4	151	53.5	203	72.0
Female	97	16.6	108	18.4	81	28.7	44	15.6
Male and female	---	---	25	4.3	1	0.4	4	1.4
Legal persons	36	6.1	17	2.9	40	14.2	20	7.1
Unknown	6	1.0	6	1.0	9	3.2	11	3.9
Total	586	100.0	586	100.0	282	100.0	282	100.0

Source: Court Registers for Provincial and Magistrates' Courts, Chiangmai Province, for 1965, 1968, 1971, and 1974.

[a] Analysis here is based only upon civil suits involving "wrongful acts" (lamoet). Elsewhere in this study civil "private wrongs" have included both "wrongful acts" and "divorce and related matters." In "divorce and related matters" the two litigants in nearly all cases must, by definition, be male and female. The distribution in such cases, based on a sample of 21 cases drawn from the records of every third civil suit processed during 1965, 1968, 1971, and 1974, is as follows: Plaintiff: male, 6 (28.6%); female, 15 (71.4%). Defendant: male, 15 (71.4%); female, 6 (28.6%).

MARITAL DISPUTES

I spoke with *Nang* Buakham as we sat beneath her mother's house on a bare wood platform. The house stood ten feet above the ground in a large and shaded bamboo grove. Nearby a neighbor drew water from a well and carried it to her home in two buckets suspended at either end of a flexible bamboo shoulder pole. A group of boys, among them *Nang* Buakham's son, played marbles on the hard packed dirt near the house. *Nang* Buakham was a shy and gentle woman, 34 years of age. While we talked, her mother sat with us, contributing an occasional comment, sometimes obscene and usually derogatory to her son-in-law. The old woman's teeth were black with betel nut, and she wore a white flower in her hair.

In April 1972, *Nang* Buakham's husband, a minibus driver, had taken a second wife and had left *Nang* Buakham and her three young sons, returning to his own village with his new wife. *Nang* Buakham remained in possession of a house her parents had assembled in their compound for the couple and their children. Friends sometimes saw the husband with the other woman and asked *Nang* Buakham why she didn't confront him or even beat him in public to embarrass him. She replied that she wasn't that type of person. She simply wanted to talk with him like an adult. He was free to leave her if that was what he wanted to do. Unfortunately, her husband showed little willingness to talk when she approached him at his minibus queue, and he refused to help support her or the three boys. The local headman was unable to influence her husband because he lived in a village outside the headman's jurisdiction. *Nang* Buakham therefore brought a civil suit against her husband in the Chiangmai court, asking that they be divorced, that she be given custody of the children, and that the marital property be divided between the two of them.

I asked *Nang* Buakham how she had decided to go to court in this matter. She told me that she had been hesitant, because she had heard that people often brought suits in court without getting good results. Many of her acquaintances advised her not to litigate but to try to settle the matter privately with her husband instead. She felt they were implying that she did not dare to sue, and this made her want to try it. A brother-in-law who lived in Chiangmai city took her from her village to see an attorney in town, and the attorney advised her to bring the suit. In the first stages of litigation, *Nang* Buakham alleged that the minibus had been purchased from the combined earnings of herself and her husband and that she was therefore entitled to 18,500 *baht,* which was half of its original purchase price. In a countersuit, her husband replied that his father had paid for the vehicle, that *Nang* Buakham had no interest in it at all, but that he himself was entitled to 6,000 *baht* representing half the value of the house in which they lived.

In the course of the proceedings, both parties abandoned their claims to assets held by the other and asked the court simply to decide who should have custody of the children and how much maintenance should be paid, if any. Two months after the complaint was filed, the court held that, because the father's employment would require him to spend much of his time away from home, *Nang* Buakham should be given custody of the children. Her husband was ordered to provide support in the amount of 200 *baht* per child each month until they became adults. The court issued an order that the two should be divorced, and if either party refused to register the divorce at the district offices, then the other could take the judgment of the court as constructive evidence of intent and obtain the divorce from the district officials.

As it turned out, *Nang* Buakham did not go to the district office to register her divorce. This was because a court official advised her that it would be more difficult to force her husband to make support payments if they were no longer married. Even when I spoke to her she was still officially married, although she had resumed the use of her maiden name. Her husband, during the two and one-half years since the court judgment, had paid only 200 *baht,* which he brought to her one month after the lawsuit ended. He had also provided clothing and books for the children since that time. *Nang* Buakham knew that she could go back to court and collect the monthly payments that her husband owed her. Her attorney had told her that if her husband failed to provide the money she could bring an enforcement action against him. But she did not think much about bringing another lawsuit. She did not especially want to go back to court.

How did *Nang* Buakham feel about her experience in the Chiangmai court? She admired the judge. He was a kind man who spoke nicely. He said some truthful things and some playful things. It was the judge, speaking directly to

Nang Buakham and her husband, who insisted on the figure of 200 *baht* per child, even when her husband said he could pay only half that amount. He tried to reconcile the two of them, and when that proved impossible he arranged a fair settlement and divorce. The lawsuit did not seem to affect the attitudes of her friends and neighbors towards her. At first her husband was very angry. He came to her house several times to ask why she wanted to waste money in court. Her father-in-law advised her to discuss the matter, not to litigate, but she told him that she had already tried to discuss it and had gotten nowhere. Did *Nang* Buakham feel disappointed now, considering the fact that she never did obtain a legal divorce nor did she receive support payments from her husband? No, she was not disappointed. She never really thought she would win, but even going to court was a victory for her. It was not a frightening experience, but it was embarrassing at the time. Looking back at it, though, she felt that it was fun, an exciting experience which showed that she was right even if she didn't gain any real advantage from it.

Marriage in Thailand, like the ownership of land, is now the subject of formal registration requirements that are often at odds with customary norms and with widespread public behavior. From a legal point of view, marriage takes place upon the signing of a few simple forms and the payment of a nominal fee at the district office.[9] No religious ceremony is required by law. In practice, however, religious rites are quite common and indeed may be observed more frequently than the legal registration requirements. In some parts of Thailand the marriage rites are primarily Buddhist in nature, but Wijeyewardene notes that for northern village Thais it is the spirit cult rather than Buddhism that provides the ritual sanction (1967:67). The young man and woman will, at the house of the woman, perform an act that indicates their interest in one another: talking affectionately, touching, holding hands, embracing, or even engaging in sexual intercourse. This act, according to the ritual, offends the spirits of the house which protect the chastity of the women in the family. Therefore the man must propitiate the spirits by paying a certain sum of money to the woman's family and by asking their permission to marry. If the woman does not wish to marry the man, however, then he must pay only half the amount normally required. (Sanguan Chotisukharat, 1969:79-82). Customary "registration" of marriages is thus effected by informing the spirits rather than by informing the government. Although there is some evidence that the customary practices are more widespread among rural people than the formal registration procedures, the latter may be observed when substantial assets are held by either party (Wijeyewardene, 1967:67-69).

---

9. "Section 1449. Marriage under this Code shall be valid only on registration being effected" (Thai Civil and Commercial Code).

The marital relationship, like other alliances in Thai society, has an important voluntary component. When either side is dissatisfied, he or she may simply abandon the relationship and leave the house. Because of the frequency of unregistered marriages, it is difficult to cite a "divorce rate" in Thai society. It appears, however, that divorce and re-marriage are very common in northern Thailand among both men and women. Marlowe reports a typical pattern to be "a short marriage or two with 'strangers' [residents of a different village] and then a lasting marriage with the boy or girl next door" (1969:17). Wijeyewardene found in one small northern Thai village that, among those persons who had ever been married, 23 out of 69 men and 35 out of 77 women had been divorced at least once (1967:68).[10]

In contrast to this customary pattern of easily achieved *de facto* divorce, however, the formal law codes require a showing of substantial cause before they will allow a judge to grant a *de jure* divorce sought by only one of the spouses. The showing that the plaintiff must make in a divorce suit is in most cases quite similar to the showing of a "wrongful act" (*lamoet*). The similarity accounts for my inclusion of these cases in the discussion of private wrongs. The law codes provide that one spouse may enter a claim for divorce in court only when one of the following preconditions exists: (1) adultery committed by the wife—adultery by the husband is not grounds for divorce; (2) "gross misconduct," bodily harm, or serious insult by one spouse to the other spouse or to his or her ascendants; (3) desertion for more than one year, failure to provide "proper maintenance and support," or the commission of acts "seriously adverse to the relationship of husband and wife to such an extent that the other cannot continue cohabitation as husband and wife"; (4) the sentencing of either spouse to a prison term for theft, snatching, robbery, gang robbery, piracy, the counterfeit or alteration of currency, or any other offense for a term exceeding three years; (5) a judgment that either spouse has disappeared, so long as the judgment has not been revoked; (6) a judgment that either spouse is incompetent because of unsoundness of mind which has lasted continuously for more than three years since the date of such judgment and which is "still incurable so that the continuance of marriage cannot be expected"; (7) the violation by either spouse of a bond of good behavior that he or she had executed; (8) a finding that either spouse suffers from a disease that is communicable, dangerous, incurable and potentially injurious to the other spouse; (9) a finding that either spouse has "defective genital organs so as to be permanently unable to cohabit as husband and wife" (Civil and Commercial Code, Section 1500).

This rigorous set of conditions for a court-ordered divorce contrasts sharply with actual patterns of behavior among discontented couples both in registered and unregistered unions. For example, a wife whose husband

---

10. Wijeyewardene includes unregistered as well as registered marriages and divorces in these figures.

became involved with another woman would have no grounds for divorce in a court of law so long as he behaved reasonably well towards her and supported her properly. In reality, however, there are some women who would refuse to accept the acquisition of a "minor wife" by their husbands and would simply leave them. It is clear that one spouse or the other often feels that there is more than enough cause to justify a *de facto* divorce while the preconditions for a divorce under law are far from satisfied.[11] The law codes in such cases have reduced the power and independence of the spouse in a registered marriage who wishes to end the marital relationship without the consent of the other spouse.

Most plaintiffs in divorce suits allege some specific form of misconduct on the part of their spouse, making tangible—and actionable—a breakdown in the relationship which may in fact be somewhat more subtle. *Nang* Buakham, in the case that opened this section, merely alleged the commission of "acts seriously adverse to the relationship of husband and wife."[12] Other suits are commonly predicated upon "gross misconduct," bodily harm, or serious insult. In a case in 1965, for example, plaintiff alleged that her husband frequently went out drinking with his friends, that he gambled, that he did not earn a proper living, that he came home drunk, beat her, and cursed her and her parents, causing them public shame. Defendant denied all of these charges, although he did allege that after his wife left him to live with her parents, her father was sufficiently angry to come after him with a gun. Ironically, in this case of violently ruptured domestic relations, unlike the less dramatic case of *Nang* Buakham, the couple was reconciled only six months after the lawsuit was filed and resumed living together at that time. A third divorce action, also in 1965, followed a different but equally common pattern. In this case it was the husband who brought the suit, alleging that his wife had become addicted to gambling and that she had taken all of their marital property—amounting to 40,000 *baht* (approximately $2,000)—together with the title deed to their house, and had lost them in an illegal lottery. The response of the wife was not to contest the action, but simply to agree to

---

11. If one spouse does leave the other because of objectionable behavior, the separation cannot later be used as grounds for divorce by the spouse who decided to leave, despite the fact that a desertion of more than one year has taken place. Desertion makes possible a divorce suit only for the spouse who was deserted. (See Sa-at Nawičharoen, 1974:170-71).

12. This particular provision of Section 1500 of the Family Law has been illustrated by Professor Sa-at Nawičharoen (1974:171) in the following terms:

> For example, if one spouse continually speaks abusively towards or drives away the other spouse, or together with his or her own relatives one spouse criticizes or ridicules the other spouse, then the victim can sue for divorce. If one spouse regularly and for a long period of time refuses to have sexual relations with the other spouse without justification, this is also a legal cause for divorce, because sexual relations are an important element in the cohabitation as husband and wife. Therefore this type of adverse act is considered serious enough to make a continuation of the marriage impossible.

register their divorce at the district office. Plaintiff therefore withdrew his suit less than three months after filing it.

The first level of mediation for marital disputes is often in the village; but when the marriage has been formally registered, the divorce must also be registered with the district authorities in order to be recognized officially. This permits the district-level officials to act as mediators as well. If one spouse in a registered marriage resists the divorce and the matter comes to court, then the judge himself is cast in the familiar role of mediator of last resort. It is commonly felt that marital disputes should be mediated in such a way as to bring about a reconciliation if at all possible. We have seen that village leaders and even the district-level officials attempt to discourage couples from divorces, both *de facto* and *de jure* (see pages 89 and 93, above). The Honorable Sanya Dharmasakti, former President of the Supreme Court and former Prime Minister of Thailand, has written that the same attitude usually prevails among judges who preside over divorce actions in court:

> The practice of the courts is to insist on a narrow interpretation of these terms [which specify the grounds for divorce], and that all reasonable efforts are made by the courts in divorce proceedings to reconcile estranged spouses; but too often the utmost efforts are in vain. (Sanya Dharmasakti and Wimolsiri Jamnarnwej, 1972:17)

This was certainly the procedure followed in *Nang* Buakham's case, where the judge arranged the terms of a settlement only after assuring himself that a reconciliation was impossible.

There are at least three reasons why the reconciliation of disputing spouses is seen as desirable among most potential mediators in Thailand. First, the attempt by mediators to preserve the marriage, rather than to let both parties go their own way, is thought to provide a healthy opportunity for husband and wife to articulate grievances to a third person which they may have been reluctant to discuss directly with one another. Even among married couples, the face-to-face assertion of one's rights may sometimes prove too unpleasant to be worth the effort. Second, it is often presumed that the attempt to dissolve the relationship is premature, the result of a rash or angry impulse in a marriage that could still be enjoyed by both spouses. Third, I would suggest, the attempt to reconcile marital disputes is almost an instinctive reflex in a society where multiple marriages and divorces give rise to bitter conflicts among rival claimants to real and personal property. Such conflicts may involve the spouses themselves, who quarrel over the proper division of the marital property or, in the case of the wife, try to prevent minor wives from usurping established claims to the common assets. These conflicts may also involve the half-brothers and half-sisters who are the children of divorced parents. This kind of rivalry and competition for property is commonly seen as one of the most compelling arguments against the taking of minor wives. It is also viewed as a good reason to try to preserve the threatened marital relationship, if possible, to prevent fragmentation and conflict between the various members of the household and their rivals.

To summarize, then, modern legal requirements concerning the registration of marriages and divorces are comparable to registration requirements concerning rights in land, in that both sets of requirements are often ignored and in some ways fail to conform to customary patterns of behavior. As a result, in both areas of law, new patterns of conflict have arisen and new legal categories have been created to frame the grievances of the disputants. Modern Thai laws have expanded the traditional process of reconciliation by, in effect, establishing new mediators with a power to reconcile feuding couples: district-level officials in charge of registering divorces, and judicial officials who must decide the divorce actions brought before them. At the same time, the modern laws have drastically limited the traditional power of either spouse to obtain a unilateral dissolution of the marital relationship. This is because, once the marriage has been registered, a strong showing of wrongful behavior must be made before the court will order a divorce. The wife, in particular, is placed at a disadvantage in this situation, because she retains all of her legal disabilities until the marriage is formally dissolved. The option of walking out of the house is still available, but this in itself will not lead to a formal divorce unless the deserted spouse wants one. Frequently, out of pride or spite, the deserted spouse will refuse to cooperate and the couple will remain legally married long after the relationship has disintegrated. The spouse who seeks a divorce must therefore make the conflict overt and concrete, alleging in court specific acts of serious wrongdoing by the other party, unless he or she can persuade the other to register their divorce peacefully.[13] In addition, the advent of the modern Thai family law drastically affected conflicts arising as a result of multiple marriages. The law codes permit only one registered marriage at a time, but customary practices may allow the husband several unregistered marriages either sequentially or simultaneously. When unregistered spouses and illegitimate children are the claimants, the courts and the district-level officials must often deny remedies which were long sanctioned both by formal law and by custom.

Despite the creation of an important new forum for the resolution of marital disputes, therefore, the reformation of the substantive law of marriage resulted in a stripping away of legal power from minor wives and occasionally from their children as well. The modern law codes have thus elevated the "major" wife, the wife whose marriage is officially registered, to a new position of power over her rivals, and they have also granted husbands in both registered and unregistered marriages greater power in relation to their wives. These shifts in status, enforceable in the courts of law, have redistributed

---

13. Or unless other, less common grounds for divorce exist, as listed in provisions 4-9 of Section 1500, cited on page 174, above.

power between the sexes even when local customs and local mediators have stood in opposition to them.

OTHER FORMS OF CONFLICT BETWEEN MEN AND WOMEN

In addition to its role in mediating marital disputes, the provincial court involves itself in relations between the sexes when it is called upon to examine private wrongs between men and women who are not necessarily husband and wife. Often such matters reach the court after mediation at a lower level has failed. The failure can usually be explained in terms which are by now familiar: factors such as age, status, ethnicity, or political power make it impossible for any local mediator to command the respect of both parties, and the provincial court must provide the crucial "crossover" point which allows negotiations to take place between the disputants. What is unique to the cases I wish to describe in this section, however, is the subject matter. In each of the following cases, a woman appeared as plaintiff to sue a man for alleged wrongful acts in which no remedy was available at the local level. In several of the cases, the woman plaintiff sought to obtain through litigation a traditional remedy to which she felt entitled. Her claim was ineffective at the local level, usually because she lacked the leverage to enforce it. The absence of leverage in some of these cases, as we shall see, resulted as much from status differences as from sexual inequities, if such a distinction can properly be made. In the concluding case, however, such status differences were overcome by the judicial enforcement of a contractual agreement binding a government official to provide support for his minor wife and illegitimate child. This final case will suggest that traditional obligations eroded by the modern legal codes can be reasserted by a determined litigant in the form of contractual duties. The enforcement power of the provincial court in such cases can nullify the political power of an adversary with higher social status and prestige who, even in the traditional society, might well have avoided liability.

The first case history presents, in a sense, a marital dispute in reverse. It is not uncommon in Thailand for an unmarried woman who alleges rape or sexual impropriety on the part of a man to demand as a remedy that the man agree to marry her. Whereas in marital disputes the wrongful act was raised as grounds for divorce, in these disputes the wrongful act is raised as grounds for marriage. The law codes, of course, provide no such remedy. A serious criminal suit for indecent behavior or rape may, however, induce the man to agree to the marriage in exchange for withdrawal of the prosecution. In this way the modern Thai Penal Code can be manipulated by the plaintiff to obtain a traditional remedy.

A 19-year-old woman, whom I shall call *Nangsao* Čhinda, brought a private criminal suit in the Chiangmai court together with her father, alleging that *Nangsao* Čhinda's former sweetheart, *Nai* Chan, had drugged and raped her in the back of a minibus. The following facts are drawn from the testimony of *Nangsao* Čhinda and her father. For two years, *Nangsao* Čhinda and *Nai* Chan had loved one another and had exchanged many letters. *Nai* Chan drove a minibus for a living and *Nangsao* Čhinda was a student. When *Nangsao* Čhinda learned that *Nai* Chan had become involved with another woman, she broke off the relationship, but the two still met occasionally as friends. More than a year later, *Nai* Chan encountered *Nangsao* Čhinda near the house where she lived while attending the local teachers' training college in Chiangmai city. He invited her to see a movie with him before she returned to her village home. As they watched the movie, *Nai* Chan gave *Nangsao* Čhinda some cold tablets which made her feel light-headed. Later they went to eat noodles and iced tea. *Nai* Chan brought the noodles to her from a stall outside the coffee shop. *Nangsao* Čhinda became very dizzy and asked *Nai* Chan to take her home. *Nai* Chan hailed a minibus and spoke with the driver before climbing in the back with *Nangsao* Čhinda. By this time, *Nangsao* Čhinda claimed to have become dazed and semi-conscious. She was aware only of the fact that *Nai* Chan began to take sexual liberties with her, that she had no strength to resist, that the minibus eventually stopped and *Nai* Chan raped her, and that he then called out to another man, whom she believed to have been the driver, who also raped her. Later when she was totally unconscious, she was taken by the driver to the home of her father's neighbor. The next day, *Nangsao* Čhinda and her father notified the police, who recorded the complaint and sent her to the Chiangmai Hospital for a medical examination. Neither the police records nor the medical records were offered in evidence, but it is possible that both were unfavorable to *Nangsao* Čhinda, for no public prosecution was ever brought. Nevertheless, the police attempted at the time to mediate the dispute. *Nai* Chan then agreed to marry *Nangsao* Čhinda when she finished her education and to formalize their engagement in four to five days. Apparently *Nai* Chan refused to honor this agreement, however, and *Nangsao* Čhinda and her father subsequently brought a criminal action against him and the driver for rape.

Plaintiff's primary goal was to force *Nai* Chan to marry *Nangsao* Čhinda in order to atone for his wrongdoing and to alleviate the shame that she was perceived to have suffered from his wrongful act. Possibly this result was still anticipated during the early stages of the lawsuit. Ultimately, however, *Nangsao* Čhinda and her father had to settle for the secondary goal of money damages. Apparently the documentary evidence against *Nangsao* Čhinda was weighty, although both she and her father claimed to have signed papers in the police station without knowledge of their contents. As it became clear that they could not hope to win the case, and as their hold on *Nai* Chan and the driver became correspondingly weaker, they were inclined to accept a compromise. Three and one-half months after filing the private criminal suit, plaintiffs withdrew their prosecution in exchange for the payment of 1,500 *baht* (about $75) by *Nai* Chan. Significantly, the payment was described by the court as *"kha siahai"*: not a payment to propitiate the spirits, not even a payment for the *khwan*-soul, but simply a payment of "damages" for an injury that was not specified. *Nangsao* Čhinda did not achieve the customary remedy of marriage because *Nai* Chan and the driver had developed a strong legal defense to the charge of rape, deriving not only from the documentary evidence but from the admitted history of affectionate relations that had formerly existed between *Nangsao* Čhinda and *Nai* Chan. This background material was strongly emphasized by the defense attorney and may well have influenced the outcome of the case. The marriage did not take place and the two men avoided criminal liability by the payment of a relatively small sum of money, which may or may not have constituted an admission of wrongdoing. The settlement was accepted by *Nangsao* Čhinda as a partial vindication for the wrong she alleged.

Wrongful acts of a sexual nature may be verbal as well as physical. In these cases marriage is not considered as a remedy, but the courts will enforce the payment of fines for seriously insulting speech—a remedy corresponding to village sanctions for the same form of wrongful behavior. We have seen that symbolic and indirect verbal communication can be a potent way to express emotion (see page 67, above). Insults with a sexual content are seen as potentially very damaging—destructive of reputation when addressed by a man to a woman and humiliating when addressed by a woman to a man. Such insults may be communicated in many ways: by the deliberate use of an inappropriate pronoun, by touching the head, shoulders, or other portions of the body, by gesturing with one's feet towards the other person, by reference to certain degrading animal terms such as dog or lizard (*hia*, literally "water monitor").

A heated exchange of insults between a woman meat-seller and a male schoolteacher is reported in a criminal case brought by the woman in the Chiangmai court. Plaintiff had accidentally dropped some of the meat she was selling and was in a bad temper when defendant came to her stall. There was a brief exchange of words between them, and apparently plaintiff spoke loudly or rudely to him. Defendant advised her to speak a little more sweetly, to use better manners. He said to her, "Didn't you hear the news that they stabbed a woman merchant in Lampang for speaking rudely?" Plaintiff retorted, "When you kill me, will you eat my vagina?" There was disagreement over what happened next, but it was admitted that defendant reached for a knife to threaten plaintiff for her insult, and that plaintiff ran from the shop crying out that defendant was trying to kill her. Defendant was later arrested, but the police inquiry official ordered that the case against him be dropped, and plaintiff therefore brought her own private criminal action for indecent behavior and attempted murder.

Defendant in this case should have avoided plaintiff until her angry mood had passed. When he spoke with her, however, her tone of voice or the pronouns she used in reply may well have provoked him into making his menacing remark about the stabbing in Lampang. Plaintiff's insulting response, with its explicit sexual reference, was considered deeply humiliating when addressed by a woman to a man (the Thai expression is stronger than my English translation). This was the reaction not only of the defendant but of the trial court which held that plaintiff's words, uttered in public, caused defendant to feel "ashamed and angry" enough to threaten plaintiff physically. The court, in dismissing plaintiff's case, appeared to balance defendant's inconclusive gesture with his knife against the humiliation and loss of face that he had suffered from her insult, finding that all in all plaintiff gave better than she got. This was the same finding, presumably, that had been made by the police when they dropped charges against defendant. The decision of the trial court was also upheld by the Court of Appeals.

Sexual insults can be judged equally potent and offensive when directed by a man towards a woman. In a private criminal suit brought by a village woman against a deputy district officer, plaintiff accused defendant of improper sexual behavior while he was riding on the back seat of her motorcycle and later of defaming her character in public. When the two disputants had met at the police station for a hearing on the allegation of sexual improprieties, defendant had ridiculed plaintiff in front of a number of other persons. Several of them later testified that he had spoken as follows:

> You claim that I felt your leg and your arm, do you? I am the deputy district officer. I certainly wouldn't behave that way with a villager If I were paid 300 *baht* to fuck someone like you, I wouldn't do it. Even if there were three more like you, I still wouldn't take them. A deputy district officer would lose his prestige if he fucked village people. If I were going to do such a thing, I'd do it with another government official. I'm the deputy district officer. Why don't you go ahead and bring this suit? You're just like a can of farts and a shit-smelling bug.

These insults were accompanied by the use of the pronouns *ku* (I) and *müng* (you), considered extremely rude when used in this context. The entire monologue is almost unbelievably crude in the original Thai, an ultimate achievement in humiliation by a man speaking to a woman and by a relatively high-ranking government official to a villager. The trial court and the appellate court found for the plaintiff with little difficulty in this matter, as well as on the separate count of indecent sexual behavior.[14] The fact that defendant was a local official with considerable status served, in the court's view, to corrob-

---

14. "Whoever insults any person in his presence, or by publication, shall be punished with fine not exceeding five hundred *baht*" (Thai Penal Code, Section 393). The court held that plaintiff's original charge of defamation, rather than insult, was inappropriate because defendant's comments were not detrimental to plaintiff's reputation nor did they convey any false information about plaintiff, but were merely curses and invective.

orate plaintiff's story, for an ordinary villager would not dare to allege such disgraceful misbehavior by the official unless it had actually taken place. Defendant's wrongdoing was especially reprehensible because of his higher status and his corresponding obligation to look after the welfare of the villagers under his care. In this case, therefore, a woman succeeded in punishing a local official by bringing her allegations to the provincial court, by phrasing her charge of verbal abuse in terms recognized by the law, and by having her case decided by a judge sympathetic to her complaint and cognizant of the difficulties faced by a woman villager who is confronted with wrongful behavior by a male official.

The final case in this section expands on the theme of conflict between male government officials and female villagers, adding the elements of multiple marriage and the power of modern contracts to alter traditional relationships. This case, like the preceding one, involves a deputy district officer, whom I shall call *Nai* Insom. He was assigned to an area where an 18-year-old woman named *Nangsao* Čhan lived with her mother. Government officials like *Nai* Insom are transferred frequently, and sometimes hold positions far from their own homes. It is not unusual for such men to acquire minor wives in the areas where they work. *Nai* Insom, who was just over 30 years old, found himself attracted to *Nangsao* Čhan while he was stationed in her district. Early in 1969 he went to speak with her mother, *Nang* Phǫn, asking that *Nangsao* Čhan come to live with him as his wife and promising that he would later register their marriage. *Nang* Phǫn agreed to the arrangement, claiming that she had been "intimidated and fearful" because of *Nai* Insom's official position. A few months later, *Nangsao* Čhan became pregnant. Her mother reminded *Nai* Insom of his promise to register their marriage, but *Nai* Insom refused, admitting at last that he already had a wife elsewhere whose marriage had been lawfully registered. At that point *Nang* Phǫn was ready to bring a civil suit against *Nai* Insom for misleading her daughter and damaging her reputation. *Nai* Insom learned of her plans and went to admit his wrongdoing. He offered to pay damages if she would drop her lawsuit.

In September 1969, *Nang* Phǫn, *Nangsao* Čhan, and *Nai* Insom signed a compromise agreement that had been prepared by *Nang* Phǫn's lawyer. This legally binding contract stipulated that *Nangsao* Čhan was at that time four months pregnant and that *Nai* Insom was the legal father. He agreed that, if she gave birth, he would register the baby as his child and would provide support payments until the child came of legal age. He promised, further, that he would provide support for *Nangsao* Čhan herself in the amount of 300 *baht* each month beginning immediately. In exchange, *Nangsao* Čhan and her mother agreed not to bring any lawsuit against *Nai* Insom as long as he abided by the terms of the contract. This agreement shows on *Nai* Insom's part some feeling of responsibility towards his minor wife and his expected child. It also indicates *Nai* Insom's realistic awareness that a lawsuit could be costly, embarrassing, and possibly detrimental to his job, regardless of its outcome. On the part of *Nangsao* Čhan, and especially on the part of her mother, *Nang* Phǫn, I would suggest that it shows more than that. *Nang* Phǫn appeared in court as the sole legal representative of her daughter, for *Nang* Phǫn's marriage had never been officially registered. She and her husband had separated some years before, and *Nang* Phǫn claimed that she alone had supported *Nangsao* Čhan during her childhood. Certainly *Nang* Phǫn's former husband was at no point involved in protecting his daughter's interests with regard to the incidents I have just described. *Nang* Phǫn, then, was a woman who had herself gone through the common process of unregistered marriage, childbirth, and informal divorce, and she had learned enough from her own experience to provide better for her daughter than she had provided for herself. When the deputy district officer wanted to take *Nangsao* Čhan as his wife, *Nang* Phǫn could hardly refuse him; but once *Nangsao* Čhan became pregnant, *Nang* Phǫn found a way to gain a legal hold on *Nai* Insom despite his superior status and power. A legal contract bound *Nai* Insom to support *Nangsao* Čhan and their child in a way that would have been purely optional under any other circumstances, subject to the good will of the male official, his future job assignments and financial fortunes.

Later events proved that *Nang* Phǫn's precautions were both wise and effective. She and *Nangsao* Čhan claimed that *Nai* Insom refused to make any support payments after January 1970. *Nai* Insom admitted that he had defaulted on the contract, but claimed that only the December payment was outstanding for 1970. In any event, *Nang* Phǫn's lawyer began to send reminders to *Nai* Insom dated as early as February 1970. In January 1971, *Nang* Phǫn and *Nangsao* Čhan brought a civil suit against *Nai* Insom to enforce the compromise agreement of September 1969, claiming that he owed 3,450 *baht* (about \$172.50) plus interest.[15] *Nai* Insom did not contest any of the allegations of fact except the precise date and amount of his default. Less than a month after the lawsuit had been filed in the Chiangmai court, a compromise agreement was reached whereby *Nai* Insom agreed to pay 900 *baht* to compensate for his contractual default. In addition, *Nai* Insom agreed to continue his payment to *Nangsao* Čhan of 300 *baht* each month, but these payments were to continue only for ten more years or until such time as *Nangsao* Čhan acquired a new husband under law. In addition, *Nai* Insom now had the right to miss one monthly payment without immediate enforcement action being taken. Only after missing two consecutive payments would the court step in to enforce the compromise agreement.

Nai Insom did obtain a slightly more favorable compromise agreement in court than the one he had signed originally with *Nang* Phǫn and *Nangsao*

---

15. It is interesting to note that this amount includes only the 300 *baht* per month that *Nai* Insom had agreed to pay *Nangsao* Čhan for her own support. Apparently he had not defaulted upon any payment for support of the baby born to *Nangsao* Čhan.

Čhan. Nevertheless, the significant fact about this case is that the minor wife—and her mother—were successful in enforcing their claims against a man who was a rather prestigious and influential local official. Moreover, at the time of their lawsuit *Nai* Insom no longer lived in their district at all. Under normal circumstances, his transfer out of their community would have been enough to discourage any claims against him. In short, the legally binding contract, enforceable in the provincial court, proved superior to the traditional factors of official status and geographical distance in vesting the minor wife with rights she had all but lost under the modern legal regime. The universality of the court's jurisdiction, and the socially equalizing effect of an enforceable contract, gave *Nang* Phǫn and *Nangsao* Čhan a unique claim against *Nai* Insom, a claim that he was unable to oppose in the Chiangmai court.

The relationships between men and women are affected in various and sometimes contradictory ways by the modern laws of Thailand. Women such as *Nangsao* Čhan and *Nang* Phon may find that, even when one area of the law is unfavorable to their interests, another legal concept such as the enforceability of contracts can be invoked to provide them with real leverage over their adversary. Modern Thai law has given and taken away power on both sides in its adjustment of the relationship between the sexes. The resulting distribution of legal authority would seem at present to provide the greatest benefits for those persons who tend to think in terms of antenuptial agreements, contractual arrangements for support, and litigation in the courts of law. For these people, even when their claims are not recognized by local mediators, the provincial court will usually offer a forum for productive negotiations. Such persons, however, are not often found or admired in Thai society, particularly when the parties involved are lovers or husband and wife.

Under Section 28 of the 1974 Constitution, a radical change was promised in the legal relationships between the sexes at all social levels. This change would have placed men and women on a far more equal plane under the law and in society generally, granting new substantive rights at the same time that it established some women in positions of local political power and leadership. While this guarantee of equal rights would not have resolved problems such as the dilemma of the illegal minor wife and her children, it would have removed many significant legal disabilities now imposed upon women and would have eliminated the need for pre-existing contractual agreements to secure certain important rights. Although these new rights were strange to local mediators, they could have been reinforced by the courts and by the women who would then be situated in positions of authority in provincial Thailand. The abolition of the 1974 Constitution could thus hinder the movement toward legal equality for men and women and return this area of the law to the kind of accommodation between code and custom that has evolved since the enactment in 1935 of

Book V of the Thai Civil and Commercial Code. It remains to be seen whether the forces that promoted Section 28 of the 1974 Constitution will be able to win renewed support for their cause from the government and the public in the more conservative climate following the military coup d'etat of 1976.

Chapter Twelve
Private Citizens and Public Officials

Disputes between private citizens and public officials constitute a third area of legal conflict that is, because of its subject matter, inherently resistant to mediation at the local level. Public officials generally have considerable status and power in the local community. This fact tends to deter victims of their wrongful acts from seeking or obtaining satisfaction through traditional procedures. The provincial court is often the only forum where the complainants can realistically hope to proceed. They must translate their grievances into the language of the legal codes and use the leverage which the law provides in order to negotiate for remedies they consider appropriate. The disputes may arrive in the court under many formal headings: official malfeasance, bodily injury, murder, trespass, defamation, indecent sexual behavior, misuse of the judicial process, or wrongful acts. The underlying issue, however, is usually the same: power, its allocation and its proper use. Such suits are not always successful, but in a significant number of cases the complainants will emerge either with a favorable judgment or with a compromise agreement that provides them at least part of the satisfaction they seek. In these cases the court constitutes a crossover point that facilitates negotiations between socially distant disputants. More important, however, the court acts as a forum that reallocates social power in a relationship traditionally weighted overwhelmingly in favor of the public official.

Government officials and private citizens, the latter group including both farmers and merchants, occupy different worlds in Thai society, governed by different aspirations and different norms of social behavior. Yet these three worlds are in constant contact with one another. Although peaceful coexistence is the rule, interaction inevitably leads to conflict, and the conflicts sometimes become lawsuits. The courts are then required to mediate and to resolve the disparate sets of norms brought to such conflicts by each of the participants. In this chapter, I propose first to sketch briefly the nature of the interaction between public officials and private citizens, with primary emphasis upon the role played by code and statute in the competition for resources and power. In the second section of this chapter, I shall then focus upon the formal litigation of private wrongs, giving particular attention to cases brought by Thai villagers, who have usually been portrayed as unwilling to challenge the authority and prestige of government officials.

GOVERNMENT AGENTS AND THE PUBLIC

With improved communication and transportation systems, with the increased power and mobility of governmental agencies, with technological development and the expansion of a cash-based economy, the outside world has increasingly impinged upon the traditional Thai village setting. Villagers have felt the influence and the power both of merchants and of government officials. Most observers agree that this process has changed village life throughout Thailand, especially since the Second World War. These changes, particularly as they relate to the legal issues that are the subject of this study, can be viewed in two ways. On the one hand, there have been some dramatic discontinuities in traditional rural life, such as the intrusion of governmental regulations and personnel into the villages and the rise of impersonal contractual relationships among villagers in their commercial dealings with one another and with outsiders. On the other hand, we see at the village level a contrary pattern equally typical of Thai society: a tough and individualistic response to these external influences, an adaptation of foreign forms for traditional ends, a strong assertion of cultural continuities in the face of social change. In the materials that follow, it may be possible to discern some of the continuities and the discontinuities that have marked the evolution of rural Thai society during the modern period.

The line between villager and government official has always been sharply drawn. The northern farmers studied by Moerman spoke in terms of "people who work" and "people who eat monthly money." There was no overlap, no gray area between these two groups:

> All villagers think of themselves as farmers; no officials, not even the lowest clerk or the poorest teacher, ever do farm work. While villagers may envy officials their leisure, they also pride themselves on being "men who work." (1968:10-11)

The villagers usually respect the status of the government officials, but are fearful of their power and sometimes skeptical of the various programs and regulations that the officials attempt to bring to the villages. Dealings with government officials tend to be uncomfortable for the villagers, best avoided if possible or handled through some capable go-between. If the villager has no personal contacts within the bureaucracy, he or she will often seek the intervention of the village chief or the *kamnan*. Even these local leaders, however, are government officials in a sense, and occasionally they must act as spokesmen for the laws and regulations of the central government rather than traditional village practices.

Many of the local leaders, as we have seen, become skilled at manipulating official regulations for the advantage of their villagers. Even when they act in this way, however, they foster certain basic changes in the village. Whether the attitude is one of compliance or avoidance, there is an implicit admission that the legal categories created by the central government now occupy the field, that the modern regulations and certification procedures have diminished the authority of the traditional practices that controlled village society over the centuries. Formerly, for example, registration of marriage, birth, death, divorce, property ownership, and other vital statistics, was performed by the ritual notification of the household or village spirits.[1] In modern times, when the government becomes involved with such matters, the ritual notification of spirits is given no formal status and only the official registration procedures are considered authoritative. One result of increased contact between village society and the national administrative system, therefore, has been that "secular power as vested in both the local village leaders and in government officials has increased at the expense of power believed to be vested in various spirits" (Keyes, 1975:205).

What has taken place, however, has not been merely a shift in the location of power, from village spirits to governmental officials. There has also been an important change in the substantive rules that the new authority figures seek to enforce. Many hitherto innocent and uncontroversial patterns of behavior among the villagers have become the objects of governmental proscription and intervention. The police and the provincial courts arrest and convict hundreds of villagers each year for crimes such as gambling, marijuana and opium violations, the production of illegal alcoholic beverages, and forestry violations, all of which involve customary practices that are now unlawful. This is not to say that the villagers are unaware of the laws they are accused of violating. Indeed, they are so well aware of certain laws that they can use them shrewdly to get an enemy in trouble with the authorities—by hiding homemade liquor on his property, for example, and then seeing that the police are informed so they can make an arrest (Klausner, 1974:49). Playing cards for money or taking a chance on an informal lottery game are universally popular activities in Thailand, yet both are forbidden by law, together with dozens of other forms of gambling found throughout Thailand (see Royal Edict Concerning Gambling, 1935).

The rationality of the "rationalized" legal system that brings such prohibitions to village society may escape local people. They do not see the total logic of the Thai legal system but only the specific rules that affect them and

---

1. Certain types of information useful in the control of provincial manpower, however, have for centuries been the subject of governmental registration requirements. See Akin Rabibhadana (1969:20-25).

often contradict their own customary practices. It is not only a social difference between villagers and officials, a matter of class or of regional background, but a difference in the fundamental normative systems that the two groups obey. The language of the law is to a large extent the language of the officials, and the categories of the law may shortchange the villagers in the distribution of social power. At the same time, however, the legal codes give certain advantages to village people in their dealings with government officials, and, as we shall see, villagers sometimes exploit these advantages with dramatic effect.

The relations between government officials and a second set of private citizens—the merchants—are also characterized by a conflicting set of behavioral norms and by competing material ambitions that can place the two groups in an adversary relationship. In recent years, proliferating governmental regulations have subjected commercial activities in Thailand to frequent intervention by state officials. The reality of this intervention is apparent in the numerous convictions for such criminal offenses as illegal slaughter and distribution of livestock, violations concerning workshops, and violations involving building regulations, and also in the multitude of statutes that regulate interest rates, tariffs, the sale of drugs, the inspection of weights and measures, the manufacture and sale of tobacco, the sale of rice, and many other commercial activities. Government officials with their discretionary power to enforce such laws and merchants with their cash resources exist in an uneasy state of symbiosis. The successful merchant may seek when necessary to use his status and wealth to make the law work in his favor. The official, on the other hand, may use his legal powers to increase his own resources at the expense of those he regulates. It is true that officials are "people who eat monthly money," but the diet is often a lean one and is sometimes supplemented by snacks between meals. The competition for financial resources and for legal power makes this relationship volatile, despite the state of mutual dependency in which both groups exist. Add to this the fact that the entrepreneurial class is composed largely of ethnic Chinese and South Asians (Indians and Pakistanis) while the government officials are largely ethnic Thais, and the potential for misunderstanding and conflict becomes even greater.

The interaction between public officials on the one hand and merchants and farmers on the other can thus result in considerable stress. With the rapid social changes of recent years, there has been a continual shift and flux in the respective wealth, power, and value systems of these competing groups. In addition, social and legal changes have brought the groups into closer daily contact, thereby multiplying the opportunities for conflict. Sometimes conflict erupts in the form of accusations by private citizens that government officials have misused their power. The nature of these charges and the manner in which the provincial court hears and resolves them will be the subject of the second section of this chapter.

PRIVATE WRONGS BETWEEN VILLAGERS AND OFFICIALS

We have seen that most villagers will try to avoid direct contact with government officials and to conduct their lives without much concern about the formal administrative bureaucracy. We have also seen, however, that it has become increasingly difficult for villagers to do this. The national government has increased its regulation of village activities, has sent its representatives out to the local level in greater numbers, has vested the village chief and the *kamnan* with more numerous official duties, has expanded and equipped its police forces and placed them in greater contact with most villages. As a result, the average villager in modern Thailand is more likely than ever before to be confronted at some point by a relatively powerful representative of the national government. How does he or she feel about such persons and react to the authority they exert at the local level? I would suggest that the answer to this question is not as simple as has sometimes been thought. In this section I shall first present the orthodox description of village attitudes towards government officials. Then I shall suggest that there are important exceptions to this orthodoxy and that the law codes and the courts can provide the means for villagers to raise unexpected and important challenges to governmental authority.

A former governor of Chiangmai, respected for his scholarship as well as his administrative abilities, has written in the following terms of village attitudes towards government officials:

> Since the people believe that the king and his government are good and superior, government officials who are the king's representatives are also believed to be good and superior.... [B]y accepting the fact that government bureaucrats are superior to them, the people accept their subordinate position without regret, resentment, or frustration. Above all, they accept entirely the authority of government officials without questioning their actions concerning efficiency and responsibility in the official performance of public affairs. (Arsa Meksawan, 1962:29-30)

This description, although written by a government official, represents the generally accepted view of villager deference towards persons of status and persons who act as agents of the royal will (*kharatchakan*, the Thai term for government official, means literally servant or slave of the king's affairs). It finds support, for example, in the empirical psychological data gathered by an American anthropologist working in the central Thai village of Bang Chan. Herbert Phillips found that the villagers were strongly disinclined to raise direct challenges to persons in positions of authority, even when those persons were obviously in the wrong:

> The data clearly confirm the generally recognized willingness of villagers to respond positively and undefiantly to authority figures. Their response is accompanied by feelings of esteem, admiration, and often

diffidence toward the authority figure. However, their behavioral and emotional responses toward the authority are not absolute: when the authority is wrong they are most likely to ignore him. They do this, however, without in any way challenging the prerogatives of his authority or pointing to his error. Their structuring of the situation indicates that they are more interested in avoiding the error, and the blame that might be associated with it, than in taking issue with him. At the same time, a large minority are willing to implement the error in order to conform to his authority demands. (Phillips, 1965:155)

Phillips goes on to speak of the "benevolent, nurturing" role that the authority figure is expected to play with regard to the ordinary villager. This sort of paternalistic bond has also been described by Moerman in his discussion of the relationship between government officials and the villagers whom they regulate:

Ideally, the official should care for the peasant as a parent cares for his child. Everyone in Chiengkham agrees that the official is wiser, wealthier, and more powerful than the villager, whom it is thus his duty to guide and protect. (Moerman, 1969b:154-55)

Despite the common perception that villagers admire government officials, that they defer to them and look to them as a source of benevolent protection, I found in my research a persistent countervailing sentiment in the village society of Chiangmai. Each year some 20 or 30 lawsuits for private wrongs, under a wide variety of headings, were brought by villagers against government officials. Despite their relatively small numbers, these lawsuits were remarkable in several respects. First, they belied any sweeping assertion that *all* villagers would always avoid direct and hostile challenges to the actions of government officials. Second, they raised the question why these particular villagers would desire or dare to sue powerful officials who could easily retaliate against them. Merely asking this question makes us aware that fear as well as admiration may contribute to the deference that most villagers have traditionally accorded to government officials. Third, the suits brought against public officials suggested that the courts of law have the latent potential to act as social equalizers, to place officials and villagers on an approximately equal footing, to provide villagers with leverage against the officials who control them, and to stimulate negotiations between the two groups when conflicts arise. If the courts can in fact perform this crucial function, then we may find them increasingly perceived by villagers as a forum in which their grievances may be articulated and their new array of legal rights vindicated.

The police are most frequently the subjects of lawsuits for private wrongs brought by villagers against government officials.[2] They sometimes are accused

---

2. In a 1975 newspaper interview, official wrongdoing by police was cited as a major cause of social unrest by Dr. Puey Ungpakorn, a respected Thai statesman and scholar:

in the Chiangmai court of misusing their powers of inspection, investigation, and arrest in order to pressure their victims into making illegal payments. One case involving this kind of unlawful procedure provides a detailed account of the manner in which defendant policemen allegedly forced the plaintiff to pay a total of 2,000 *baht* (approximately $100) in order to avoid prosecution for illegal lottery activities. Plaintiff's account in this case, although uncorroborated, is worth presenting here to exemplify a type of accusation occasionally brought against policemen in the Chiangmai court.[3] Plaintiff and his friend, after their arrest, were being taken to the police station on police motorcycles when the group came to a stop along the roadside. The suspects were then told that all charges would be dropped if they paid 3,000 *baht* to the police. Plaintiff offered to pay only 1,000 *baht,* but this was refused on the grounds that it would be insufficient for the six or seven policemen who had to share it. A second offer of 1,500 *baht* was likewise rejected, and the group went on to the station. Rather than entering the police station itself, they were led to the nearby house of a police lieutenant. One of their group went inside to talk with the lieutenant, and then they were all ushered in. Plaintiff explained to the lieutenant that he was willing to pay as much as 1,500 *baht*, but that the arresting officers still demanded 3,000 *baht*. He said that he lived far away and did not know where he could find such a sum of money. The police lieutenant responded, "If you don't have the money, you will have to go to the station to be booked. It is already late." Plaintiff became frightened and offered 2,000 *baht*. The lieutenant told him to ask the other officers. Plaintiff asked them if they would agree to accept 2,000 *baht*. They decided that they could be satisfied with that amount. Plaintiff explained that he would have to go and try to persuade his boss to provide him with the necessary funds. The lieutenant ordered a police private to accompany him, warning plaintiff that if he did not return with the money that same day, he would be booked on the original charges.

Later that night, plaintiff returned with 1,300 *baht*. His boss had advised him that this amount would be sufficient, since the police had already confiscated 828.25 *baht* belonging to the illegal lottery operation and could apply that sum towards the 2,000 *baht* they had demanded. The police lieutenant did not agree to this, however, saying that the money that had been confiscated was the property of the state and must be sent to the central offices. Plaintiff was ordered to bring another 700 *baht*. Because it was rather late at night, the police officials were persuaded to postpone the final payment until

---

There has been considerable lawlessness on the part of officials, the killing of people without authority, without the processes of law, atrocities committed, suspicion cast on so many people, dividing the nation against itself. Therefore the Police Department will have to be shaken up, and the police better paid. I have always advocated this. (*The Nation,* April 26, 1975).

3. I have already mentioned this particular case in a different context in chapter 5, page 74, above.

the following morning. Plaintiff returned again to his boss's home where he spent the night and obtained the additional 700 *baht*. The next morning, around 8:00, plaintiff presented the final 700 *baht* to one of the officers who had arrested him. All charges were dropped and plaintiff was allowed to go on his way. The only reason the case ever came to court was that plaintiff sought to recover compensation by suing the entire group of police officials for malfeasance and fraud. His private criminal action resulted in an unspecified out-of-court settlement.

Allegations of police corruption can take many different forms. A number of cases charged the police with abuses arising from their duties as inspectors at highway checkpoints. The defendants in these cases were police officers who accused truck drivers of transporting illegal lumber products, stolen charcoal, even illicit opium. They would allegedly seize the goods and demand the payment of a sum of money, threatening otherwise to arrest and imprison the victim. In most cases, according to the lawsuits later brought against the police, the items seized were perfectly innocent and lawfully obtained. The police, however, were in a position to manipulate the facts and force their victims to pay them the money they demanded. Most of these lawsuits for malfeasance by checkpoint inspectors were promptly settled out of court.

Another common complaint was that the police would stop an automobile driver for one reason or another and then retain his driver's license. In order to get his license back, the driver would have to go to the police station, locate the officer, and pay him an illegal fee. This procedure backfired in one instance when a young police sub-lieutenant in Chiangmai unwittingly confiscated the license of a retired police lieutenant-colonel. The senior officer was angered by the affront to his status and dignity. He promptly sued the arresting officer for official malfeasance, methodically listing the police regulations that the sub-lieutenant, through his unlawful and coercive acts, had allegedly violated. Such insulting behavior towards a high-ranking superior officer, even a retired one, could well be grounds for demotion and reassignment. In this instance, however, the lieutenant-colonel appears to have been appeased. The sub-lieutenant must have made a satisfactory apology to the retired lieutenant-colonel, for the suit was dropped in less than a month, even before a preliminary hearing could be held.

The assignment of police officers to outlying highways and to village fairs and other functions has brought them into frequent contact with villagers who previously saw little of such officials. Friction has sometimes resulted from these increased contacts. The checkpoint cases provide one example of how such friction can lead to formal litigation, and, on occasion, to the vindication of claims presented by villagers against police officials. Another example is provided by a pair of lawsuits brought by several village teen-agers against a group of police officers assigned to supervise a village fair in their neighborhood. In the first case, the 18-year-old son of a former village school headmaster sued five police officers for bodily injury, offenses against liberty, and malfeasance by a government official. *Nai* Bunmi accused the police of dragging him down from a dance stage at the fair, kicking and beating him, handcuffing his hands behind his back, slapping him, throwing him on the stairs of the dance stage so that he hit his head, and then forming a circle around him, threatening onlookers with their guns, and beating and kicking him until he lost consciousness. They took *Nai* Bunmi unconscious to the police station but lodged no charges there and allowed him to be carried home. *Nai* Bunmi made clear his intention to file a complaint against the men who had allegedly beaten him. He and his intermediaries contacted the policemen's superiors and later *Nai* Bunmi went to the police station with his lawyer. The police lieutenant who was duty officer at the district police station asked how much *"kha tham khwan"* (payment to propitiate the *khwan*-soul) *Nai* Bunmi would like. *Nai* Bunmi demanded 5,000 *baht* (about $250) from each of the five policemen who participated in the alleged beating. Otherwise, he added, he intended to bring a lawsuit against them. As negotiations were pending, the principle defendant allegedly approached *Nai* Bunmi's aunt and uncle, threatening them with serious consequences if they did not dissuade *Nai* Bunmi from pressing his case.

Negotiations failed and the case finally came to the Chiangmai court. Defendants denied that they had beaten *Nai* Bunmi and alleged that he had been drunk and had acted in an offensive manner towards some of the women on the dance stage. His actions, they claimed, had angered a group of onlookers, and when *Nai* Bunmi jumped down from the dance stage a fight had broken out. One of the policemen had intervened at that point, leading *Nai* Bunmi away from the melee. He testified that he had arrested *Nai* Bunmi in an extraordinarily gracious manner: "You are very drunk. May I invite you to go to the police station?" He denied beating *Nai* Bunmi, although he claimed that the latter had struggled violently while being detained. *Nai* Bunmi, on the other hand, testified that he had not been drunk at all and in fact had been unconscious from the beating during most of the time that he was under arrest. Plaintiff's story was corroborated by some soldiers who were also on duty at the fair. They testified that the police had indeed beaten *Nai* Bunmi. Defendants called as witnesses an assistant village chief and several residents of the village in which the fair was held, but their testimony as to the alleged beating was inconclusive.

No settlement was reached in court, and the judge himself rendered a verdict favorable to *Nai* Bunmi on the count of bodily injury. Three of the policemen were sentenced to six months in prison, while the remaining two were given suspended sentences of three months each. The judge was impressed primarily with two factors that he considered favorable to *Nai* Bunmi. The first was that plaintiff's version of the facts was supported by the disinterested testimony of the soldiers, whereas defendants' version was self-serving and uncorroborated by any neutral witness. The second factor was that plaintiff and several of plaintiff's witnesses were villagers living under the jurisdiction of defendants and their fellow police officers. The court found that it would be most unusual for villagers to bring false allegations against government officials with such status and power. Despite the fact that *Nai* Bunmi had sought an informal settlement at the police station, this did not tend to prove that he had invented the entire incident to extort money from defendants, "because it is impossible to believe that an ordinary citizen would fabricate a criminal case against five defendants, who are policemen assigned to his own locale, solely to force them to pay money to him." Moreover, the court found, if defendants were truly innocent of *Nai* Bunmi's accusations, they would have been angered by his lies and would have sued him for lodging false charges against a government official. Neither the defendants nor the police inquiry officer ever brought such a suit, however, and this fact made *Nai* Bunmi's case all the more credible.

One year after this verdict was rendered, while the case was still pending before the Appeals Court in Bangkok, the same police officer who was the principal defendant in *Nai* Bunmi's suit became involved in another incident with a fellow villager of *Nai* Bunmi whom I shall call *Nai* Chai. When *Nai* Chai went to an outdoor movie that was playing in a schoolyard, he encountered this policeman searching all persons who entered through the schoolyard gate. The officer patted down *Nai* Chai, and then allegedly struck him hard in the stomach. When *Nai* Chai protested, the policeman became angry and slapped him. Then he asked *Nai* Chai where he came from. *Nai* Chai told him the name of the village, which the policeman recognized immediately as the home of his former antagonist, *Nai* Bunmi. He uttered more obscenities and had his partner strike *Nai* Chai on the back of the neck. *Nai* Chai ran away and immediately went to notify the police at the district station house. He then returned with his father and his friend to retrieve a bicycle that he had left at the school. The policeman saw him there and asked where he had been. *Nai* Chai's father replied that they had just lodged an official complaint at the police station. The officer thanked them sarcastically, and then told them he would have to seize *Nai* Chai's bicycle because the license had expired. At the same time he announced in front of the onlookers that the residents of *Nai* Chai's village were cunning indeed, and that they must be fought until one side or the other was totally destroyed.

When *Nai* Chai's lawsuit for bodily injury and official malfeasance reached the Chiangmai court, defendant's fighting spirit seems to have left him. Probably because of his prior conviction on a similar charge, he was more inclined to compromise than to try to vindicate himself. The court played the role of mediator, and the parties reached a settlement shortly after the preliminary hearing had been held.[4] Ironically, only four months after this settlement was reached, the Appeals Court reversed the policeman's conviction in the suit brought against him by *Nai* Bunmi. The appellate court relied entirely on its own interpretation of the facts, giving particular emphasis to the testimony of the assistant village chief which was favorable to defendants with regard to *Nai* Bunmi's alleged misconduct on the dance stage. The Appeals Court discounted the testimony of the soldiers in support of *Nai* Bunmi's story, because one of them testified that defendants had "punched" *Nai* Bunmi, a term never used by *Nai* Bunmi himself. Finally, the Appeals Court ignored the most interesting point in the trial court's decision: the holding that plaintiff's story was inherently credible because he was a mere villager, subject to the power and influence of the five government officials he had accused of criminal wrongdoing. The Supreme Court of Thailand, after a similar scrutiny of the factual findings of the trial court, affirmed the decision of the Appeals Court and found defendants innocent of all charges.

These two cases are, I think, interesting and rather significant. The readiness of the villagers to challenge these police officers in court is indeed surprising. The fact that the plaintiff's attorney in both suits was a man distantly related by marriage to *Nai* Bunmi may have increased the complainants' awareness of the provincial court as a viable option for them in their struggle with the police officials. Nevertheless, the decision to sue was a dramatic and a potentially dangerous one for the plaintiffs in both cases. The trial judge explicitly recognized this fact, and he considered it an element in support of plaintiff's case. The conviction that he rendered gave the villager, *Nai* Bunmi, a share of the legal power that he sought to obtain in his conflict with the police. It also set the stage for the second suit, brought by *Nai* Chai, in which the same defendant was apparently induced to settle without resisting the charges brought against him. The later reversal on appeal, based upon a different interpretation of the testimony at trial, did not touch upon the interesting issue of the inherent credibility of lawsuits brought by villagers against powerful government officials. The judge in the suit brought against a deputy district officer by a village woman for sexual misconduct, it may be recalled, had also raised this issue in his decision for the plaintiff.[5] If the provincial courts indeed recognize the dangers risked by villagers who sue public officials, and if they give evidentiary weight to this particular factor,

---

4. Since no record is provided for settlements of most private criminal suits, it is always possible that *Nai* Chai withdrew his suit as the result of threats by the defendant, or for some other reason, rather than as the result of an agreement by the defendant to pay compensation. I have assumed that this was not the case here, while acknowledging that the possibility exists, because similar threats were allegedly made in *Nai* Bunmi's case without any such result, and because *Nai* Chai knew of these threats even before he brought his suit. If they did not deter him in the early stages of litigation, it seems unlikely that they would deter him after a preliminary hearing had already been held.

5. See chapter 11, page 181.

Private Wrongs between Villagers and Officials

then the courts may encourage villagers to brave such risks and call government officials to account more often for their wrongful acts. If, on the other hand, the courts give greater credence to the testimony of government officials, because of their status as public servants and their duty to protect the interests of the state and the king, then villagers would remain strongly disinclined to challenge officials in court, even when they believe them to be guilty of serious wrongful actions.

I have tried to show elsewhere in this study that government officials other than the police sometimes appear as defendants in actions for private wrongs. In the preceding chapter, for example, we saw two lawsuits directed against deputy district officers by women whom they had allegedly mistreated. Government officials of all ranks have in fact appeared from time to time in the Chiangmai court to defend themselves against charges of private wrongs brought by villagers. Most commonly, however, the defendants in such actions, if not police officers, are village chiefs or *kamnan*—the administrative officers closest to the ordinary lives of the villagers. The village chief and the *kamnan* also have the duty to apprehend and discipline criminal offenders, a duty that inevitably involves them in situations of conflict with other villagers. These community leaders are thus involved frequently in local disputes, both as would-be mediators and as participants. Despite their prestige and status at the village level, their involvement in situations of conflict can result in accusations of wrongful acts. Such accusations may lead to mediation, often conducted by their administrative superiors; yet many cases prove impossible to mediate for lack of a mutually acceptable go-between. In those cases, the village chief and the *kamnan* may appear like other government officials as defendants in lawsuits brought by villagers in the provincial court. The court is then required to adjust relationships at the village level itself, between individual villagers and their elected representatives.

In the final portion of this chapter, I shall describe two private criminal suits brought by villagers against their own village leaders. In both cases, the local leaders were accused of acting together with the police to betray the interests of their villagers for their own personal gain. The dual role of the village chief and the *kamnan*—part villager and part government official—became a liability for the defendants; they came to be seen more as "them" than as "us." The alleged abuse of their official powers violated their implicit duty to protect and nurture their villagers. The villagers felt that it was necessary to seek a remedy from the court of law, where official standards of conduct could be officially enforced.

Late in March 1968, a group of villagers far from the city of Chiangmai came upon a wonderful find. As they were out gathering vegetables in the forest, they found a river full of fish floating lifeless on the surface of the water. The group of 36 villagers joined others already on the scene, plunging into the river and scooping out great numbers of fish with baskets and with their bare hands. Soon there were huge piles of fish on the river bank, weighing altogether some 1,000 kilos. The 36 villagers agreed to help one another transport the fish back to the village where they planned to divide them equally among themselves. They loaded the fish on bicycles, motorcycles, and minibuses and rushed them down the road to a central gathering spot in the village. There they began to sort the fish into 36 separate piles according to size and number. How had these fish come to give their lives for the benefit of the villagers? The village chief and the police, who were soon at the scene, concluded immediately that the fish had been poisoned, in violation of Thai law. The villagers would say only that they did not know how the fish had died, that they themselves had not poisoned them but had innocently found them floating in the river.

The events that followed would later form the basis of a lawsuit by four of the villagers and a countersuit for false prosecution by the ranking police officer. The villagers alleged that their own village chief had joined with the police in threatening to arrest the villagers for poisoning the fish. The four officials had then confiscated the fish, supposedly pursuant to a criminal investigation. They drove off with the entire catch in a truck and had the fish sold the next day in the market, dividing the profits among the four of them. The total value of the fish was estimated by the villagers at 9,400 *baht* (approximately $470). No formal police investigation into the alleged poisoning ever took place. The villagers were outraged and their representative promptly went to consult an attorney. In the meantime, it became known that the village chief had taken his share of the profits and donated 1,605 *baht* to the local temple. This conspicuous form of merit-making was apparently designed by the headman to blunt public criticism, to remind the villagers of his virtue and his piety, and to cleanse any guilt that might have attached itself to him.

The village chief and the police presented a very different version of the same events. They maintained that, when the officials had asked the villagers whether or not the fish had been poisoned, their leader had replied that they did not know. None of them had used poison, but in any case they had merely collected the fish in order to sell them and donate the money to the local temple. At that point, all the villagers had shouted their pleasure and approval of this proposal for community merit-making. A truck was obtained and the fish were taken to a local fish seller. It is true that the officials had ridden away in the truck, but that was only so that they could hitch a ride back to the police station. They had had nothing at all to do with the fish once they left the village. The village chief had carefully recorded the weight of the fish, and the sale brought a total profit of 1,605 *baht*, all of which had been donated to the temple according to the decision of the villagers.

The final result of the litigation in this dispute was concealed by the participants. We know only that the suit and countersuit were both withdrawn on the same day, after the court found that a *prima facie* case existed on each side. Villagers and officials announced simply that they had reached a satisfactory agreement and they wished to bring an end to the litigation. One suspects that the officials made some kind of an offer to the villagers. They had more to lose than the villagers, because their official positions had been placed in jeopardy by the litigation; and it seems unlikely that the villagers, daring to carry their grievance to the provincial court, would abandon it at that point without achieving any of their goals. In any case, the situation was an interesting one. The villagers had participated in an exhilarating group activity, but their excitement had been chilled by an encounter with government officials including their own village chief. The officials exerted pressure on the villagers by means of their formal law-enforcement powers and by reference to statutory prohibitions against fishing with poison. The villagers retaliated by their own resort to the law, challenging the propriety of the allegedly official acts and citing the Thai Penal Code with its provisions prohibiting the use of official position to extort money from private citizens.[6] To obtain leverage over their adversaries, the villagers took their complaint to the provincial court. The assertion of official power at the local level was countered by an assertion of legal power at the judicial level, and negotiations were apparently initiated between the two groups in the provincial court that would not otherwise have occurred in the village setting.

The preceding case pitted a group of villagers against four officials who were accused of extortion and malfeasance in office, crimes detrimental to the village as a whole. In the final case of this chapter, one woman—a 60-year-old farmer—challenged her own *kamnan*, assistant *kamnan*, and three police officers, accusing them of murdering her 36-year-old son. *Nang* Nian's son, *Nai* Soei, had formerly held the position of village chief in the village where they lived. Two years before his death he had resigned. None of the disputants indicated that there had been any quarrel or hard feelings associated with his resignation, but it is possible that some resentment existed between *Nai* Soei and the local village leadership and that this resentment was somehow associated with his death and with the events that followed.

The testimony of *Nang* Nian and her witnesses showed that *Nai* Soei had left his house alone at six in the evening in search of two stray cattle. He

---

6. "Section 157. Whoever, being an official, wrongfully exercises or omits to exercise any of his functions to the injury of any person, or dishonestly exercises or omits to exercise any of his functions, shall be punished with imprisonment of one to ten years or fine of two thousand to twenty thousand *baht*, or both.

"Section 337. Whoever compels any person to give or promise to give him or any other person any pecuniary benefit by committing any act of violence or threatening to cause injury to life, body, liberty, reputation or property of the compelled person or of a third person, and thereby causes the person so compelled to submit to such compulsion, is said to commit extortion, and shall be punished with imprisonment not exceeding five years and fine not exceeding ten thousand *baht*. . ." (Thai Penal Code).

carried with him only an ax, a blanket, and a sash or loin cloth (*pha khao ma*). *Nang* Nian's neighbor, *Nai* Bunchu, came to her house at seven that evening to tell her that he had encountered *Nai* Soei in the woods on the way home from collecting mushrooms. He had seen *Nai* Soei in the custody of the five defendants, who were leading him in handcuffs under armed guard towards the police station some 20 kilometers away. At midnight, *Nang* Nian heard more than ten loud gunshots coming from the woods in the direction of the police station. She assumed at the time that villagers were merely hunting in the woods. The next morning, another neighbor prepared food and clothing for *Nai* Soei and left to visit him at the police station. At seven that same morning, the neighbor returned to *Nang* Nian's house and told her that *Nai* Soei had been shot to death and that two of the police officers were guarding the body, which lay across a path in the middle of the forest. The officers kept the small group of onlookers at a distance from the body. They could see only the bloody gunshot wounds and the ax still tucked into the back of his pants. The neighbor asked the officers why they had arrested and shot *Nai* Soei like a dog or a pig. They replied that he should return home or he himself would be shot. *Nai* Soei's body was buried by defendants in the forest where he was shot. It was never turned over to his relatives for the customary funeral rites. *Nang* Nian learned later, from newspapers and from the official post mortem inquest, that *Nai* Soei's death had been caused by the five defendants. Declining to bring the case through the police and public prosecutor, *Nang* Nian filed a private criminal suit for murder in the Chiangmai court.

Defendants at trial presented a rather different version of the facts. They claimed that the three police officers had been called to the area by a report that three missing water buffalo had been taken toward the village where plaintiff lived. The officers enlisted the help of the *kamnan* and his assistant and began to search for the buffalo. Late in the afternoon they learned from a villager that the buffalo had been recovered by their owner. After dinner they all began the trip back to the police station. At about two in the morning, as they reached the top of a hill, they saw four people coming toward them on the path, leading a bull. One of the defendants announced that they were police and ordered the four to stop. Immediately the officials were fired upon, and they ran for cover. When the four strangers continued to shoot at them, they returned the fire for three or four minutes until there was silence on the other side. They went to look and found one man lying dead, a home-made handgun near his body and a bull standing some 20 yards away. The other strangers had all escaped. Three defendants remained with the body, while the other two took the bull to the *kamnan*'s house and then reported the incident to the police chief. A medical official inspected the body, which witnesses had identified as that of *Nai* Soei. The body was then turned over to the *kamnan* and the village chief of *Nang* Nian's village. The bull was claimed by the resident of a neighboring village, who reported that it had been missing since the day of the incident.

The case is one of the most problematic I encountered in my research. Both versions raise serious questions that were never answered in the course of the trial. Why had five officials spent the better part of a day searching for three missing water buffalo, a vastly disproportionate response by the police to a rather mundane occurrence? What evidence was there to link *Nai* Soei to the disappearance of the bull he supposedly led through the forest, and who were his three alleged accomplices? What was the origin of the weapons they had supposedly used to fire on the officials? Most suspicious of all, why had *Nai* Soei been buried in the forest by the defendants instead of being returned to his family? *Nang* Nian's version also presented certain difficulties, however. Above all, what motive had the defendants to shoot *Nai* Soei? The police officers scarcely knew him, and *Nang* Nian produced no evidence of bad feeling between *Nai* Soei and the *kamnan*. She makes a very strong case of official wrongdoing and violence against her son, the former village chief, except that we have no idea why such a killing would take place.

Feelings apparently ran too high during the trial to permit any compromise between the adversaries, and finally the judge rendered a carefully crafted opinion exonerating the five defendants. The court stated that the crucial question was whether or not defendants had arrested *Nai* Soei and were in fact taking him through the forest to the police station. In support of this contention, plaintiff had only one witness, *Nai* Bunchu. He testified that he had passed *Nai* Soei on the forest path, led in handcuffs by the defendants. He had not spoken to *Nai* Soei to ask where he was going or why he had been arrested. The court also noted that *Nai* Bunchu was an opium addict with a history of arrests for possession and addiction. His personal appearance was thin and pale, typical of an addict who might testify to anything in return for money. For this reason, the court did not attach great weight to the testimony of *Nai* Bunchu. Moreover, *Nai* Bunchu had testified that, after meeting *Nai* Soei in the forest, he had taken his mushrooms home and had bathed and eaten dinner before going to tell *Nang* Nian of her son's predicament. *Nang* Nian, on the other hand, had testified that *Nai* Bunchu had come to her house still perspiring from his journey through the woods and was carrying a full bag of mushrooms with him at the time. She testified, moreover, that he had carried the mushrooms in a bag, whereas *Nai* Bunchu had testified that they were wrapped in large leaves. The court based its acquittal on factors such as these—contradictions in the testimony of plaintiff and her witnesses.

On appeal, plaintiff argued that opium addiction was common among villagers in the area and should not automatically discredit the entire testimony of plaintiff's key witness. The silence between *Nai* Soei and *Nai* Bunchu in the woods was understandable, she argued, because they were afraid of the defendants and the weapons they were carrying. As for the mushrooms and the timing of *Nai* Bunchu's bath, the one fact of overriding importance was that *Nang* Nian and *Nai* Bunchu agreed as to the time and the substance of their conversation. The Appeals Court, however, upheld the decision of the trial court in all respects, emphasizing that little weight could be given to the testimony of a convicted opium addict. The Supreme Court affirmed the verdict without comment two years after the death of *Nai* Soei.

The case is a difficult one. It is true that *Nang* Nian suggested no motive for the murder which she alleged. It is always possible, however, that a word, a glance, an imagined insult, could have sparked the killing, if some deeper rivalry was not in fact the cause. More important, *Nang* Nian herself had no apparent motive to bring a false prosecution against these five officials. Her determination in this matter was remarkable. An ordinary and rather elderly village woman dared to bring a charge of murder against five powerful and potentially dangerous local officials. Not content with the verdict rendered by the provincial court in Chiangmai, she took the case all the way to the Supreme Court of Thailand. Ultimately, the court seemed simply to have concluded that there was reasonable doubt as to the guilt of the defendants, despite the fact that *Nang* Nian's case was in many respects the more credible.[7]

The remarkable thing about this lawsuit, however, is the tenacity of the villager in her confrontation with the government officials. This case, and the others before it, sharply contradict the orthodox view that villagers "accept entirely the authority of government officials," that they respect and admire government officials by virtue of their superior status, that wrongful acts by government officials are inevitably accepted or overlooked. We have evidence in these and other lawsuits that, despite a strong cultural aversion to hostile confrontation and despite the dangers inherent in direct challenges to official authority, a significant number of villagers each year are willing to take government officials to court when they believe them to have committed wrongful acts. The courts, moreover, do not reject such challenges out of hand. Although they sometimes support the officials over the villagers, they may find merit in the villagers' claims as well, occasionally concluding that their evidence is credible simply because of the risks they must run in prosecuting such powerful opponents. Whether through judicial mediation or formal adjudication, the villagers who litigate private wrongs against government officials have sometimes found the provincial court to be a place where official rules can be enforced against governmental agents and where local figures of

---

7. "... Where any reasonable doubt exists as to whether or not the accused has committed the offense, the benefit of the doubt shall be given to him" (Criminal Procedure Code, Section 227).

status and power may be brought to terms through the provisions of the Thai legal codes.

Before the reforms of King Chulalongkorn, the ruling officials in Chiangmai were the nobility. They not only administered the province but presided over the courts of law as well. Since the establishment of the modern judicial system, the adjudicative and administrative functions have been made independent of one another, and the local nobility have been replaced by modern government bureaucrats. Nevertheless, the ordinary citizens of Chiangmai, like most Thai people, still retain strong feelings of respect for government officials because of their status, their power, and their ideal function of benevolent protection for the village people. What happens, then, when these status superiors betray their paternalistic obligations, when they act in their own self-interest to the detriment of their clients? While most villagers seem willing to ignore a certain amount of self-serving behavior among local officials, they can be angered when such behavior becomes excessive and the price that they must pay becomes too high. The status superior has then betrayed the reciprocal relationship that should bind him to his inferiors. There is an unfairness, even a kind of treachery in such behavior, and when it is accompanied by violence or insult it becomes intolerable.

The court records show that some villagers view the provincial court as a forum in which such wrongs can occasionally be righted. When the public official betrays his obligations as a person of authority, some villagers are willing to take the matter to court. They seek, in short, to shatter the traditional hierarchical bonds between themselves and the government official, to step outside the traditional world of local status hierarchies, and to enter an environment where disputes can be mediated by a representative of the state and resolved according to neutral and universal rules of law. This is not to say that the provincial judge, whether acting as a mediator or adjudicator, will inevitably disregard the status of the litigants who appear before him. In some cases, however, the judges tend to favor the villager over the public official for the very reason that the villager's inferior status makes his case against a powerful adversary inherently credible. The fact that villagers continue each year to sue public officials in the provincial court indicates that they believe the status of the official will not immunize him from liability in every instance.

At least on some occasions, then, the court is perceived by villagers as a mechanism to modify the overwhelming power of government officials in their dealings with private citizens. The symbolic importance of this redistribution of power at the local level, even in isolated and intermittent cases, could prove important in the social struggles now underway in Thailand. An awareness appears to be spreading at the village level of an alternative to the traditional system of reciprocal hierarchical relationships, an awareness cultivated in recent years by politicians, students, and farmer leaders.[8] After many years, we may be witnessing the beginning of an era in which certain nontraditional norms supported by the legal codes are filtering down to the village level, where they are seen by some villagers as a justification for challenges directed against established authorities. The lawsuits by villagers against government officials indicate that the attitude of village people is not always one of subservience, that they are willing to challenge official misbehavior or exploitation which they deem excessive, and that they perceive the national judiciary as a forum in which the rules of law can be used to give voice to their grievances. The response of the provincial courts to the competing claims of villagers and officials in Thai society will remain an important factor that could shape the course of the social and political battles still being waged in Chiangmai and in Thailand as a whole.

---

8. I am here emphasizing the use of litigation as a form of cultural discontinuity to be contrasted with the traditional system of status hierarchies and deference towards authority. This is not intended to contradict my earlier emphasis upon cultural continuities within the process of litigation itself. The interaction between the two systems of justice is clearly a process that cuts both ways at once. My point is simply that these particular challenges against official authority for the most part could not be raised *at all* in the traditional setting. They depend for their very existence upon the substantive legal norms of the modern law codes. Were it not for the law codes, most of these disputes could not be prosecuted in any forum by the complainant.

Conclusion

The transformation of Thai law during the past hundred years has been undertaken in part for symbolic purposes and in part to achieve specific practical ends. The recurring hope has been that the new laws somehow—through moral example, through governmental regulation, or through judicial enforcement—could be translated in Thai society into new patterns of behavior, new distributions of power, new systems of relationship and obligation, and new understandings of justice. In Part I of this study, I have traced the history of some of these changes and described the establishment of the modern Thai legal system and the provincial setting in which it has functioned. In Part II, I have elaborated some of the customary beliefs and procedures related to the handling of private wrongs: the undercurrent of traditional legal culture that has persisted into the modern era despite the broad-ranging legal reforms enacted by the Bangkok government. In Part III, I have described specific areas in which the traditional and the modern systems of law have interacted and reshaped one another in the Chiangmai provincial court. Finally, in Part IV, I have examined some areas in which the new legal precepts have produced changes in the traditional social order and in which the court has redistributed power and rearranged social relationships to accord with particular provisions of the modern law.

Obviously, there is no perfect "fit" between the idealized norms of the codified law and the customary norms of the society in which the Chiangmai court functions. Important divergencies appear with regard to many basic legal concepts, such as the definition of a "private wrong" and the question of how the victims of wrongful acts should respond. There are discrepancies regarding the appropriate remedy for a legal injury and the procedures by which remedies should be pursued. Code and custom also differ over questions of scope of liability and standing, over methods to determine the worthiness of contending claims and the nature of the evidence to be taken into account. Finally, there are divergencies regarding the punishment or compensation to be required and the ways in which the formal and informal systems will take cognizance of solutions obtained through rival procedures.

It is not at all surprising that such differences should exist between the indigenous legal culture and the new laws promulgated in Bangkok over the past hundred years. It seldom happens that the national law of a modern state is founded upon legal principles derived solely from the traditional norms and practices of its own people and its own society. Rather, the emergence of modern nation-states throughout the world has been marked by "the transfer of whole legal systems across cultural boundaries," resulting in a situation where "large portions of the globe are subject to laws the principles of which are drawn from a number of widely differing cultures" (Hooker, 1975:1). Thailand is not unique in its reliance upon foreign legal models that are in many ways alien to the environment in which they were established.

There exist in the lowlands of Chiangmai province two pervasive systems of justice, each founded upon a different set of concepts regarding injury and obligation, guilt and innocence, and social organization and behavior. These two systems come into frequent contact with one another, as the formal laws and regulations of the Thai government reach out to local village societies, and as customary village practices influence the formal proceedings of the provincial court. In many instances, a particular set of events or relationships comes to be ordered and understood according to both of these systems of social order and law. When lawsuits for private wrongs are brought to the Chiangmai court, the subject matter typically must flow from one system to the other, must be "translated," as it were, from one language to another before it can enter the new environment. Only after this process of translation has occurred can the law codes act upon the subject matter of the dispute. In order to articulate particular grievances in the provincial court, litigants must abandon, for example, the world of patron-client relationships for a world in which liability is premised upon the rules of principal and agent. Broad considerations of merit, status, and fate must be replaced by narrow considerations of negligence and intended harm in specific interactions between individuals.

The process of translation is marked, too, by an apparent shift from one set of goals and strategies to another. Thus, rather than forcing the wrongdoer to make merit for his victim or to help recover the lost *khwan*-soul, the plaintiff now requests the state to impose a prison sentence upon the wrongdoer or to compel him to pay a fine or to make restitution in an amount unrelated to the traditional rituals for rectifying wrongful acts. New procedures and remedies are an intrinsic part of the new environment into which the subject matter has been translated. As we have seen, however, the plaintiff typically adopts these new legal theories and objectives primarily for the sake of form. The underlying goals and perceptions of justice remain in large part traditional. In a case in which plaintiff formally requests the imprisonment of

Conclusion

defendant, for example, he will abandon his private criminal action with its implied goal of state punishment as soon as he receives traditional compensation for the injury he has suffered.

Plaintiff utilizes this strategy in order to gain leverage over the defendant, to tap new sources of power that can be exerted in the local community. The leverage exists because of the plurality of legal systems. The modern legal system in Chiangmai offers remedies for many private wrongs that would go unresolved in the traditional society, if, indeed, they were perceived as wrongful at all. The alternative legal systems thus fill in gaps and provide new procedures and solutions that are missing in either system by itself. The discrepancies between the two systems create a form of potential energy that is released by the leap from one environment to the other. The release of energy produces new distributions of power, new forms of relationship, and new perceptions of justice in the local community. This process is possible only because the two systems coexist in such close proximity.

Divergencies between the two systems of justice are thus a source of change in Chiangmai province. If there were perfect congruency between the formal laws and local customs, then we would expect to find more stability in the social order than now exists. Change would occur only in the context of a single, universally-accepted model of obligation and relationship. As it is, however, the process of translation from one system to another results in the modification of both systems by extrinsic contacts. The resulting changes should not necessarily be understood as an evolution of Thai law from one typical form to another or from one level of advancement to another—the stereotype of "modernization." Rather, it should be understood as a process of mutual adaptation in which the two distinctive systems of justice interlock and interact with one another over time. The significance lies not so much in the evolutionary changes that occur within either of the individual systems as it does in the evolution of the relationship itself.

It is the evolving relationship between two different systems of justice that produces the distinctive patterns of justice in Thailand—a situation that is not properly symbolized by the seal of Yama nor the scales of justice, but by the dynamics of interaction between the two ideal types. The interaction is marked, as we have seen, by friction, by mutual accommodation, and by the interpenetration of rival theories of law and justice, a process taking place upon a stage that is itself changing, shifting, and turning. Impetus for change in this dyadic relationship comes not only from its internal dynamics but also from external factors. The province of Chiangmai has undergone dramatic changes during the past hundred years, and these changes in turn have had an effect upon legal developments at the local level. The educational system has been transformed and centralized. Local languages and cultural traditions have begun to merge into the central Thai mainstream. The provincial economy has been transformed and linked to markets in distant parts of the country and the world. National elections and parliamentary debates have attracted the attention of a growing segment of the provincial population. Radio and television have joined remote towns and villages to the capital, as have new highways and bus, rail, and air routes. Visitors to Chiangmai from other regions and other nations have become more numerous, and natives of Chiangmai have also travelled and become familiar with foreign languages and foreign traditions.

All of these changes have influenced the evolving relationship between new and traditional concepts of justice. They have challenged the traditional world-view of villagers in Chiangmai province, they have disseminated new concepts of law and social structure, and they have increased the interaction among individuals outside of familiar village contexts, beyond the reach of village-level mechanisms for handling conflict. Changes in the provincial setting have, in these and other ways, stimulated changes in the legal culture and have made villagers more ready to step outside the traditional system of justice and to explore alternative procedures and remedies when private wrongs occur.

Changes in Thailand's political climate have also influenced the direction and pace of legal development. Among the many governments that have held power in Thailand during the past century there have been sharp differences of perspective regarding the structure and theory of political control. There have been varying degrees of emphasis placed upon egalitarian ideals, upon the rights of poor and powerless members of Thai society, upon the accountability of government officials to the citizenry, upon public debate and free elections. During the most recent experiment with parliamentary democracy from 1973 to 1976, for example, movement away from the traditional legal system was promoted by legislation granting new rights to tenant farmers, women, laborers, and others. New kinds of lawsuits began to appear in the Chiangmai court involving litigants whose relationships had formerly been regulated by informal customary practices. As the dispositions of these suits were determined by the new legal standards, the consequences were felt throughout the province. Significant new perceptions of justice were promoted by law and reinforced in some instances by judicial action.

Political trends of this kind, however, have consistently been checked by a contrary tendency towards authoritarian rule in contemporary Thailand. During periods of social upheaval, strikes, and public demonstrations, considerable sympathy is generated in support of governments that justify themselves with reference to the idealized image of a strong and righteous ruler who promotes *dharma* and ends social turmoil through the sacred use of force. When governments based upon such principles prevail in Bangkok, the political climate throughout the country is usually characterized by an emphasis upon order, obedience, and the primacy of established authority. Neither legislation nor governmental policies are then likely to encourage the evolutionary movement away from traditional concepts of justice in

Conclusion

provincial Thailand. At such times, the process of legal development at the local level is left largely to its own internal dynamics, without the added external stimuli that are present under other political conditions.

In recent years the interaction between rival theories of law and justice has become increasingly hostile and abrasive. The gulf has widened between those who would promote new systems of relationship and obligation and those who would preserve the more traditional configurations. Conflict between the contending factions in Chiangmai province has led to bitter debate, to public demonstrations and private recriminations, to violence and bloodshed. The challenge has become more difficult than ever before to harmonize the rival systems of law and to reconcile the competing perceptions of justice that are at large in the local community. The relationship between the two systems of justice has reached a crucial stage in its evolution. Whether their interaction will continue to balance and blend the various constituent elements or will lead to further confusion and disintegration depends in large part upon the flexibility, wisdom, and understanding displayed by the provincial judiciary and the national government. Their response to the demands and expectations of the people of provincial Thailand will determine the outcome of the process of legal change first set in motion by King Chulalongkorn to bring justice, progress, and unity to provincial Thailand.

Bibliography

A. Books and Articles in Thai and English*

Abel, Richard L. (1973a) "A Comparative Theory of Dispute Institutions in Society," *Law & Society Review*, 8(2): 217-347.
────── (1973b) "Why Go To Court: A Historical and Comparative Study of Patterns of Local Court Use in Kenya," unpublished working draft.
Adul Wichiencharoen and Luang Chamroon Netisastra (1968) "Some Main Features of Modernization of Ancient Family Law in Thailand," in David C. Buxbaum, ed., *Family Law and Customary Law in Asia: A Contemporary Legal Perspective*. The Hague: Martinus Nijhoff, pp. 89-106.
Akin Rabibhadana (1969) *The Organization of Thai Society in the Early Bangkok Period, 1782-1873*. Ithaca, N.Y.: Southeast Asia Program, Cornell University.
Anderson, J. N. D., ed. (1963) *Changing Law in Developing Countries*. London: George Allen & Unwin.
Anuman Rajadhon, Phraya (1950) *Rüang phrarachalančhakǫn lae tra prachăm tua prachăm tamnaeng* [Royal Thai Seals, Heraldry, and Insignia]. Bangkok: Phra Chan Press.
────── (1968) *Essays on Thai Folklore*. Bangkok: Social Science Association Press of Thailand.
Arsa Meksawan (1962) *The Role of the Provincial Governor in Thailand*. Bangkok: Institute of Public Administration, Thammasat University.
Basham, A. L. (1963) *The Wonder That Was India: A Study of the History and Culture of the Indian Sub-Continent Before the Coming of the Muslims*. New York: Hawthorne Books.
Benedict, Ruth (1952) *Thai Culture and Behavior: An Unpublished War Time Study Dated September, 1943*. Ithaca, N.Y.: Southeast Asia Program, Cornell University.
Bennett, Paul J. (1971) *Conference Under the Tamarind Tree: Three Essays in Burmese History*. New Haven, Conn.: Yale University Southeast Asia Studies.
Bowring, Sir John (1969) *The Kingdom and People of Siam* [1856]. 2 vols. London: Oxford University Press.
Brailey, Nigel J. (1973-74) "Chiengmai and the Inception of an Administrative Centralization Policy in Siam," *Southeast Asian Studies*, 11(3): 299-320; 11(4): 439-69.
Burling, Robbins (1965) *Hill Farms and Padi Fields: Life in Mainland Southeast Asia*. Englewood Cliffs, N.J.: Prentice-Hall.
Burtt, E. A., ed. (1955) *The Teachings of the Compassionate Buddha*. New York: New American Library.

*Thai authors are listed by given names; others are listed by surname.

Carter, A. Cecil (1904) *The Kingdom of Siam*. New York: G. P. Putnam's Sons, Knickerbocker Press.
Chakrit Noranitipadungkarn (1963) *Somdet phrac̆hao bǫrommawongthoe krom phrayadamrong rachanuphab kap krasuang mahatthai* [Prince Damrong Rachanupab and the Ministry of Interior]. Bangkok: Faculty of Public Administration, Thammasat University.
—— and A. Clarke Hagensick (1973) *Modernizing Chiengmai: A Study of Community Elites in Urban Development*. Bangkok: Research Center, National Institute of Development Administration.
Chitti Tingsabadh, David E. Allan, Mary E. Hiscock, Derek Roebuck (1974) *Credit and Security in Thailand: The Legal Problems of Development Finance*. St. Lucia: University of Queensland; New York: Crane, Russak & Co.
Chulalongkorn, King (1927) *Phraratchadamrat song thalaeng phrabǫrommarachathibai kaekhai kanpokkhrǫng phaendin* [Speech Explaining the Governmental Reforms]. Bangkok: Sophonphiphatthanakǫn Press.
Coedès, G. (1968) *The Indianized States of Southeast Asia*. Walter F. Vella, ed., Susan Brown Cowing, trans. Honolulu: East-West Center.
—— (1969) *The Making of South East Asia*. H. M. Wright, trans. Berkeley: University of California Press.
Cohen, Jerome Alan (1966) "Chinese Mediation on the Eve of Modernization," *California Law Review*, 54(3): 1201-26.
Colson, Elizabeth (1974) *Tradition and Contract: The Problem of Order*. Chicago: Aldine Pub. Co.
Committee on Legal Services to the Poor in the Developing Countries (1974) *Legal Aid and World Poverty: A Survey of Asia, Africa, and Latin America*. New York: Praeger Publishers.
Conze, Edward (1959a) *Buddhism: Its Essence and Development*. New York: Harper & Row.
——, ed. and trans. (1959b) *Buddhist Scriptures*. Baltimore: Penguin Books.
Crawfurd, John (1967) *Journal of an Embassy to the Courts of Siam and Cochin China* [1828]. Kuala Lumpur, London, New York: Oxford University Press.
Damrong Rachanuphab, Prince (1933) *Laksana kan pokkhrǫng prathet sayam tae boran* [The Administration of Siam from Ancient Times]. Bangkok: Sophonphiphatthanakǫn Press.
Davis, Richard (1974) "Muang Metaphysics: A Study in Northern Thai Myth and Ritual," Ph.D. dissertation, University of Sydney.
Derrett, J. Duncan M. (1963) "Justice, Equity and Good Conscience," in J. N. D. Anderson, ed., *Changing Law in Developing Countries*. London: George Allen & Unwin, pp. 114-53.
—— (1968) *Religion, Law and the State in India*. New York: Free Press.
de Young, John E. (1966) *Village Life in Modern Thailand*. Berkeley: University of California Press.
Engel, David M. (1975) *Law and Kingship in Thailand During the Reign of King Chulalongkorn*. Ann Arbor: Center for South & Southeast Asian Studies, University of Michigan.
Epstein, A. L. (1967) "The Case Method in the Field of Law," in A. L. Epstein, ed., *The Craft of Social Anthropology*. London: Tavistock Publications, pp. 205-30.
Esmein, A. (1913) *A History of Continental Criminal Procedure with Special Reference to France*. John Simpson, trans. Boston: Little, Brown & Co.
Evers, Hans-Dieter, ed. (1969) *Loosely Structured Social Systems: Thailand in Comparative Perspective*. New Haven, Conn.: Yale University Southeast Asia Studies.
Felstiner, William L. F. (1974) "Influences of Social Organization on Dispute Processing," *Law & Society Review*, 9(1): 63-94.
—— (1975) "Avoidance as Dispute Processing: An Elaboration," *Law & Society Review*, 9(4): 695-706.
Friedman, Lawrence M. and Robert V. Percival (1976) "A Tale of Two Courts: Litigation in Alameda and San Benito Counties," *Law & Society Review*, 10(2): 267-301.

Galanter, Marc (1966) "The Modernization of Law," in Myron Weiner, ed., *Modernization*. New York: Basic Books, pp. 153-65.
────── (1968) "The Displacement of Traditional Law in Modern India," *Journal of Social Issues*, 24(4): 65-91.
────── (1972) "The Aborted Restoration of 'Indigenous' Law in India," *Comparative Studies in Society & History*, 14(1): 53-70.
────── (1974) "Why the 'Haves' Come Out Ahead: Speculations on the Limits of Legal Change," *Law & Society Review*, 9(1): 95-160.
────── (1975) "Afterword: Explaining Litigation," *Law & Society Review*, 9(2): 347-68.
Gerini, G. E. (1895) "Trial by Ordeal in Siam and the Siamese Law of Ordeals," *Asiatic Quarterly Review*, 2d series, 9: 415-24; 10: 156-75.
Gervaise, Nicolas (1928) *The Natural and Political History of the Kingdom of Siam* [1688]. Herbert Stanley O'Neill, trans. Bangkok: Siam Observer.
Gluckman, Max, ed. (1972) *The Allocation of Responsibility*. Manchester: Manchester University Press.
Haas, Mary R. (1964) *Thai-English Student's Dictionary*. Stanford, Cal.: Stanford University Press.
Hahm, Pyong-Choon (1969) "The Decision Process in Korea," in Glendon Schubert and David J. Danelski, eds., *Comparative Judicial Behavior: Cross-Cultural Studies of Political Decision-Making in the East and West*. New York: Oxford University Press, pp. 19-47.
────── (1971) *The Korean Political Tradition and Law: Essays in Korean Law and Legal History*. 2d ed. Seoul: Royal Asiatic Society, Korea Branch.
Hall, D. G. E. (1964) *A History of South-East Asia*. 2d ed. London: Macmillan & Co.
Hallett, Holt S. (1890) *A Thousand Miles on an Elephant in the Shan States*. Edinburgh and London: William Blackwood & Sons.
Hanks, Jane Richardson (1963) *Maternity and Its Rituals in Bang Chan*. Ithaca, N.Y.: Southeast Asia Program, Cornell University.
────── (1965) "A Rural Thai Village's View of Human Character," *Felicitation Volumes of Southeast-Asian Studies, Presented to His Highness Prince Dhaninivat Kromamun Bidyalabh Bridhyakorn on the Occasion of His Eightieth Birthday*. Bangkok: Siam Society, vol. I, pp. 77-84.
Hanks, Lucien M. (1962) "Merit and Power in the Thai Social Order," *American Anthropologist*, 64(6): 1247-61.
────── (1965) "Two Visions of Freedom: Thai and American," *Felicitation Volumes of Southeast-Asian Studies, Presented to His Highness Prince Dhaninivat Kromamun Bidyalabh Bridhyakorn on the Occasion of His Eightieth Birthday*. Bangkok: Siam Society, vol. I, pp. 85-90.
────── (1966) "The Corporation and the Entourage: A Comparison of Thai and American Social Organization," *Catalyst*, 2: 55-63.
────── (1972) *Rice and Man: Agricultural Ecology in Southeast Asia*. Chicago: Aldine Pub. Co.
────── (1975) "The Thai Social Order as Entourage and Circle" in G. William Skinner and A. Thomas Kirsch, eds., *Change and Persistence in Thai Society; Essays in Honor of Lauriston Sharp*. Ithaca, N.Y.: Cornell University Press, pp. 197-218.
────── (1976) "Banditry in a Southeast Asian Setting," unpublished manuscript.
──────, Jane Richardson Hanks, and Lauriston Sharp, eds. (1965) *Ethnographic Notes on Northern Thailand*. Ithaca, N.Y.: Southeast Asia Program, Cornell University.
Hatton, Howard A. (1973) "Translation of Pronouns: A Thai Example," *Bible Translator*, 24(2): 222-34.
Henderson, Dan Fenno (1968) "Law and Political Modernization in Japan," in Robert E. Ward, ed., *Political Development in Modern Japan*. Princeton, N.J.: Princeton University Press, pp. 387-456.
Ho, Robert and E. C. Chapman, eds. (1973) *Studies of Contemporary Thailand*. Canberra: Research School of Pacific Studies, Australian National University.
Holdsworth, Sir William (1965-72) *A History of English Law*. 17 vols. A. L. Goodhart and H. G. Hanbury, eds. London: Methuen & Co.

Hooker, M. B. (1975) *Legal Pluralism: An Introduction to Colonial and Neo-colonial Laws.* Oxford: Clarendon Press.

Hudson, Roy (1973) *Hudson's Guide to Chiang Mai and the North.* Chiangmai: Hudson Enterprises.

Ingersoll, Jasper (1966) "The Priest Role in Central Village Thailand," in Manning Nash et al., *Anthropological Studies in Theravada Buddhism.* New Haven, Conn.: Yale University Southeast Asia Studies, pp. 51-76.

Ingram, James C. (1971) *Economic Change in Thailand, 1850-1970.* Stanford, Cal.: Stanford University Press.

Kaufman, Howard Keva (1960) *Bangkhuad: A Community Study in Thailand.* Locust Valley, New York: J. J. Augustin (Monographs of Association for Asian Studies).

Kawashima, Takeyoshi (1963) "Dispute Resolution in Contemporary Japan," in Arthur T. von Mehren, ed., *Law in Japan: The Legal Order in a Changing Society.* Cambridge, Mass.: Harvard University Press, pp. 41-72.

Keyes, Charles F. (1971) "Buddhism and National Integration in Thailand," *Journal of Asian Studies,* 30(3): 551-67.

——— (1975a) "Buddhist Pilgrimage Centers and the Twelve-Year Cycle: Northern Thai Moral Orders in Space and Time," *History of Religions,* 15(1): 71-89.

——— (1975b) "The Northeastern Thai Village: Stable Order and Changing World," *Siam Society Journal,* 63(1): 177-207.

Kingkeo, Attagara (1967) "The Folk Religion of Ban Nai: A Hamlet in Central Thailand," Ph.D. dissertation, Indiana University.

Kingshill, Konrad (1960) *Ku Daeng—The Red Tomb: A Village Study in Northern Thailand.* Chiangmai: Prince Royal's College.

Klausner, William J. (1974) *Reflections in a Log Pond: Collected Writings.* Bangkok: Suksit Siam.

Kraisri Nimmanahaeminda (1965a) "The Irrigation Laws of King Mengrai," in Lucien M. Hanks et al., *Ethnographic Notes on Northern Thailand.* Ithaca, N.Y.: Southeast Asia Program, Cornell University, pp. 1-5.

——— (1965b) "Put Vegetables into Baskets, and People into Towns," in Lucien M. Hanks et al., *Ethnographic Notes on Northern Thailand.* Ithaca, N.Y.: Southeast Asia Program, Cornell University, pp. 6-9.

——— (1967) "The Lawa Guardian Spirits of Chiengmai," *Siam Society Journal,* 55(2): 185-225.

Kunstadter, Peter, ed. (1967) *Southeast Asian Tribes, Minorities, and Nations.* 2 vols. Princeton, N.J.: Princeton University Press.

Lal, P., trans. (1967) *The Dhammapada.* New York: Farrar, Straus & Giroux.

La Loubère, Simon de (1969) *The Kingdom of Siam* [1691]. London: Oxford University Press.

Lawson, Frederick H. (1955) *A Common Lawyer Looks at the Civil Law.* Ann Arbor: University of Michigan Law School.

LeBar, Frank M., Gerald C. Hickey, and John K. Musgrave (1964) *Ethnic Groups of Mainland Southeast Asia.* New Haven, Conn.: HRAF Press.

le May, Reginald (1924) "Legends and Folklore of Northern Siam," *Siam Society Journal,* 18(1): 1-49.

——— (1926) *An Asian Arcady: The Land and Peoples of Northern Siam.* Cambridge: W. Heffer & Sons.

Lingat, Robert (1935) *Prawatsat kotmai thai (kotmai ekkachon): lamoet* [History of Thai Law (Private Law): Private Wrongs]. Bangkok: Thammasat University.

——— (1950) "Evolution of the Conception of Law in Burma and Siam," *Siam Society Journal,* 38(1): 9-31.

——— (1973) *The Classical Law of India.* J. Duncan M. Derrett, trans. and additions. Berkeley: University of California Press.

Low, James (1847) "On the Laws of Mu'ung Thai or Siam," *Journal of the Indian Archipelago & Eastern Asia,* 1: 327-429.

McFarland, George Bradley (1944) *Thai-English Dictionary.* Stanford, Cal.: Stanford University Press.

Bibliography

McGilvary, Daniel (1912) *A Half Century Among the Siamese and the Lao: An Autobiography*. New York: Fleming H. Revell.

Marlowe, Gertrude Woodruff (1969) "Economic Variety in a North Thai Village," in *Tribesmen and Peasants in North Thailand; Symposium of the Tribal Research Centre, 1967*. Chiangmai: Tribal Research Centre, pp. 15-25.

Marut Bunnag (1971) *Kan triam khadi aya lae kan sak phayan* [The Preparation of Criminal Cases and the Examination of Witnesses]. Chiangmai: Saengsin Press.

Masao, Tokichi (1905) "Researches into Indigenous Law of Siam as a Study of Comparative Jurisprudence," *Siam Society Journal*, 2(1): 14-18; reprinted in *Yale Law Journal*, 15(1): 28-32.

—— (1908) "The New Penal Code of Siam," *Siam Society Journal*, 5(2): 1-14, Comments: 15-23; reprinted in *Yale Law Journal*, 18(2): 85-100.

Massell, Gregory J. (1968) "Law as an Instrument of Revolutionary Change in a Traditional Milieu: The Case of Soviet Central Asia," *Law & Society Review*, 2(2): 179-228.

Moerman, Michael (1966a) "Ban Ping's Temple: The Center of a 'Loosely Structured' Society," in Manning Nash et al., *Anthropological Studies in Theravada Buddhism*. New Haven, Conn.: Yale University Southeast Asia Studies, pp. 137-74.

—— (1966b) "Kinship and Commerce in a Thai-Lue Village," *Ethnology*, 5(4): 360-64.

—— (1968) *Agricultural Change and Peasant Choice in a Thai Village*. Berkeley: University of California Press.

—— (1969a) "A Thai Village Headman as a Synaptic Leader," *Journal of Asian Studies*, 28(3): 535-49.

—— (1969b) "Western Culture and the Thai Way of Life," in Robert O. Tilman, ed., *Man, State, and Society in Contemporary Southeast Asia*. New York: Praeger Publishers, pp. 145-61; reprinted from *Asia*, 1: 31-50 (1964).

Moore, Frank J. with Clark D. Neher (1974) *Thailand—Its People, Its Society, Its Culture*. New Haven, Conn.: HRAF Press.

Moore, Sally F. (1972) "Legal Liability and Evolutionary Interpretation: Some Aspects of Strict Liability, Self-Help and Collective Responsibility," in Max Gluckman, ed., *The Allocation of Responsibility*. Manchester: Manchester University Press, pp. 51-107.

Mosel, James N. (1959) "Thai Administrative Behavior," in William J. Siffin, ed., *Toward the Comparative Study of Public Administration*. Bloomington: Indiana University Press, pp. 278-331.

Nader, Laura, ed. (1969) *Law in Culture and Society*. Chicago: Aldine Pub. Co.

Nash, Manning, et al. (1966) *Anthropological Studies in Theravada Buddhism*. New Haven, Conn.: Yale University Southeast Asia Studies.

Neale, Frederick Arthur (1852) *Narrative of a Residence at the Capital of the Kingdom of Siam*. London: Office of National Illustrated Library.

Neher, Clark D. (1974) *The Dynamics of Politics and Administration in Rural Thailand*. Athens, Ohio: Papers in International Studies, Southeast Asia Series, Ohio University.

Nusit Chindarsi (1970) "Blue Meo Religion," M.A. thesis, University of Sydney.

Organ, Troy Wilson (1974) *Hinduism: Its Historical Development*. Woodbury, N.Y.: Barron's Educational Series.

Phillips, Herbert P. (1965) *Thai Peasant Personality: The Patterning of Interpersonal Behavior in the Village of Bang Chan*. Berkeley: University of California Press.

Phornphun Chongvatana (1974) "The Disputes of British Subjects Against the Chiefs of Chiengmai Resulting in the Siamese Government Taking over the Administration of North West Siam (Payab Circle) (1858-1902)," M.A. thesis [in Thai], Chulalongkorn University.

Piker, Steven (1968) "The Relationship of Belief Systems to Behavior in Rural Thai Society," *Asian Survey*, 8(5): 384-99.

Prani Sirithǫn Na Phatthalung (1963) *Phet Lanna* ["Diamonds" of Lanna]. 2 vols. Chiangmai: Suriwong Press.

Prisna Sirinam (1973) "Relations Between Siam and the Tributary States in Lanna Thai During the Early Bangkok Period," M.A. thesis [in Thai], College of Education, Thailand.

Rahula, Walpola (1959) *What the Buddha Taught.* New York: Grove Press.
Ramsay, James Ansil (1971) "The Development of a Bureaucratic Polity: The Case of Northern Siam," Ph.D. dissertation, Cornell University.
Reynolds, Craig J. (1976) "Buddhist Cosmography in Thai History, with Special Reference to Nineteenth-Century Culture Change," *Journal of Asian Studies,* 35(2): 203-20.
Reynolds, Mani and Frank, trans. (1978) *The Three Worlds According to King Ruang: A Thai Buddhist Cosmology.* Stanford, Cal., and Bangkok: Stanford University Press & Siam Society.
Rudolph, Lloyd I. and Susanne Hoeber Rudolph (1967) *The Modernity of Tradition: Political Development in India.* Chicago: University of Chicago Press.
Saint-Hubert, Christian de (1965) "Rolin-Jaequemyns (Chao Phya Aphay Raja) and the Belgian Legal Advisors in Siam at the Turn of the Century," *Siam Society Journal* 53(2): 181-90.
Sanguan Chotisukharat (1969) *Prapheni thai phak nüa* [Customs of Northern Thailand]. Bangkok: Sanitphan Press.
────── (1971) "Supernatural Beliefs and Practices in Chiengmai," *Siam Society Journal,* 59(1): 211-31.
Sanya Dharmasakti and Wimolsiri Jamnarnwej (1972) *Status of Women in Thailand.* Bangkok: Women Lawyers Association of Thailand.
Sathian Laiyalak *et al.*, comps. (1935-53) *Prachum kotmai pračham sok* [Collected Laws, Arranged Chronologically]. 69 vols. Bangkok: Daily News; Peng Heng (Kim Li Nguan); and Nitiwet Press.
Sawada, J. Toshio (1968) *Subsequent Conduct and Supervening Events: A Study of Two Selected Problems in Contract Jurisprudence.* Tokyo: University of Tokyo Press; Ann Arbor: University of Michigan Law School.
Siffin, William J. (1966) *The Thai Bureaucracy: Institutional Change and Development.* Honolulu: East-West Center Press.
Silcock, T. H., ed. (1967) *Thailand: Social and Economic Studies in Development.* Canberra: Australian National University Press.
Skinner, G. William and A. Thomas Kirsch, eds. (1975) *Change and Persistence in Thai Society: Essays in Honor of Lauriston Sharp.* Ithaca, N.Y.: Cornell University Press.
Smith, Harold E. (1973) "Polygyny and Marriage Registration in Thailand," *Southeast Asia,* 2(3): 291-99.
Srivisarn Vacha, Phya (1954) "Kingship in Thailand," *Siam Society Journal,* 42(1): 1-10.
Starr, June and Jonathan Pool (1974) "The Impact of a Legal Revolution in Rural Turkey," *Law & Society Review,* 8(4): 533-60.
Steinberg, David Joel, ed. (1971) *In Search of Southeast Asia: A Modern History.* New York: Praeger Publishers.
Sternstein, Larry (1966) "Bangkok at the Turn of the Century; Mongkut and Chulalongkorn Entertain the West," *Siam Society Journal,* 54(1): 55-71.
Sutčharit Thawǫnsuk, comp. (1964) *Kan chǎt san huamüang khrang raek* [Establishment of the First Provincial Courts]. Bangkok: Ministry of Justice.
Tambiah, S. J. (1968) "Literacy in a Buddhist Village in North-East Thailand," in Jack Goody, ed., *Literacy in Traditional Societies.* Cambridge: Cambridge University Press, pp. 86-131.
────── (1969) "Animals Are Good to Think and Good to Prohibit," *Ethnology,* 8(4): 423-59.
────── (1970) *Buddhism and the Spirit Cults in North-East Thailand.* Cambridge: Cambridge University Press.
Tanin Kraivixien (1968) *Kan patirup robop kotmai lae kan san nai ratchasamai phrabat somdet phračhunlačhǫmklao čhaoyuhua phrapiyamaharat* [Transformation of the Legal System and the Judiciary During the Reign of King Chulalongkorn]. Bangkok: Government House Printing Office.
Thailand (1964) *Official Yearbook, 1964.* Bangkok: Government House Printing Office.
Thailand, Ministry of Finance, Department of General Statistics (1922) *Statistical Year Book of the Kingdom of Siam, 1922, English Edition.* Bangkok.

Bibliography

Thailand, Ministry of Interior, Department of Local Administration; U.S.O.M.; National Statistical Office (1969) *Amphoe-Tambon Statistical Directory of Fifty-five Changwats.* Bangkok.
Thailand, Ministry of Justice (1943) *Watthanatham thang kan san* [Judicial Lore]. Bangkok.
Thailand, National Statistical Office, Office of the Prime Minister (1964) *Bulletin of Statistics,* 12(2). Bangkok.
—— (1970) *1970 Population and Housing Census; Changwat Chiangmai.* Bangkok.
Thailand, The Supreme Court (1969) *Record of the Third Asian Judicial Conference, Bangkok, 19th-27th November, 1967.* Bangkok: Supreme Court.
Thamsook Numnonda (1974) "The First American Advisers in Thai History," *Siam Society Journal,* 62(2): 121-48.
Thompson, P. A. (1906) *Lotus Land; Being an Account of the Country and the People of Southern Siam.* Philadelphia: J. B. Lippincott.
Tilman, Robert O., ed. (1969) *Man, State, and Society in Contemporary Southeast Asia.* New York: Praeger Publishers.
Tribal Research Centre (1974) *Directory of Tribal Villages in Thailand.* Chiangmai: Tribal Data Project.
Van Roy, Edward (1965) "Structure of the Miang Economy," in Lucien M. Hanks et al., eds., *Ethnographic Notes on Northern Thailand.* Ithaca, N.Y.: Southeast Asia Program, Cornell University, pp. 21-30.
—— (1967) "An Interpretation of Northern Thai Peasant Economy," *Journal of Asian Studies,* 26(3): 421-32.
—— (1971) *Economic Systems of Northern Thailand: Structure and Change.* Ithaca, N.Y.: Cornell University Press.
van Vliet, Jeremias (1910) "Translation of Jeremias van Vliet's *Description of the Kingdom of Siam"* [1692], L. F. van Ravenswaay, trans., *Siam Society Journal,* 7(1): 1-105.
Vella, Walter F. (1955) *The Impact of the West on Government in Thailand.* Berkeley: University of California Press.
—— (1957) *Siam Under Rama III, 1824-1851.* Locust Valley, New York: J. J. Augustin (Monographs of Association for Asian Studies).
Vickery, Michael (1970) "Thai Regional Elites and the Reforms of King Chulalongkorn," *Journal of Asian Studies,* 29(4): 863-81.
Virada Somswasdi (1974) "Comparative Studies in Matrimonial Property Laws of the United States and Thailand," M.C.L. thesis, Cornell University.
Wales, H. G. Quaritch (1931) *Siamese State Ceremonies: Their History and Function.* London: Bernard Quaritch.
—— (1934) *Ancient Siamese Government and Administration.* London: Bernard Quaritch.
Weber, Max (1968) *Economy and Society: An Outline of Interpretive Sociology.* 3 vols. Guenther Roth and Claus Wittich, eds.; Ephraim Fischoff et al., trans. New York: Bedminster Press.
Wenk, Klaus (1968) *The Restoration of Thailand Under Rama I, 1782-1809.* Greeley Stahl, trans. Tucson: University of Arizona Press (Monographs of Association for Asian Studies).
Wichitmattra, Khun [Sanga Kančhanakphan] (1970) *Samnuan thai* [Thai Idioms]. Bangkok: Bamrungsat Press.
Wijeyewardene, Gehan (1965) "A Note on Irrigation and Agriculture in a North Thai Village," *Felicitation Volumes of Southeast-Asian Studies, Presented to His Highness Prince Dhaninivat Kromamun Bidyalabh Bridhyakorn on the Occasion of His Eightieth Birthday.* Bangkok: Siam Society, vol. II, pp. 255-59.
—— (1967) "Some Aspects of Rural Life in Thailand," in T. H. Silcock, ed., *Thailand: Social and Economic Studies in Development.* Canberra: Australian National University Press, pp. 65-83.
—— (1968a) "Address, Abuse and Animal Categories in Northern Thailand," *Man,* n.s. 3(1): 76-93.

——— (1968b) "The Language of Courtship in Chiengmai," *Siam Society Journal,* 56(1): 19-32.
——— (1970) "The Still Point and the Turning World: Towards the Structure of Northern Thai Religion," *Mankind,* 7(4): 247-55.
——— (1971) "A Note on Patrons and Pau Liang," *Siam Society Journal,* 59(2): 229-33.
——— (1972) "Review of Edward Van Roy, *Economic Systems of Northern Thailand,*" *Siam Society Journal,* 60(1): 424-27.
Wilson, Constance M. (1970) "State and Society in the Reign of Mongkut, 1851-1868: Thailand on the Eve of Modernization," Ph.D. dissertation, Cornell University.
Wilson, David A. (1962) *Politics in Thailand.* Ithaca, N.Y.: Cornell University Press.
Wood, W. A. R. (1965) *Consul in Paradise: Sixty-Nine Years in Siam.* London: Souvenir Press.
Wǫraphakphibun, Phra (1969) *Prawatsat kotmai thai* [History of Thai Law]. 2d ed. Bangkok: Faculty of Political Science, Chulalongkorn University.
Wyatt, David K. (1967) "The Thai 'Kaṭa Maṇḍiarapāla' and Malacca," *Siam Society Journal,* 55(2): 279-86.
——— (1968) "Family Politics in Nineteenth Century Thailand," *Journal of Southeast Asian History,* 9(2): 208-28.
——— (1969) *The Politics of Reform in Thailand: Education in the Reign of King Chulalongkorn.* New Haven: Yale University Press.
Yano, Toru (1968) "Land Tenure in Thailand," *Asian Survey,* 8(10): 853-63.
Young, Ernest (1907) *The Kingdom of the Yellow Robe.* 3d ed. London: Archibald Constable & Co.

B. Legal Texts and Commentaries*

I. Constitution

Constitution of the Kingdom of Thailand, 1974 [*Ratthathammanun haeng ratcha-anačhak thai, B.E. 2517*]. Bangkok.

II. Law Codes, Edicts, and Regulations

Lanna Custom Law; Transliteration Series 2 [*Kotmai lanna; phak pariwat lamdap thi 2*], by Sommai Premchit in collaboration with Puangkam Tuikheo. Chiangmai: Chiangmai University, 1975.
Lanna Custom Law; Transliteration Series 3 [*Kotmai lanna; phak pariwat lamdap thi 3*], by Sommai Premchit in collaboration with Puangkam Tuikheo. Chiangmai: Chiangmai University, 1975.
Law for the Organization of the Courts of Justice, 1934 [*Phrathammanun san yuttitham, B.E. 2477*]. With amendments. (In Thai and English.) Suchat Chiwachat, comp. Bangkok: Rajadaromp Printery, 1962.
Law of the Courts of Justice, 1908 [*Phrathammanun san yuttitham, R.S. 127*]. In Sathian Laiyalak *et al.,* comps., *Prachum kotmai pračham sok* [Collected Laws, Arranged Chronologically]. Bangkok: Daily Mail, 1935-53, vol. 22: 238.
Law of the King of Nan [*Kotmai phračhao nan*]. Singkha Wannasai, trans. and ed. (in Central Thai). Unpublished manuscript. Lamphun, Thailand, 1971.
Law of Local Administration, 1914 (*See* Royal Edict Concerning the Law of Local Administration, 1914).
Law of the Provincial Courts, 1896 [*Phrathammanun san huamüang, R.S. 114*] In Sathian Laiyalak *et al.,* comps., *Prachum kotmai pračham sok* [Collected Laws, Arranged Chronologically]. Bangkok: Daily Mail, 1935-53, vol. 15: 54.
Law of the Three Seals [*Kotmai tra sam duang*]. In Sathian Laiyalak *et al.,* comps.,

*All texts are in Thai unless otherwise noted.

Bibliography

Prachum kotmai pračham sok [Collected Laws, Arranged Chronologically]. Bangkok: Daily Mail, 1935-53, vols. 1 & 2.

Mangrai Custom Law; Transliteration Series 1 [*Mangraisat; phak pariwat lamdap thi 1*], by Sommai Premchit in collaboration with Puangkam Tuikheo. Chiangmai: Chiangmai University, 1975.

Police Regulations Concerning Cases [*Rabiap kan tamruat kiao kap khadi*]. Police Lieutenant Colonel Samroeng Singhawara, comp. Thonburi: Krungthai Press, undated.

Royal Edict Concerning Attorneys, 1965 [*Phraratchabanyat thanaikhwam, B.E. 2508*], as amended in 1971. Royal Thai Government Gazette [*Ratchakitčhanubeksa*], vol. 82(1), section 58 (July 24, 1965) and vol. 88(1), section 44 (April 27, 1971).

Royal Edict Concerning Gambling, 1935 [*Phraratchabanyat kan phanan, B.E. 2478*]. With amendments and related regulations. Sathian Wichailak, comp., with Süpwong Wichailak. Bangkok: Nitiwet Press, 1973.

Royal Edict Concerning Regulations for Judicial Officials, 1954 [*Phraratchabanyat rabiap kharatchakan fai tulakan, B.E. 2497*]. With amendments and related regulations. Sathian Wichailak, comp., with Süpwong Wichailak. Bangkok: Nitiwet Press, 1974.

Royal Edict Concerning the Law of Local Administration, 1914 [*Phraratchabanyat laksana pokkhrong thongthi, B.E. 2457*]. With amendments and related regulations. Sathian Wichailak, comp., with Süpwong Wichailak. Bangkok: Nitiwet Press, 1973.

Royal Edict Concerning the Sale of Rice, 1946 [*Phraratchabanyat kan kha khao, B.E. 2489*]. With amendments and related regulations. Sathian Wichailak, comp., with Süpwong Wichailak. Bangkok: Nitiwet Press, 1973.

Royal Edict Concerning Violations Arising From the Use of Checks, 1954 [*Phraratchabanyat waduai khwamphit an koet čhak kan chai chek, B.E. 2497*]. In Sawaeng Suntharakalam, *Kham athibai phraratchabanyat waduai khwamphit an koet čhak kan chai chek* [An Explanation of the Royal Edict Concerning Violations Arising From the Use of Checks]. Bangkok: Phraephitthaya, 1971.

Royal Edict to Control the Rental of Riceland, 1974 [*Phraratchabanyat khuapkhum kan chao na, B.E. 2517*]. Sathian Wichailak, comp., with Süpwong Wichailak. Bangkok: Nitiwet Press, 1975.

Royal Edict to Prohibit Excessive Interest Rates, 1932 [*Phraratchabanyat ham riak dokbia koen attra, B.E. 2475*]. Sathian Wichailak, comp., with Süpwong Wichailak. Bangkok: Nitiwet Press, 1972.

Royal Edict to Prohibit Prostitution, 1960 [*Phraratchabanyat pram kan kha praweni, B.E. 2503*]. With related regulations. Bangkok: Sutphaisan Press, 1974.

The Thai Civil and Commercial Code, Books I-VI [*Pramuan kotmai phaeng lae phanit, bap 1-6*]. With amendments and glossary. (In Thai and English). Kamol Sandhikshetrin, comp. Bangkok: Nitibannakan Press, 1972.

The Thai Civil Procedure Code [*Pramuan kotmai withi phitčharana khwam phaeng*]. With amendments. (In Thai and English). Bangkok: Odeon, 1968.

The Thai Criminal Procedure Code [*Pramuan kotmai withi phitčharana khwam aya*]. With amendments. (In Thai and English.) Suchat Chiwachat, ed. Thonburi: Nitibannakan Press, 1969.

The Thai Land Code of 1954 [*Pramuan kotmai thi din, B.E. 2497*]. With amendments, related regulations, edicts, and sample forms. In Michai Rüchuphan, comp., *Kham athibai kotmai thi din* [An Explanation of the Land Law]. Bangkok: Kasembannakit Press, 1970.

The Thai Penal Code [*Pramuan kotmai aya*]. With amendments. (In Thai and English). Watana Ratanawichit, comp. and trans. Bangkok: Odeon, 1969.

III. Commentaries

Michai Rüchuphan (1970) *Kham athibai kotmai thi din* [An Explanation of the Land Law]. Bangkok: Kasembannakit Press.

Sa-at Nawičharoen (1974) *Kham athibai pramuan kotmai phaeng lae phanit bap 5 waduai khropkhrua* [An Explanation of the Civil and Commercial Code, Book V, Concerning the Family]. Bangkok: Nitibannakan Press.

Sanya Dharmasakti and Praphas Uaichai (1975) *Kham athibai pramuan kotmai withi phitčharana khwam aya* [An Explanation of the Criminal Procedure Code]. Bangkok: Saengthong Press.
Sawaeng Suntharakalam (1971) *Kham athibai phraratchabanyat waduai khwamphit an koet čhak kan chai chek* [An Explanation of the Royal Edict Concerning Violations Arising from the Use of Checks]. Bangkok: Phraephitthaya.
Woraphakphibun, Phra (1970) *Kham athibai kotmai laksana lamoet* [An Explanation of the Law of Wrongful Acts]. Bangkok: Phraephitthaya.
―――― (1971) *Kham athibai pramuan kotmai phaeng lae phanit waduai bukkhon* [An Explanation of the Civil and Commercial Code, Concerning Persons]. Bangkok: Watcharin Press.
Yut Saeng-uthai (1971) *Kham banyai pramuan kotmai aya* [An Explanation of the Penal Code]. Bangkok: Odeon.

Index

CASE DESCRIPTION INDEX

McGilvary protects family accused of witchcraft, 34-35
landowner unwilling to evict squatter, 64
police demonstration in Lamphun, 67
revenge murder of coconut thief, 67
arrest of agent for illegal lottery, 74-75, 192-93
injured woman sues minibus driver and owner of vehicle, 75
theft of wood by village youth, 85-86
village bully fights with vendor, 86-87
village chief mediates drunken fight between two friends, 87
automobile driver prosecuted after village-level settlement, 88
village chief persuades discontented husband not to leave wife, 89
"lucky" minibus driver wins lottery but loses in court to former wife, 90
dispute over ownership of land to be purchased for highway, 92-93
bus collision in village mediated by policeman, 94-95
policeman mediates "civil" dispute over purchase of livestock, 95
injured pedicab driver negotiates settlement in attorney's office, 97-98
murdered woman's family sues suspected killer for defamation of deceased, 106
out-of-court settlement in bad check litigation, 108-9
civil suit brought after defendant convicted for fighting, 112
student confession in motorcycle accident, 113
dispute over stolen rooster, 113
civil suit stayed until criminal liability for drunken fight established, 113
collapse of partnership to buy and sell livestock, 114-17
runaway ox cart case, 120-24, 131
parental responsibility for teenage motorcycle driver, 124-25, 131
gambling suspect accuses police of coercing payment, 125-26
trespass suit in which plaintiff fails to sign complaint, 127
pregnant woman sues for breach of betrothal contract, 127-29

alleged rape of six-year-old girl by neighbor, 129
postal official takes daughter of local merchant as minor wife, 130
settlement of accident case involving American official, 131-32
tobacco field irrigation dispute, 138-39
former village chief in brawl with incumbent village chief, 139
schoolteacher's widow refuses to vacate house, 139-40
elderly villager's livestock allegedly destroy neighbor's crops, 140-41
daughter of village chief injured by truck, 141-42
Vietnamese sausage-maker in motorcycle accident, 145-46
Burmese trader sues Thai border police, 146
hill tribe murder case, 146-48
villager alleges fraudulent certification of land by brother, 154-55
elderly woman and her brother accuse her son and others of land fraud, 158
trespass suit by holdover tenant against landlord, 159-60
widow seeks return of land from ungrateful niece, 161-62
survey and boundary dispute involving two landowners, 162
father sells land although children are registered as owners, 163-64
divorce suit by village woman against unfaithful husband, 171-73
divorce suit against abusive husband, 175
husband seeks divorce of wife who gambles, 175-76
student accuses former boyfriend of rape, 178-80
woman meat-seller allegedly insulted and attacked with knife, 180-81
insults and sexual impropriety by deputy district officer, 181-82
minor wife sues deputy district officer for breach of contract to provide support, 182-84
retired police lieutenant-colonel accuses sub-lieutenant of malfeasance, 193
village teenager alleges beating and wrongful arrest by group of police at fair, 193-97
village teenager alleges misconduct by policeman at outdoor movie, 195-97
dispute over fish caught by villagers, 197-99
village woman accuses officials of murdering her son, 199-203

SUBJECT INDEX

Agency, law of, 119-20
Astrology and personality, 60
Attorneys
  in Chiangmai and Thailand, 96
  in the courtroom, 14-15, 135-37
  mediation by, 96-98, 99

Brahmin legal advisers, 23
Buddhism
  and concept of injury, 61, 62-63, 64-66, 68
  and human personality, 57-60
  monks as mediators, 82-83
  in northern Thailand, 38, 173

Checks, violations involving. *See also* Royal Edict Concerning Violations Arising from the Use of Checks (1954)
  cultural factors, 145
  frequency of litigation, 57, 108
  strategy of litigation, 108-10
Chiangmai (city), 30, 31, 36-37
Chiangmai (province)
  attorneys in, 96
  modern features, 36-42
  rental of land and housing in, 158
  site for juvenile and mobile courts, 16
  social and political development, 25n, 29, 30-36, 207-9
Chiangmai Provincial Court. *See also* Courts; Judges; Litigation
  caseflow characteristics, 43-53, 57
  courthouse and courtroom, 13-15, 30
  as forum for mediation, 133-49
  and Ministry of Justice, 15-18
  records of, 6-7, 14-15
Chinese, in Thailand, 189

Chulalongkorn, King (Rama V), 4, 32-33, 36, 203
  and transformation of Thai law, 1, 2, 6, 18, 24, 29, 153, 155-56
Civil and Commercial Code. *See* Thai Civil and Commercial Code
Civil litigation. *See* Litigation
Civil Procedure Code. *See* Thai Civil Procedure Code
Codes. *See names of individual law codes*
Colonization, avoidance of, 1, 18, 32-33
  influence on legal culture, 133
Compoundable offenses, 108
"Compromise agreements," 52, 95, 111-12, 117, 164-65, 182-84
Confessions, 14, 113
Contracts
  as basis for civil actions, 47, 52, 112
  for betrothal, 127-29
  determine liability of principal for acts of agent, 119-20
  involving land, 40, 158-60
  and private prosecutions for bad checks, 109-10
  See also "Compromise Agreements"
Convictions, 51
"Coolness," 64, 68, 149
Court costs, 111, 114
Courts. *See also* Chiangmai Provincial Court; Litigation
  Appeals Court, 16
  Civil Court, 16
  Criminal Court, 16
  international (consular) courts, 18, 33, 34n, 135n
  juvenile courts, 16
  magistrates' courts, 15, 16, 25, 44

225

military courts, 44-45
mobile courts, 16
monthon courts, 25
provincial courts generally, 15, 17, 25-26
Supreme (*Dika*) Court, 16
Criminal litigation. *See* Litigation
Criminal Procedure Code. *See* Thai Criminal Procedure Code

Damrong Rachanupab, Prince, 11, 18, 25, 26-27, 29, 36, 104-5
Daṇḍa, 23
Death sentence, historically, 24, 33-34
Defamation, 106, 181n
Dharma (thamma), 1, 4, 23, 65, 208
Disputes
    processing of
        litigation. *See* Litigation
        by local ruler and council, 22-24
        mediation. *See* Mediation
        ordeal and oath, 20-21
        in patron-client hierarchies, 22, 75-78
        witchcraft proceedings, 21-22
    types of
        contracts, 41, 109-10
        family and marital, 40-41, 83, 87, 89, 91, 93, 124, 171-78
        insult and defamation, 67, 180-81
        land and water, 40, 82, 88-89, 91, 155-65
        official malfeasance, 35, 95-96, 186-87, 191-204
        physical injury, 83, 85, 87
        sexual wrongs, 178-82
        theft, 83, 85
        traffic, 95
        witchcraft, 21-22, 34
    See also Case Description Index
District officials, 36, 90-93, 99, 156, 176. *See also* Government officials

Edicts. *See names of individual royal edicts*
Education and educational system, 2, 41-42, 207
Elements, 59, 60
Employer liability for acts of employee, 119-20
Entourage. *See* Hierarchy and social organization; Patron-client relationships
Execution of civil judgments or orders, 112, 117
Explanation of the Establishment of the Provincial Courts (Prince Damrong Rachanupab), 11, 26-27, 104-5

Fate, 55, 59, 206

Gambling, 60, 67, 87-88, 188. *See also* Case Description Index
Government officials
    allegations of wrongs by, 125-26, 190-204. *See also* Case Description Index
    prosecution of, by villagers, inherently credible, 181-82, 195, 196-97, 202, 203
    relations with private citizens, 130, 180-84, 186-89
    villager attitudes toward, 190-91, 203-4
Governor, provincial, 11, 22-24, 33, 36, 51

Habit, 59, 60
Heart, 59-60
Hierarchy and social organization, 69-78
    See also Patron-client relationships; Reciprocity
Hill tribes, 38, 146-48

Indians, in Thailand, 145, 189
Individualism, 69-70, 75
Injured person (*čhao thuk*)
    identification of, by code and custom, 118, 120-26
    right to bring private criminal suit, 104-8
    traditional concepts of, 63-68
Injury, traditional concepts of, 61-68
Inquiry officials. *See* Police
Insult, 67, 68, 175, 180-82. *See also* Defamation
Interior, Ministry of, 16, 17, 25, 36, 153
International (consular) courts, 18, 33, 34n, 135n
Irrigation headman, 82

Joint prosecution, 107
Judge-Commissioner in Chiangmai, 32-33, 34-35
Judges
    attitudes of, toward prior informal settlements, 131
    before reforms of King Chulalongkorn, 18-20
    in the courtroom, 13-15
    differentiated from administrative officials, 11, 26-27
    organization and ranking of, 15-18
    role as mediator, 134, 136-37, 148-49, 164-65
    women as, 170
Judicial Service Commission, 17
Justice
    administration of, before Ministry of Justice, 18-24
    concepts of, 1, 3-6, 36, 126, 127, 205-9

Subject Index

and *dharma*, 23, 65, 208
and force, 23-24, 208-9
three modes of, 51-53
two symbols of, 4, 207
Justice, Ministry of, 5, 15-18, 25

Kamnan. *See also* Case Description Index
enforcement role of, 94, 197
mediatory role of, 78, 84-90, 99, 139, 140-41, 144
and the provincial administration, 25, 36, 187-88, 190
and registration of land, 156
Karma, 66. *See also* Fate
Khwan, 58, 62, 68, 206
payment to propitiate, 62, 63, 141, 194,
Kinship, 69-70. *See also* Parent-child relationship
liability of kin for individual wrongs, 74
Krengčhai, 64, 140, 142, 144

Lamoet. *See* Wrongful act
Land. *See also* Case Description Index
conflict involving, 40, 88-89, 91, 112, 155-65
cultivation of, in Chiangmai, 37-40
ownership of, 39-40, 153-60
registration of, 88-89, 91, 153-58, 160-65
rental of, 40, 47, 158-60
shortage of, among hill tribes, 38, 146-47
Land Code. *See* Thai Land Code (1954)
Lannathai, 31
Law, in Thailand
application of, in court, 134-37, 148-49
before reforms of King Chulalongkorn, 18-24, 153, 155, 168-69, 203
King Chulalongkorn and, 1, 2, 6, 18, 24, 29, 32-33, 153, 155-56, 203
concerning civil and criminal actions. *See* Litigation
concerning contracts
for betrothal, 127-29
for employment, 119-20
for rental of land, 40, 47, 158-60
concerning defamation and insult, 106, 175, 180-82
concerning land, 47, 88-89, 91, 153-65
concerning marriage, 91, 93, 123, 173-78
and court system, 15-18, 25, 33, 34-36, 44-45
Prince Damrong Rachanupab and, 11, 18, 26-27, 29, 104-5
and *dharma*, 1, 4-5, 23, 65, 208

differentiation of judicial and administrative functions, 11, 24, 26, 33-34
and dispute processing. *See* Disputes
divergence between code norms and customary norms
causes of, 206
as source of social change, 151-52, 207-8
edicts. *See names of individual royal edicts*
enforcement of, by government officials. *See also* Case Description Index
district officials, 90-93, 99, 176
kamnan, 84-90, 94, 139, 140-41, 156, 187-88, 190, 197
police, 74, 86, 87, 88, 91, 93-96, 99, 140-41, 179, 191-203
village chief, 84-90, 94, 155, 156-57, 187-88, 190, 197
interaction of legal norms in litigation
norms concerning merit, status, and personality, 5, 136, 148, 206
norms concerning remedies, 126-32
norms concerning standing and liability for injury, 118-26, 206
and justice. *See* Justice
law codes. *See names of individual codes*
and legal culture. *See* Traditional legal culture
and literature of modernization, 2
and litigation. *See* Litigation
King Mangrai and, 31, 153n
martial law, 45, 106
and mediation. *See* Mediation
private wrongs, 51-52, 57, 104-10, 111-14, 114-17
Prince Ratburi Direkrit and, 18, 25, 29
recodification of, 2-3, 24-27, 33, 155-57, 168
registration requirements and procedures. *See* Registration
used as instrument of modernization, 2, 28-29
women and, 167-71, 174-78, 184-85
Lawa, 30
Law codes of Thailand, drafting and promulgation of, 1, 25, 33, 154, 168
Law of Local Administration (1914). *See* Royal Edict Concerning the Law of Local Administration (1914)
Law of the Courts of Justice (1908), 25, 33, 46
Law of the Provincial Courts (1896), 11, 25, 26
Law of the Three Seals, 20n, 23n, 27n

Lawyers. *See* Attorneys
Liability for private wrongs, 118-25, 131
   in civil and private criminal suits, 111
   liability of parents for children, 120-25
   within patron-client hierarchies, 73-75
Literacy, 41-42, 167
Litigation. *See also* Case Description Index
   alleging witchcraft, 34-35
   before Ministry of Justice established, in provinces, 22-24
   choice between civil and criminal, 95, 112
   civil
      goals and strategies of, 103, 111-14
      mediation of, by district officials, 91
      types of, in Chiangmai court, 47, 52, 57
   costs of, 111, 114
   criminal (public prosecutions)
      outcomes of, 51
      types of, in Chiangmai court, 47
   joint civil and criminal suits, 114-17
   participants in, 134-37, 148-49
   private criminal prosecutions
      Prince Damrong Rachanupab discusses, 104-5
      distinguished from public prosecutions, 47
      goals and strategies of, 103, 104-10, 122-23, 129
      outcomes of, 51-52
      types of, in Chiangmai court, 57
   private wrongs
      brought as civil suits, 111-14
      brought as criminal suits, 104-10
      brought as joint civil and criminal suits, 114-17
      defined, 51-52
      frequency of litigation, 57
      litigation of, as departure from normal mediation process, 137-38, 142-48
   rates of, in Chiangmai court, 43-53, 57, 142-44
   three modes of, 51-53
   values concerning, 3, 46, 98, 133-35, 144-45
Luck, 60, 63, 90

McGilvary, Daniel, 34-35
Magistrates' court. *See* Courts
Mangrai, King, 31, 153n
Mangraisat, 31, 153n
Marriage. *See also* Case Description Index; Matrimonial property; Women
   marital conflict, 40-41, 52n, 83, 89, 91, 93, 171-78
   registration of, 41, 91, 123, 173, 177-78

Martial law, 45, 106
Matrimonial property, 41, 168-69
Mediation. *See also* Case Description Index
   attitudes toward, 3, 79-81, 98-99
   by attorneys, 96-98
   by clergy, 82-83
   in court, 42, 131-32, 133-49, 164-65, 176
   of criminal infractions, 91
   by district officials, 90-93, 161, 176
   effect on use of judicial system, 57, 133-34
   by headmaster of school, 140
   inhibited by distance, 142-44
   inhibited by ethnic differences, 144-48
   by irrigation headman, 82
   levels of, 79-99
   by *phuyai*, in general, 22, 52, 75-77, 81-82, 137-38
   by police, 91, 93-96, 99, 131, 140-41, 179
   by spirit medium, 65-66, 81
   by village chief and *kamnan*, 84-90, 139, 140-41, 157, 197
Merchants, and government officials, 189
Merit, 4-5, 58-59, 60, 62, 64, 65, 66, 68, 198, 206
Ministry of Justice. *See* Justice, Ministry of
Minor wives, 130, 167, 168, 175, 176-77, 182, 184

Nakleng (strong man or bully), 24, 66, 86-87
Non-assertiveness, 64, 98
Northwest *monthon*. *See* Phayap *monthon*

Oath, 14, 20, 21, 34
Oral advocacy, 135
Ordeal, 20-21, 34

Parent-child relationship, 69-70, 120-25
Patron-client relationships, 70-78, 99, 119-20, 142, 206
Penal Code. *See* Thai Penal Code
Personality, 57-61
Phayap *monthon*, 33, 46n
Phuyai ("big person," person of status and authority), 22, 52, 55, 76, 98, 137-48
Police. *See also* Case Description Index
   in Chiangmai court, 13-15
   interaction with villagers, 74, 190, 191-203
   mediation by, 91, 93-96, 99, 131, 140-41, 179
   on strike in Lamphun, 67
   and village authorities, 86, 87-88
Politeness, 64

Subject Index

Prachot, 67
Preliminary hearings, 109
Private criminal suits. *See* Litigation
Private wrongs. *See* Litigation, private wrongs
Prosecutor
   and decision to prosecute, 125-26
   establishment of, under Prince Damrong Rachanupab, 26-27, 104-6
   and private criminal actions, 104-8
   and Public Prosecution Department, 16
   and settlements of criminal cases mediated by police, 94
Public officials. *See* Government officials

Rama V. *See* Chulalongkorn, King
Ratburi Direkrit, Prince, 18, 25, 29
Reciprocity, 41, 70-75, 99, 119, 203-4
Registration
   governmental procedures and village rites, 173, 188
   of land, 88-89, 91, 153-58, 160-65
   of marriage, 41, 91, 123, 173, 177-78
   of paternity, 123n, 168n
Remedies, traditional conceptions of, 61-63, 121-23, 126-32
Retaliation, 66-67, 68, 129, 144
Royal Edict Concerning Attorneys (1965), 96n. *See also* Attorneys
Royal Edict Concerning Gambling (1935), 188. *See also* Gambling
Royal Edict Concerning Regulations for Judicial Officials (1951), 17n
Royal Edict Concerning the Law of Local Administration (1914), 84, 91, 93
Royal Edict Concerning Violations Arising from the Use of Checks (1954), 108. *See also* Checks, violations involving
Royal Edict to Control the Rental of Riceland (1974), 160

Sexual offenses, 178-82. *See also* Case Description Index
Sharecropping, 40, 158, 160
Spirits
   hierarchy of, 60-61
   injuries and, 21-22, 34-35, 61-62, 65-66
   marriage rites and, 129, 173, 188
   origins of, 58
   ritual notification of, 41, 173, 188
Standing, 118, 120-26

Thai Bar Association, 96
Thai Civil and Commercial Code, 25, 95, 153-54, 184-85
   § 38-39, 169
   § 138, 111
   § 420, 47, 128

§ 424, 114n
§ 425, 119
§ 429, 124
§ 569, 159-60n
§ 820, 119
§ 823, 119
§ 1435, 128n
§ 1438, 128
§ 1449, 173n
§ § 1463-64, 169n
§ 1500, 174, 175n
§ § 1529-30, 168n
§ 1538, 123n
§ 1541, 123n
Thai Civil Procedure Code, 25, 111n, 112
   § 198, 116
Thai Criminal Procedure Code, 25, 129
   § 2, 125
   § 5, 47, 122
   § 28, 47, 105
   § 30, 107
   § 34, 105-6
   § 35, 108
   § 36, 108
   § § 37-38, 94
   § 39, 94, 106-7
   § 40, 114
   § 41, 114
   § § 46-47, 112, 114n
   § 158, 127
   § 161, 127n
   § 227, 202n
Thai Land Code (1954), 89, 153-57, 158
Thai Penal Code, 25, 46, 110, 122, 123
   § 78, 51
   § 90, 106n
   § 157, 199n
   § 281, 108
   § 284, 108
   § 321, 108
   § 333, 108
   § 337, 199n
   § 351, 108
   § 356, 108
   § 360, 108
   § 361, 108
   § 365, 108
   § 366, 108
   § 393, 181n
Thesaphiban system, 25, 26, 33, 36
Traditional legal culture
   avoidance of colonization and, 133
   concepts of injuries and remedies, 61-63
   concepts of justice, 1, 3-6, 126, 127, 205-9
   confronts new legal system in provincial Thailand, 3
   new courts reject some traditional

procedures and causes of action, 34-36
evolving relationship of traditional legal culture and formal legal system, 207-9
hierarchy and liability for wrongs, 73-75
hierarchy and negotiation of disputes, 75-78, 137-49
influence of, upon judicial mediation, 133-37
interaction of legal norms in litigation
    norms concerning merit, status, and personality, 5, 136, 148, 206
    norms concerning remedies, 126-32
    norms concerning standing and liability for injury, 118-26, 206
and legal procedures before reforms of King Chulalongkorn, 18-24
litigation and failure of traditional mediation, 137-48
and mediation. *See* Mediation
non-litigiousness, 3, 45-46, 98-99, 113, 133, 145
norms concerning ownership and rental of land, 40, 88-89, 153-60
norms concerning public officials, 190-91, 203-4
norms concerning status and rights of women, 40-41, 166-70, 173-77
and responses to injury, 63-68
and seal of Yama, 4-5
tendency of "modern law" to destroy or absorb, 28-29

Treaty of 1874, 32, 34
Treaty of 1883, 33

Village chief. *See also* Case Description Index
    enforcement role of, 94, 197-99
    mediatory role of, 78, 84-90, 99, 139, 144, 155
    and the provincial administration, 25, 36, 187-88, 190
    and registration of land, 156-57

Winyan, 58, 60
Witchcraft proceedings, 20, 21-22, 34-35
Women. *See also* Case Description Index
    Constitution of 1974 and, 170, 184-85
    education and literacy of, 167
    frequency of litigation involving, 170-71
    historical legal status of, 168-69
    in legal profession, 166, 170
    matrimonial property and, 41, 168-69
    minor wives, 130, 167, 168, 175, 176-77, 182, 184
    as negotiators for husbands in disputes, 87, 155
    in northern Thailand, 166-71
Wrongful act (*lamoet*), definition of, 47, 128

Yama, 4-5, 207
Yokkrabat, 23
Yommarat, *Phraya. See* Yama

MONOGRAPHS OF THE ASSOCIATION FOR ASIAN STUDIES
Published by and available from: The University of Arizona Press
Box 3398, Tucson, Arizona 85722

XXXIV. *Code and Custom in a Thai Provincial Court*, by David M. Engel. 1978. $10.50 cloth; $4.95 paper.

XXXIII. *Philippine Policy Toward Sabah: A Claim to Independence:* by Lela Garner Noble. 1977. $10.50 cloth; $4.95 paper.

XXXII. *Political Behavior of Adolescents in China: The Cultural Revolution in Kwangchow*, by David M. Raddock. 1977. $8.95 cloth; $4.50 paper.

XXXI. *Big City Government in India: Councilor, Administrator, and Citizen in Delhi*, by Philip Oldenburg. 1976. $9.50 cloth; $4.95 paper.

XXX. *The New Jerusalem: Aspects of Utopianism in the Thought of Kagawa Toyohiko*, by George B. Bikle, Jr. 1976. $8.95 cloth; $4.95 paper.

XXIX. *Dōgen Kigen—Mystical Realist*, by Hee-Jin Kim. 1975. $8.95 cl, $4.95 p.

XXVIII. *Masks of Fiction in DREAM OF THE RED CHAMBER: Myth, Mimesis, and Persona*, by Lucien Miller. 1975. $7.95 cloth; $3.95 paper.

XXVII. *Politics and Nationalist Awakening in South India, 1852–1891*, by R. Suntharalingam. 1974. $7.95 cloth; $3.95 paper.

XXVI. *The Peasant Rebellions of the Late Ming Dynasty*, by James Bunyan Parsons. 1970. $7.50.

XXV. *Political Centers and Cultural Regions in Early Bengal*, by Barrie M. Morrison, 1970. $7.50.

XXIV. *The Restoration of Thailand Under Roma I: 1782–1809*, by Klaus Wenk. 1968. $7.50.

XXIII. *K'ang Yu-wei: A Biography and a Symposium*, translated and edited by Jung-pang Lo. 1967. 541 pp. $14.50.

XXII. *A Documentary Chronicle of Sino-Western Relations (1644–1820)* by Lo-shu Fu. 1966. xviii + 792 pp. $14.50.

XXI. *Before Aggression: Europeans Prepare the Japanese Army*, by Ernst L. Presseisen, 1965. O. P.

XX. *Shinran's Gospel of Pure Grace*, by Alfred Bloom. 1965. $2.50 paper.

XIX. *Chiaraijima Village: Land Tenure, Taxation, and Local Trade, 1818–1884*, by William Chambliss. 1965. $5.00.

XVIII. *The British in Malaya: The First Forty Years*, by Tregonning. 1965. O. P.

XVII. *Ch'oe Pu's Diary: A Record of Drifting Across the Sea*, by John Meskill. 1965. $4.50.

XVI. *Korean Literature: Topics and Themes*, by Peter H. Lee. 1965. O. P.

XV. *Reform, Rebellion, and the Heavenly Way*, Benjamin Weems. 1964. $3.75.

XIV. *The Malayan Tin Industry to 1914*, by Wong Lin Ken. 1965. $6.50.

Earlier-published AAS Monographs

XIII. *Conciliation and Japanese Law: Tokugawa and Modern*, D. F. Henderson, Univ. Washington Press, 1965.

XII. *Maharashta Purana*, Dimock, and Gupta. East-West Center Press, 1964. O. P.

XI. *Agricultural Involution: The Process of Ecological Change in Indonesia*, C. Geertz. Univ. California Press, 1963.

X. *Bangkhuad: A Community Study in Thailand*, H. K. Kaufman. Augustin, 1959. O. P.

IX. *Colonial Labor Policy and Administration, 1910–1941*, J. N. Parmer, Augustin, 1959.

VIII. *A Comparative Analysis of the Jajmani System*, T. O. Beidelman. Augustin, 1959.

VII. *The Traditional Chinese Clan Rules*, Hui-chen Wang Liu. Augustin, 1959.

VI. *Chinese Secret Societies in Malaya*, L. F. Comber. Augustin, 1959.

V. *The Rise of the Merchant Class in Tokugawa Japan: 1600–1868*, C. D. Sheldon. Augustin, 1958. O. P.

IV. *Siam Under Rama III, 1824–1851*, W. F. Vella. Augustin, 1957. O. P.

III. *Leadership and Power in the Chinese Community of Thailand*, G. W. Skinner. Cornell Univ. Press, 1958. O. P.

II. *China's Management of the American Barbarians*, E. Swisher. Yale, 1951. O. P.

I. *Money Economy in Medieval Japan*, D. M. Brown. Far Eastern Pubs., Yale, 1951. O. P.